White's Flight

White's Flight

An Australian pilot's epic escape from Turkish prison camp to Russia's Revolution

Fred and Elizabeth Brenchley

Fred Brenchley
Elizabeth Brenchley

WILEY
John Wiley & Sons Australia, Ltd

First published 2004 by
John Wiley & Sons Australia, Ltd
33 Park Road, Milton, Qld 4064

Offices also in Sydney and Melbourne

Typeset in 11.5/15 pt Berkeley

National Library of Australia
Cataloguing-in-Publication data

Brenchley, Fred, 1942– .
White's flight: an Australian pilot's epic escape from Turkish prison camp to Russia's Revolution.

Bibliography.
Includes index.
ISBN 1 74031 100 0.

1. White, T. W. (Thomas Walter), Sir, 1888–1957. 2. World War, 1914–1918 — Prisoners and prisons, Australian. 3. World War, 1914–1918 — Prisoners and prisons, Turkish. 4. Escapes — Turkey. I. Brenchley, Elizabeth. II. Title.

940.472561

Cover photograph:
T. W. White in a Maurice Farnham 'rumpety', Mesopotamia.

Printed in Australia by
Griffin Press Pty Ltd

10 9 8 7 6 5 4 3 2 1

In memory of
Leading Aircraftman Frederick Arthur Brenchley
38th Squadron, Milne Bay, WWII

R U S S
Mariople
SEA OF AZOV
Ekaterinodar
R. Dniester
R. Dnieper
ODESSA
CRIMEA
Novorissisk
Sevastopol
RUMANIA
BLACK SEA
BUCHAREST
R. Danube
Varna
Sinope
TREBIZOND
Germeli Su
Kizil Irmak
Kastamouni
Changri
Sivas
BULGARIA
Adrianople
CONSTANTINOPLE
The Bosphorus
Scutari
Ishmidt
TURKEY
ANGORA
Yoshgard
SEA OF MARMARA
Brussa
Eskishehr
Kutaia
Tuz Cheullu
Gallipoli
Suvla Bay
Chanak
Lemnos
Mudros
Dardanelles
Afion KaraHissar
Egirdir Geul
Beyshehr Geul
Tarsus
ADANA
TAURUS MTS.
Mitylene
Yeni Fotcha
SMYRNA
Chios
Adalia
Gulf of Adalia
Budrum
Rhodes
CYPRUS
Nicosia
Beirut
Antioch
G. of Alexandretta
AEGEAN SEA

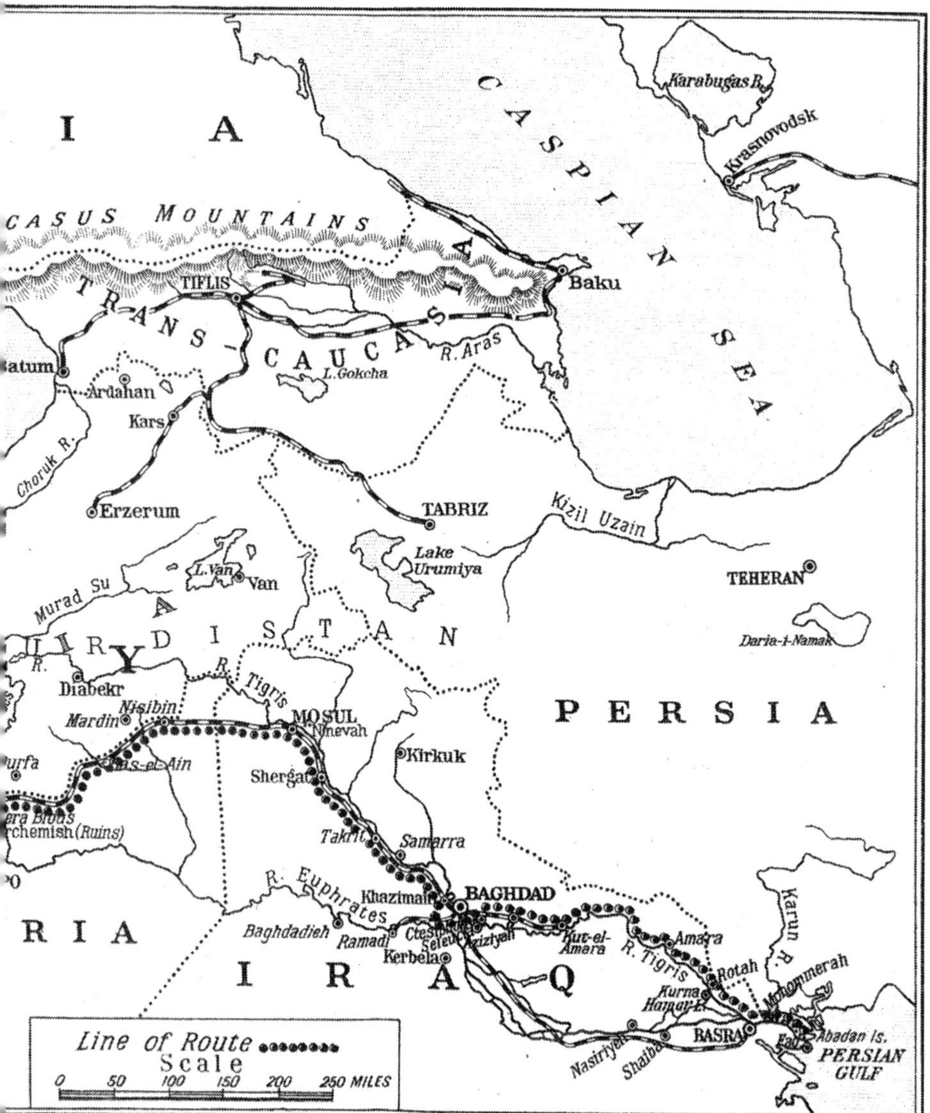

The Richards Press Limited, London, W.1

Authors' note

Tom White — pioneer wartime aviator, prisoner of war, escapee, businessman, politician and diplomat — packed a lot into one lifetime. His epic wartime adventures include stories of harsh conditions, cruelty and quixotic kindness, mixed with bravery and sheer determination to escape, whatever the risks. White's experiences ranged from the tragic to high farce.

Modern readers may find some descriptions by White and his colleagues a touch insensitive, even derogatory of wartime opponents. But this bygone era did not reflect today's cultural understanding.

Contents

Prologue

Unlucky Friday the 13th

The bullets kicked up dusty mounds as they thudded into the sand around the airplane. The Australian pilot struggled desperately with a can of petrol as he watched the approaching Arabs shooting at him.

But would the plane fly even if he did manage to refuel it? On landing some sixty miles behind enemy lines he had unluckily clipped a telegraph post, damaging a wing. The pilot glanced anxiously towards his observer, who had raced to shimmy up another telegraph pole to attach the explosive charge.

Their mission was to cut Turkish communications so their forces in Baghdad could not summon reinforcements as the British attacked. The stakes were high: the capture of Baghdad would compensate for the unfolding defeat at Gallipoli. It could hasten the withdrawal of Turkey from the war as a Germany ally, which had also been the aim of the disastrous Gallipoli landings. It could even shorten the war.

Blasts from behind him signalled the observer's success, but wires from the crashing telegraph pole now lashed around the airplane, enmeshing it and making escape impossible.

Then the Arabs were upon them. The first, a huge, shaggy-haired man was naked except for two bandoliers of cartridges across his chest.

The pilot cursed his bad luck. It was Friday, 13 November 1915.

Early airmen, like many mariners, were superstitious. Some carried mascots, such as toy black cats. The pilot had put his faith in his whistling propeller. Hit by a bullet from the ground, it had not split, the damage merely adding an eerie whistling note to the engine's exhaust. Only recently had he reluctantly changed this propeller, he remembered.

Flying on Friday the 13th was deemed particularly unlucky in the early Australian air corps. The very first batch of pilots were told that headquarters had specifically banned even flight training on that day. To add to the superstitious aura around 13, the pilots' composite force of British, Indian and Australian air crews had specifically numbered their airplanes in Mesopotamia from 1 to 12, and then 12A and 14.

Superstitious 13 carried right through to the officers' mess at their Mesopotamian desert base. It had been noticed during a recent dinner that thirteen officers were seated at the mess table.

'It is the first to rise who dies first, isn't it?' asked one. Nobody was in a hurry to rise. Drinks circulated again. Eventually, the senior officer declared, 'Then we had better rise together on the count of three!'

At three, all officers rose smartly, except for one. 'I thought you said you would count to four,' the embarrassed airman remarked. Within a year he would be the only officer who had not been killed in action, taken prisoner, or evacuated as a result of injury or sickness.

If the curse of the thirteenth had struck the two airmen that day, leading to their capture, luck would turn full circle over three years. After a Turkish prison camp commandant plotted to have the pilot and other captured officers assassinated in the desert, they were miraculously saved by the bizarre intervention of a South American soldier of fortune.

In a further twist, on another Friday the 13th in 1918 the pilot, by now a desperate fugitive in Constantinople, finally secured the money he needed to escape Turkey and flee to Russia. It would make him the only Australian prisoner of war to successfully escape from a Turkish POW camp in the First World War. But what he escaped to — Odessa and the Russian Revolution — may have been worse than a POW camp.

Fate stepped in again. Only a mischance prevented his embarking on a desperate mission to fly for the doomed anti-Bolshevik army in Siberia in order to secure passage to freedom.

Such is the luck of war.

1

Empire's child

On Mafeking Day in Melbourne, 23 May 1900, the city went wild. 'A mad orgie of popular fervour', the *Age* called it. Crowds thronged the streets, chanting and singing 'God Save the Queen' to celebrate the relief of the South African town of Mafeking after an eight-month siege by the Boers.

Australian forces played a direct role in the war. A Queensland detachment was among the force that had lifted the siege of Colonel Robert Baden-Powell's British troops. Now the whole Empire rejoiced, and 'Marvellous Melbourne' was not to be left out. Fireworks exploded and cable trams were overturned in an eruption of patriotic frenzy, a phenomenon thereafter known as 'mafficking'.

As historian Manning Clark noted, no displays of dissent were tolerated. 'Woe to the man who did not "doff his cady" while the national anthem was being chanted,' reported the *Age*. 'Off it went for him in a twinkling. If he demurred the crowd roughed him up.'

Thirteen-year-old army cadet Tommy White was swept up in the jingoism as crowds mobbed his unit in their excitement. Tommy and his fellow cadets had difficulty retaining their hats and rifles as the crowd jostled and cheered them on their march up Bourke Street to the formal ceremony at Parliament House. The day's excitement gave the tow-headed, fresh-faced youth a new resolve: he was determined to take part in the Boer War. Tommy White was a product of his era, and the South African war was emblematic of the compass points that were to guide his life — the British Empire, strong military defences, Empire trade preference and a White Australia.

Thomas Walter White was born in North Melbourne on 26 April 1888, the centenary of Australia's first British settlement, a coincidence White happily noted in later life. Tommy's father, C. J. White, then a school teacher, had come to Australia from England in 1856 as a one-year-old child with his parents on the barque *Samarang*. His mother, Emily (née Jenkins), was the Australian-born daughter of assisted English migrants.

Signs that the boy had a military bent showed early, although they may have passed undetected by his parents. 'Willie wouldn't let me push barrow, so I hit him with a stick,' were the first coherent words his parents remembered him saying. Willie was a next-door neighbour, whose mother evidently did not approve of young Tom's direct approach. School began at what White later described as the 'discerning age of three'. On his first day he won the teacher's prize of a 'bird shooter', two whittled sticks that could be used to shoot at birds. 'Apparently I used the sticks to better purpose on Willie,' he recalled.

Yet young Tommy was a small, sickly child, who suffered from asthma and bronchitis. 'Being weak-chested, my parents decided to move from the less salubrious region of North Melbourne to Moreland, a suburb four miles north at the terminus of the newly arrived cable trams; a trek in covered wagons with the family and our chattels that seemed quite an adventure then.' Moreland then had no made roads or pathways. People found their way by following the new surveyor's markers between paddocks or the cow tracks to Sydney Road. Wildflowers bloomed in summer, while in winter rain turned the ground into a quagmire. Children walking to school could be lost for hours in the frequent heavy fogs.

Moreland State School proved a blessing for Tommy. The headmaster, Mr Bottrell, was kind, if puritanical, while the head teacher,

Mr Badiford, was an excellent teacher. Both had a high success rate in achieving above-average scholarship results from their charges, and Tommy White was a good student.

Bottrell was an ardent teetotaller and strongly opposed to gambling. White was reminded of him some sixty years later when standing in the totalisator payment queue at Ascot Racecourse in England as a fellow punter in a top hat identified himself as a former school chum. 'Wouldn't our old schoolmaster turn in his grave if he could see us now!' exclaimed his old friend. Perhaps, but he would also have been proud of White's subsequent achievements. In 1937, when Moreland celebrated its fiftieth anniversary, the school listed Tom White as its 'most distinguished scholar'.

When Tommy was four his father opted for a career change, giving up teaching to open a small metal workshop in Little Collins Street in the heart of Melbourne. While he had some brass-founding experience — he had made a brass death mask of his hero Napoleon — this was still a very risky venture. By then the Whites had four children, three boys and a girl, and the Australian economy was heading into the depression of the 1890s.

Melbourne was particularly hard hit.

'Marvellous Melbourne' had experienced a sustained boom. The gold rush of the 1850s was followed by a manufacturing and rural boom that saw Melbourne grow from a small town to become the nation's financial capital. Through the 1880s Melbourne was substantially rebuilt, sprouting many prestigious eight- to ten-storey buildings and a cable tram system that facilitated a suburban property boom. This growth came to a shuddering halt in the early 1890s, with bank crashes, prolonged drought and industrial upheaval as the union movement flexed its new-found muscle. Forty-one land and finance companies in Melbourne and Sydney collapsed between July 1891 and August 1892. All Victoria's banks bar one small one went into reconstruction. Directors of land credit banks committed suicide in what the *Age* described as 'the coolest and most deliberate manner'. In what would be Australia's most severe depression before the 1930s, unemployment soared and families starved.

Such was the inauspicious background for the opening of C. J. White & Sons. 'He had a hard struggle to pay his way,' Tom White remembered of his father's new venture. 'But for the thrift, enterprise and tireless work of my mother, and her north-country determination and grit, we would have fared hardly at school in those straitened times, whereas we never knew want.'

Sport quickly captured young Tommy's enthusiasm and transformed his indifferent health. The local creek provided a swimming hole, and football and cricket matches against other schools helped him throw off the debilitating asthma. Running was a favourite activity, although sometimes involuntary. 'Football matches were sometimes hostile meetings, and one side or the other might be chased home,' he recalled. 'And I wasn't very good at fights.'

Not initially, at least. Self-defence became important only when he was persuaded to take on the local bully who had been scaring his school friends. Though still quite small and slight, Tommy was doing well in this scrap until the bully's father intervened. His own father, however, later gave him a pair of boxing gloves, and he took up boxing with zeal. 'On Saturdays at Cole's Book Arcade where free reading was available, I read the boxing books, practised left leads assiduously on the empty air, and in my early teens joined a boxing club, where the heavyweight professional boxing champion, Bill Squires, was instructor.'

His boxing confidence soared, to the extent that after a few clashes on the football field, and two exhibition bouts against unknowns, he believed he could win a state championship. After successful lead-up fights he made the championships, but then he was pitted against a well-known boxer with a bent nose and crumpled ear who had returned to the ring after some years.

As if his opponent was not intimidating enough, the bout became very rough. In those days rabbit killer punches, backhanders and kidney punches were allowed. Tommy decided that as his left hand was his best asset — he had no heavy right — he should concentrate on rapid left leads to the head. In clinches, however, he took some heavy hits. A blacksmith friend who acted as his second related afterwards how his big opponent had brought his chin down on Tommy's face, causing his nose to bleed profusely.

Tommy felt he was being badly beaten. At one break he sat in his corner with blood streaming, wondering whether to throw in the towel. But moments later it was his opponent's towel that floated into the ring. 'Which taught me that often in life things are not as bad as they seem.'

'Now the only decent nose in the family has been ruined,' wailed his horrified sister. He was forbidden by a doctor to fight in the remaining rounds, and when he returned to boxing two years later his nose was disjointed again. That ended any prospect of a boxing career.

Meanwhile the school cadets had opened up new horizons. With no local boy scouts, his father, a former member of the Rifle Volunteers, had encouraged him to join. For young Tommy there were attractions beyond the rifle practice in a disused municipal quarry and battalion parades at a seaside park. The cadets could slip away after parades for a swim in the seaside baths, and then entertain themselves at the sideshows and shooting galleries of the Eastern Market. Such 'unofficial training' was great fun for twelve-year-olds.

The duties of cadet bugler fell to Tommy. He soon mastered the instrument, playing the school into their classes every morning while also sounding 'suitable calls' for the martially inclined headmaster at assembly and retreat.

The Boer War was now in full swing. Youths in gangs raided each other in mock warfare. Tommy heard that trumpeters were needed by the militia battery of Garrison Artillery at North Melbourne, and applied for the job with the idea of using it as a step to fulfilling his ambition to participate in the war in South Africa, even if as a bugler. Following some tests he was selected and sworn in with the rank of 'boy'. There was only one hitch. The minimum age for this lowest rank in military life was fourteen, and Tommy had not disclosed that he was a few months short of requirements.

'It was a very scared recruit, height five feet, chest 28 inches, who had to appear before the formidable battery sergeant-major, to be told that he had been sworn in by mistake,' he recalled. 'But as he would be 14 before long, in this case it would be overlooked.'

Tommy went to Government House Domain, where Victorian volunteers were being tested for horsemanship before being sent to South Africa as reinforcements. But riding was then a novelty for him, and the 'troublesome boy' was warned to stay outside the fence. He later hinted that his father had in any case refused permission for the boy to go to war.

A bid to join the navy was similarly thwarted. The Royal Navy's HMS *Euryalus*, on a visit to Port Melbourne, was opened to the public in a bid to drum up naval enlistment. With his little brother Percy in tow, and clutching the enlistment information, Tommy boarded the ship, where their enthusiasm evidently got the better of them, for they promptly climbed the mast to the crow's nest, where Tommy experimented with the messaging system, receiving startling replies from all quarters of the ship.

'Seeing the crowd gazing upward with a policeman beckoning, we came down, to be led down the gangway by the ear,' White recalled. 'My father's refusal to let me apply as bugler or naval cadet was scarcely necessary in this case.'

The Boer War ended a few days after Tommy's fourteenth birthday, so for the time being he decided to seek military glory on the home front. But he quickly found that trumpeters and 'boys' in Garrison Artillery were the dogsbodies of the battery who, besides doing their turn at guard and orderly duty at weekends and camps in the forts around Port Phillip Bay, also had to serve as bandsmen and signallers. Tommy was fortunate. His father was a talented flautist and had taught him the fife. A maiden aunt gave him piano lessons, so band music came fairly easy. Signalling appealed to him too, and after his father made him a heliograph (the moveable mirror system used for flashing messages) he soon acquired army badges for proficiency in flags, lamps and heliograph.

Playing in the band, however, presented its own problems. 'It seemed to me at the time that more beer was drunk by the older bandsmen, and especially trombone players, than any other human.' On one memorable parade the first trombone player missed the cue to counter-march, stepping away on his own. When he hastily rejoined the band he managed to knock the drum-major's helmet off with his trombone slide, causing great amusement among the audience.

In the Signal Corps, Tommy showed the initiative that would later mark him out in wartime. As signaller on a tugboat used for gunnery practice, it was his duty to mark with a pointer on a graduated arc the distance a muzzle-loaded eighty pounder would fire, and flag this back to headquarters. This gave him an idea that he would later use to invent an apparatus for aerial mapping in the Mesopotamian desert. One day when the tugboat captain was ill, Tommy took command, steering the boat up and down the range. 'What more could a lad want?' he thought.

While he enjoyed the cadets, Tommy felt the pressures of the precarious state of his father's business. 'From an early age I had had a haunting uncertainty as to what would happen to my mother and my sisters and brothers if my father died,' he later wrote. 'I can remember at the age of six mentally computing my own and the family resources.'

During 1902, the year he turned fourteen, school leaving age, Tommy had to decide whether to pursue higher education or start work. His father made it clear that he expected a Leaving (Merit) Certificate, and Tommy attained this, winning a scholarship to attend either University High School or Carlton College. But he was not keen, apparently more concerned with the family's finances. He persuaded his father to let him go to work on the promise that he would resume his studies later. With one hundred and fifty others — the city was still pulling out of depression — he lined up for a job with the city merchant Henry Berry's at a starting salary of six shillings for a 48-hour week. Tommy won one of the twelve positions on offer.

'Like Gilbert's First Lord when a lad, I had to "clean the windows and sweep the floor, and polish up the handle of the big front door",' he recalled. Sales and deliveries were also among his duties. With his first savings he bought a secondhand bicycle from a school mate for ten shillings so he could save on fares. Later, with his first half-crown saved, he made a deposit on a block of land in a suburban subdivision. 'My first assay into capitalism,' he said.

Tommy greatly enjoyed business life, even at his low level. 'It is often the rule in non-success to blame one's bad luck or one's parents for leaving school too early or the social system that permitted wage slavery conditions,' he wrote later. 'Yet I do not remember experiencing any such inhibitions, finding that every day there was much to do and to learn, though the rewards did not seem commensurate with the labour. It was a stimulating exercise to memorise the cost book, and be able to reel off the costs of machinery and merchandise to the firm's travellers, and selling prices to the customers.'

While he acquired some useful business skills, young White was unhappy with his salary. With no increase in two years, and with his department manager afraid to act, he cheekily approached the formidable chairman of directors. He secured an immediate increase to eight shillings and four pence a week, raised to twelve shillings and sixpence a year later. As part of his salary rise he was expected to work some nights on stocktaking for a small extra payment. But this soon interfered with his growing military duties, and on one special training night he refused store work, and was promptly sacked.

'A happy release,' he claimed. Perhaps, but jobs were not easy to come by, and a period of unemployment gave him a lifelong sympathy for the unemployed and for welfare schemes for those willing but unable to work. He haunted the docks looking for a berth on a sailing ship for some overseas experience. Then, after a course of fitting and turning at Melbourne's Technical College, he took a short-term job with the engineer of his former store employers before joining his father's workshop.

With both Tommy and his younger brother Percy now working for the firm, C. J. White & Sons was starting to live up to its name. It was not a happy period for the family, however. In 1905 the Whites' youngest child, Vera, died suddenly, aged eleven. The family long believed she died of hydatids, and for years the children were forbidden to play with cats. More likely it was meningitis, then reaching epidemic levels in the city.

Tommy greatly admired his father, a strong Mason and soft-hearted towards his friends, who often sought loans. The little metal workshop, now with five employees, began to specialise in locks and builders' hardware. His father was punctilious about finances, calling on each of the company's creditors every month to pay them in cash, regardless of the self-denial needed to raise the funds. As young Tommy introduced the sales skills he had learned in his store job, the business began to show better results. By 1909 it was firmly established, later winning the prestigious job of casting the bronze finials that top the spires of St Paul's Cathedral.

Tommy's military career also blossomed. By 1910 he had been eight years in the ranks of the militia with the signallers and artillery. He decided it was time to move up, and applied for a commission. His commanding officer, however, made it plain that he set more value on the old school tie than experience, and he would not even consider young White, who had dropped out of school at fourteen.

Undaunted, White turned to the volunteer forces. He secured a probationary second lieutenant's spot in the senior cadets, then one of three volunteer regiments. He memorised the regulations and duties, and passed top in the test for the appointment. 'Approaching the battalion that previously rejected me, I was this time accepted on probation, the Colonel having got over his prejudice,' said White.

Securing a good pass mark in an infantry officers' course that required no formal educational standard other than his previous training, White was appointed a major in the 5th Australian Infantry Regiment. He volunteered for the post of machine-gun officer. In 1910 the .303 Vickers machine gun and the .606 pompom gun were carried on wheeled vehicles like artillery pieces. Riding on weekend parade improved his horse handling skills. Although the horses had milk cart and delivery wagon beats during the week, this was a privilege not to be despised, especially during long marches and annual manoeuvres.

White's military career began to benefit from the defence initiatives of the Deakin Government in 1908, including the foundations for an Australian navy and the first system of compulsory military training in the British Empire. The influx of eighteen-year-olds into a citizen military force meant new training and command positions for the 'old' hands.

For White, however, promotion also necessitated smoothing ruffled feathers caused by his natural enthusiasm and drive, which often spilled over into pugnacity. As a machine-gun officer, he won an early enemy by unwisely taking on the adjutant at the battalion conference on machine-gun tactics. This was none other than H. E. Elliott, later nicknamed 'Pompey Elliott' by the men he brilliantly led on the western front. At this stage Elliott was still a very ambitious officer, anxious to become commander of the new 58th Battalion, which was being formed under the new universal training scheme. The petty squabble degenerated into an incident that saw White arrested for disobeying orders, and it may have played a part in his subsequent failure to pass a further promotional exam. White later called it a '*comedie militaire*', but at the time it was deadly serious, and the subject of mountains of army paperwork.

After being appointed commander of Company D of the 60th Infantry, and sensing rightly that the new conscription scheme would mean new battalions and new commands, White applied for a commission in the permanent military forces. This meant serious examinations, including some at matriculation standard. While on study leave he heard that Major Elliott, then second-in-command of the battalion, was manoeuvring in the company apparently with the aim of becoming its commander when, as likely, it emerged as a new battalion during the army's expansion.

Before study leave White and his fellow officers had planned a 'smoke night' for the company's rifle club, a popular event involving prizes and entertainment. But at a meeting called by Elliott, at which offers of new commands for junior officers were bandied about, he cancelled the smoke night, promising a bigger and better one once the company was under his command. Furthermore, Elliott claimed that since he had not given permission for the smoke night, as the company's commanding officer White personally would have to bear any expense involved in the cancellation. Having arranged to attend the meeting even though on study leave, White strongly objected, informing Elliott that their battalion commander, Colonel F. A. Foxall, had given verbal permission, and that the venue and entertainment were already booked.

Next day White reported Elliott's extraordinary performance to Foxall, who complained of other problems he was encountering as a result of the major's ambition. 'Go ahead with the smoke night, but see that it's in plain clothes, and see that he [Elliott] is not invited,' Foxall directed.

Whether inadvertently or mischievously, Elliott did receive an invitation. He called on White the next morning. 'You're under arrest,' he said.

'On what charge?' replied White, laughing.

'For not cancelling a smoke night when I ordered you to.'

Elliott then visited other officers involved, some at their workplace, placing them 'under arrest' too. White reported these events to Colonel Foxall. He learned later that the Colonel had sought legal counsel, who advised him to put Elliott himself under arrest and 'release' the other officers. Foxall now advised White to invite Elliott to the smoke night. When he did, Elliott threatened to frog-march White before the commanding officer. White stormed off, saying, 'I'm too busy to worry further about you,' leaving Elliott in no doubt about what he thought of him. Elliott then made it an issue of discipline, and succeeded in intimidating Foxall to the point that only hours before the function he ordered White to cancel it.

That night events degenerated into high farce. First Elliott locked the hall adjacent to Essendon Town Hall where the function was booked. As White peered in through a window he saw the major rushing up and down the tables collecting buns and bottles of lemonade and packing them into boxes. A perplexed town clerk offered White the use of the town hall itself, where he assembled the men and told them the distribution of prizes would have to be done informally out in the street. With the men gathered under a lamppost outside, and as the booked artists milled around and Elliott guarded the buns and drinks inside, White handed out the prizes.

Elliott then stormed up, demanding White send the men home.

'I'm distributing prizes,' White told him.

'Well, keep the men in hand.'

'They are in hand.'

A local newspaper reported the night's affray under the headline 'Lemon Squashaliers'. Elliott threatened a libel suit against the newspaper, but wisely did not proceed. White sought and gained a military inquiry, then disputed the evidence put to it, seeking a second inquiry. Eventually White also dropped the issue, although his allegations that Foxall had inappropriately reprimanded him indicated he was still seething well after the event.

Pompey Elliott's biographer, Ross McMullin, termed the episode 'cringingly petty'. Both men came out of it poorly. For McMullan it confirmed Elliott as an absolute stickler for discipline, who was even prepared to make himself look ridiculous in the process. For White, it may have cost him a promotion, as we shall see.

Pompey Elliott went on to serve with distinction at Gallipoli and on the western front, later becoming a federal senator. In Canberra, he and White became quite good friends. 'Perhaps he had been too dictatorial in the past,' White later reflected. 'Perhaps I had been too young and rash.'

Elliott did gain command of the new battalion, and compensation of a sort followed for White when he was invited to take up the post of area officer at Bendigo, the former goldmining town north of Melbourne. White accepted. The post would give him more time for study.

Bendigo and nearby Kerang had been tough and enterprising towns in the heyday of the gold rush, and White quickly found that independent spirit still pervaded the area. No sooner had he arrived than a local meeting was called at which Bendigo parents were urged to defy authorities and keep their sons away from military training. White attended, and told the inflamed meeting that training had great benefits for the nation's defence and democracy. The motion was defeated.

Kerang's cadets tended to be more militant, with a reputation for disregarding authority. After correcting their sloppy dress, White marched them to a local park for extended drill, telling the older cadets there would be no 'stand easy' in the heat until their performance improved. His deliberate martinet performance attracted immediate murmuring in the ranks.

'He must have been a warder,' said one. 'I'd like to deal with him,' said another.

'You can stay behind and see to that,' White told the second. In the local drill hall later the two donned boxing gloves and, with the colour sergeant as referee, fought a spirited few rounds.

'Fortunately I got the better of it, though I felt some of the punishment for a week after,' rued White. 'For unluckily I had chosen the budding district hopeful as a boxer. But this gesture to a group of youths who were essentially sportsmen seemed to have better results than all the parade ground instruction. They became a crack rifle unit, while the percentage of their enlistment and casualties in World War 1 was among the highest.'

White still had exams to pass. He did very well in his militia captaincy, gaining a special certificate for 'distinction in all subjects'. The medical for the permanent army administration staff proved a bigger hurdle, however. On the first medical he had been passed out. His chest measurement had to equal half his height. White felt the tape measure was too low, and pushed it higher.

'Why did you touch that?' glowered the medical officer.

'I thought it was rather low down,' replied White.

The MO pushed it back down. 'You're a quarter of an inch short,' he said scathingly. White had to wait another year to pass, putting on some weight and expanding his chest through exercises.

The practical examination proved tougher still. Having passed the written exams in engineering, topography and infantry, he had little concern about passing the practicals, including drill for brigade and light horse, but his timing was unlucky. The government had just begun to retrench, and as fewer officers were being selected, the odds had turned against him. White missed out by just four marks in a thousand.

This temporary setback stung. 'I was unknown, except perhaps adversely over the smoke-night incident, whereas the officers who passed were a son and son-in-law of serving staff officers,' he wrote. It would have been the second time the middle-class self-achiever had been blocked by either nepotism or the 'old school tie' factor.

Transferred back to Melbourne from Bendigo, White took up the post of area officer at Carlton, an inner suburb. Carlton was rife with street gangs, and White believed the local drill hall helped keep underprivileged kids off the streets. It certainly produced some crack riflemen. Carlton gave White time for the family business again, and for two new interests as well — aviation, and a young woman.

Details of White's meeting and romance with Flora Bien from Mornington near Melbourne are not known, but at some point before the outbreak of the war he proposed marriage and she accepted. The relationship is not mentioned in any of White's writings.

Aviation, however, had been on White's mind since he read a street billboard in December 1903 that two unknown mechanics in the United States, the Wright brothers, had successfully flown a powered glider. In 1910, like other Australians, he was thrilled by the airplane flights in Australia of the famous American escapologist Harry Houdini. Houdini flew two miles, gaining a height of 300 feet above Diggers' Rest in Victoria. The Aerial League of Australia presented Houdini with a plaque for making the first controlled flight in a powered aircraft in Australia. Four months later John Duigan, a Victorian farmer, made the first flight in an Australian-made powered aircraft. In May 1914 White and other Melburnians were amazed when the French airman Maurice Guilliaux took off from the Melbourne Show Grounds and landed on the Government House lawn, flying upside down and looping the loop during the short flight.

White was bitten. 'On the strength of having built a glider — which never flew — having some technical training, possessing a motor car licence, not so common in those days, and being an enthusiastic motorcyclist, I applied to join any flying corps unit that might be formed,' he said.

That typified Tommy White. On the outbreak of war, at twenty-six years old, he had matured into a handsome, shortish man with bright blue eyes, an open face and thick black wavy hair parted on one side, with a cowlick that occasionally fell across his forehead. He was pugnacious and impatient for success, with a disdain for authority and a suspicion of 'elites' born of his comparatively humble background, small-business family and limited education. White's anti-authoritarian streak and his belief in a 'fair go' were evident in the embarrassing spat with Pompey Elliott. His small-business, self-motivated orientation would later show in hostility to both big business and big unions.

More importantly, his military training had inspired in him a hankering for overseas service for the Empire and a fascination with the new technology of aviation. In April 1888, in the very month of Tommy White's birth, the poet Henry Lawson lamented in the *Republican* monthly newspaper that most Australian schoolchildren knew more of English history than of their own. He hoped the next generation would learn to love the flag of the Southern

Cross, to sing their own national anthem and to believe in 'Australia for Australians' — in short, to be republicans.

If Tommy White was representative of that new generation, Lawson's words had fallen on deaf ears. For White, like so many of his contemporaries, was an Australian child of the British Empire.

2

Flying backwards

Tom White leapt at the chance to serve overseas when war was declared on 4 August 1914. No-one was surprised.

'Of course you will be going,' his mother said without any visible emotion. She realised the futility of trying to dissuade him. He didn't hesitate, joining the throng of young men applying for overseas service the very day war was declared. Many of them believed the war would last only a few months and were determined to see some of the action. Opposition Leader Andrew Fisher summed up the public mood with his promise that the mother country would be helped to the 'last man and last shilling'.

White was initially rejected, however. As area commander at Carlton he could not apply for enlistment — that was the rule. Impulsively, White fixed that by resigning on the spot. Stressing his machine-gun training and the need for officers capable of taking charge of a brigade's guns, he was immediately appointed machine-gun officer of the 5th Battalion, AIF, with the rank of captain.

Due to report for camp the following morning, he returned home to pack his kit. Here a letter awaited him with exciting news: White was one of four men chosen as the first pilot trainees for the new Australian Flying Corps. He was to report in a fortnight to Point Cook, near Melbourne, where the Central Flying School had recently put up a single hangar and some tents on a tract of sheep grazing land.

'It was too good to miss,' he said. Apart from the prospect of actually flying, and joining a new, untried arm of the service, he could also spend a few weeks at home with his father, who was critically ill.

When war broke out, eleven years after the Wright brothers' first powered flight, Australia had barely put a toe into military aviation. The United States and Britain acquired their first military aircraft in 1909; by 1914 all three main combatants — France, Germany and Britain — had small air arms.

Not that the airplane was universally regarded as a military breakthrough in an era dominated by the power of the navy's huge dreadnoughts. Like submarines, the other major weapons advance of the First World War, aircraft were initially derided as mere playthings. As late as 1914, France's General Foch reportedly declared, 'the aircraft is all very well for sport — for the army it is useless'.

Initially, aircraft were used mainly for reconnaissance, with pilots occasionally dropping handfuls of poisoned darts or small bombs over the side. As the war progressed they became both fighters and bombers, and by the end of the war air power, like submarine power, was firmly established as a deadly new military weapon. The dreadnought was consigned to history.

The outbreak of hostilities found Australia with two military aviation instructors employed to run the new service and train pilots, and just four, newly assembled planes, but no trained pilots. In Sydney, two newly ordered submarines, the *AE1* and *AE2* had just arrived, and joined the early Australian action to force the Germans out of New Guinea. *AE1* was lost while on patrol, never to be found; *AE2* went on to serve at Gallipoli.

Military aviation in Australia probably dawned in 1909 when the government announced a £5,000 prize for 'a flying machine ... for military purposes'. While that prize was never awarded, following an Imperial Conference in London in December 1911 the Australian government decided to create an air arm, complete with aircraft and aviators. The Commonwealth observed cautiously that it would 'accept no responsibility for accidents'.

Over the next two years money was set aside for four airplanes — two Deperdussin monoplanes and two BE2a (short for Bleriot Experimental) biplanes. Both models were constructed largely of wood, wire and fabric; the BE2a was powered by a Renault tractor engine. Two trainers were hired in Britain. Henry Petre, an English solicitor, and Eric Harrison, an Australian, were both civilians who had gained pilot's licences in England. They were given honorary military commissions, with Petre, the first to arrive, also assigned the task of locating a new flying school.

Canberra, where the new army officer training school had been created at Duntroon, was seen as the logical choice, but Petre opted instead for the flatter terrain around Melbourne. Whether or not Canberra's hills were the determining factor, Petre later told Richard Williams, one of the first graduates and a future air force chief, that he was 'not going to be isolated in the bush'.

An elementary Bristol Boxkite more suitable for beginner training was added to the school's inventory. When the Boxkite and Deperdussins were unloaded in Sydney it was found that tropical weather had rotted part of their wings. After repairs, on 17 August 1914 Central Flying School welcomed its first course of four pupils to the muddy campsite at Point Cook. It was two weeks after the outbreak of war. Selected as trainee pilots along with Tom White were Richard Williams, then an army lieutenant, Lieutenant D. T. W. Manwell of the 16th Light Horse and Lieutenant G. P. Merz of the Melbourne University Rifles, a young medical graduate from Ballarat in Victoria.

One of the trainees' first fascinations was Petre's pet bulldog. The dog chased the aircraft engines, surviving two charges through the slow-turning propeller of the Boxkite, before finally being run over and killed by the school's truck. One wag commented that the new Australian air force had gone to the dogs before it had even got off the ground.

Both Point Cook and the training regime were primitive. Apart from the corrugated iron hangar and an aircraft container converted into a galley, it was a tented camp in the long grass of sheep country. The trainees were kept well clear of the BE2a's and the single Deperdussin — Petre had already crashed one. The aptly named Boxkite was their focus. The 'beginners' bus', as it was known, was little more than a kite with a small engine, somewhat akin to a modern ultralight. There was no cabin, fuselage, instruments or even safety belts. The pilot sat in a small wooden seat perched up front, with the rotary 'pusher' engine behind. Boxkites, however, were quite safe, and when the Gnôme engine stalled the aircraft fell out of the sky like a leaf. Trainee pilots in crashes — and they were numerous — usually walked away.

In retrospect, training was like something out of a comic silent movie. While White had a dome helmet such as dirt track riders wear and a pair of goggles, Williams seems to have missed out on any flying clothing. He wore a greatcoat and turned his army cap back to front. Inevitably the cap blew off and was mashed in the propeller.

The Boxkite flew only in very still conditions. Williams recalled their morning routine:

'The usual procedure was for a pupil to awake at daylight, hold a handkerchief in the air by one corner, and if there was sufficient breeze to move it he went back to bed; if not, he woke the instructor, and if the latter approved it as a good flying morning, the commotion commenced. The orderly mechanic was awakened, the Commer truck started up, and a party went off to the hangar and got the Boxkite out.'

The Boxkite had no dual controls as on modern training aircraft. The trainee initially sat in a second seat immediately behind the pilot, rather like a pillion passenger on a motorbike. His legs straddled the pilot as he stretched to reach the instructor's grip on the control stick to learn the tricks of flying. The two would swap these tandem positions until the pilot judged the trainee ready to go solo.

White later looked back with a sense of wonder. 'Our labouring Boxkite, capable of only forty-five miles per hour, was provided with no instruments other than a barometer, and lacked the enclosing fuselage and floor that give that feeling of security one experiences in a modern machine.

'The senses took the place of instruments. One's ears did duty as engine counters; the rush of air in the face told whether the climb or glide was at the right angle. The Gnôme engine could not be throttled, so ran "all-out" or not at all, but a powered approach was made by switching on and off while descending, without "losing" the engine.'

Occasional disasters were inevitable. As they were responsible for recovering the downed planes, the mechanics grumbled that the new pupils always landed well out on the aerodrome, away from all obstacles.

'Tommy White was one to notice these things and he decided to land closer to the hangar, but misjudged his speed and in trying to get off again ... struck the hangar and the aircraft finished up in a heap right in the hangar doorway,' said Williams. 'The mechanics certainly did not have to run out into the aerodrome and swing the prop; all they had to do was to move the whole thing a few feet under cover and rebuild it.'

'Overconfidence' was White's explanation. It was his first solo flight — after one hour fifty-five minutes' flying training. The dent in the hangar remains to this day, with a plaque attached.

The pupils constantly nagged their two instructors to be allowed to fly the more sophisticated BE2a's. Only when you can take the Boxkite up to a thousand feet and bring it down in a spiral descent, they were told. This was a risky feat, right at the limit of the Boxkite's height ceiling. Training flights were at only 50 to 200 feet.

The typically adventurous White was keen to be first to give it a go. 'We talked it over and thought it could be done,' he said. 'So I had a shot at it. But having no fuselage [the Boxkite] could not be spiralled effectively, and for the last 400 feet after I had tipped it up on its wing-tips, it spun and slipped to the ground, the front elevator and port wing-tip hitting the earth with a crash, shaking off the tanks and engine, and catapulting me, followed by the seat, clear of the plane.'

His pride was hurt more than his body. 'It was facetiously said in those days that if a canary were let loose in a Boxkite and could not escape through the wires, then the plane was properly rigged,' he joked. 'Nevertheless I went through them, and they broke my fall so that I had nothing more than a few cuts and scrapes. We shouldn't have taken the instructor too literally.'

The trainees were a happy lot. Stanley Brogden, in his *History of Australian Aviation*, wrote that they often timed their crashes for Friday afternoon so they could enjoy a weekend in Melbourne while the 'beginners' bus' was repaired.

After three months and a written exam, the four trainees faced a final flying test for their new pilot's commission, or 'brevet', then issued by the Royal Aero Club under tests laid down by the Federation Aeronautique Internationale. Williams later claimed the four drew matchsticks to see who would go first. 'Each of us wanted to be the first to qualify,' he said. 'To settle this question Harrison arranged for us to draw lots. Tommy White was drawn first and I was second.'

One of the test flights required the trainee to complete a number of 'figures of eight' within a reasonable radius, and then land the airplane in a glide and come to rest within a circle about fifty yards in diameter marked on the ground. According to Williams' story, White completed two figures of eight and landings, but on the third failed to stop within the circle. 'Bad luck!' Williams said. By this time a breeze was developing and flying was called off for the day.

Next day, with calm conditions, the Boxkite was wheeled out and, according to Williams, White jumped into the pilot's seat. 'This raised a storm of protest from the other pupils,' he said. 'We took the view that nobody should have a second try until all had had one. Much to Tommy's disappointment the supervising officer ruled in our favour and I took the aircraft. I was fortunate enough to complete all three tests and so luckily became the first to qualify as a pilot at Point Cook.'

White strongly disputed Williams' recollection of the graduation of Australia's first military pilot, with its drawing of matchsticks. Williams first made the claim publicly in 1955, and White, although saying he hated to spoil a good story, said Williams simply did not give the facts. White's version of events ran like this:

'There was no drawing of matchsticks for who was to fly first. We flew in the order of the day before, which means that I flew last. Lieutenants Merz and Manwell overshot and had to fly again later; Lieutenant Williams passed and I followed him and passed too. He [Williams] makes up a story of my having failed, which, of course, is untrue.'

Interestingly, Williams stuck by his version of events, repeating the drawing of matchsticks story in his curiously titled autobiography, *These Are Facts*, published in 1977. It was not the only sign of a certain friction between the two men. Williams, as we have seen, publicly noted White's anxiety to please colleagues by landing close to the hangar, and his consequent crash. For his part, White later noted that Williams was not selected for the first overseas flying unit to Mesopotamia. As well, says White, both he and Merz were offered posts as instructors after graduation, while Williams 'was returned to the Infantry depot at Broadmeadows'. Williams later wrote a negative report about White's bid for higher awards after the war. However, he helped White return to the air force in the early days of the Second World War.

Whatever the truth behind the selection of Australia's first air force pilot, all four airmen were upset at the delay in Royal Aero Club confirmation of their brevets. With no airmail at the time it took almost two months for the test results to go to England and be returned. That meant all four missed out on being among the first one thousand British Empire pilots to graduate. Australia's first two pilots, Williams and White, became numbers 1024 and 1025 under the international system. The delay prompted White to advocate the formation of an Australian Aero Club. He called a meeting of the four new pilots and their two instructors. Petre was elected president and White, secretary. Members of the next course were invited to their inaugural function.

Like Williams, White was dead keen to fly the BE2a, with its greater power and speed, proper fuselage and pilot's cabin. Williams' flight ended when he ran out of petrol as he was taxiing back to the hangar. A minute or so more in the air could have been disastrous. White's first flight was equally hairy. It was so exhilarating after the Boxkite that he decided to defy orders not to leave the aerodrome precinct and to take a look at Melbourne from the air. While admiring the view, he tried to pump more petrol into the forward tank, but the gauge glass remained empty, which meant he had only a few minutes of fuel remaining. He spied a stony field in Newport, and successfully negotiated his first landing in a strange aircraft, startling some field workers. On inspection, he found that the mechanic who had swung the propeller had forgotten to switch on the petrol tap. White pumped up the tank, took off and returned without mentioning the near disaster.

A dilemma now faced the four new recruits. Although they were qualified pilots, Australia had no plan to send a flying unit abroad in the war. 'Though we had pilot's wings on our chests after completing the course, we could find no active service openings where we might be usefully employed,' lamented White. 'Glory had to be sought elsewhere.'

With no chance of active flying service, the logical step was to return to the army. Merz, who had just completed his medical degree at Melbourne University, planned to go overseas as a regimental medical officer, and in the meantime was keeping his flying hand in as an assistant instructor at Point Cook, a post also offered to White. Williams and Manwell both returned to the army, while White decided to join his friend Merz's battalion.

Then, completely out of the blue, in February 1915 the Indian colonial government asked Australia if it could supply aircraft and pilots to support the Anglo-Indian invasion of southern Mesopotamia, now Iraq but then still part of the Ottoman Empire.

Indian forces, with British components, had landed at Al Faw at the head of the Persian Gulf only days after Turkey and Britain declared war in October 1914. Gunboats were sent into the Shatt al-Arab waterway, and within a few weeks Basra, some seventy miles inland, was captured. Could the British now capture Baghdad and split the Turkish empire?

The Mesopotamian campaign has slipped under history's veil, overshadowed by the Gallipoli disaster and the later success of the mounted horse in Palestine, yet it was the unlikely birthplace of the Australian air force.

While the original aim of the campaign was to protect vital oil pipelines of the Anglo-Persian Oil Company, the invasion also held strategic significance. At one level a march on Baghdad would complement the allied landings at Gallipoli in the strategy of driving Turkey out of the war. At another, it was part of the plan to dismember the Ottoman Empire, with Britain, France and Russia competing over the spoils. India's colonial regime also wanted a slice to act as a buffer against Russian encroachments.

All this was beyond the grasp of the Australian government. Yes, it was happy to supply airmen, mechanics, trucks and even donkeys, but it had no aircraft. No problem, replied India, we will supply them. White claimed two of the Maurice Farman aircraft supplied secondhand were generously supplied by the Rajah of Gwalior. The Australian Flying Corps' first overseas fighting mission certainly had a colourful birth — attached to the Indian Army with aircraft supplied by a wealthy Indian potentate.

Of the seven available pilots in Australia — two instructors, four new graduates and Lieutenant W. H. Treloar, who had learned to fly in England and had only recently returned to Australia — four were selected. Captain Petre was given command, with White, Merz and Treloar as the other pilots. The Mesopotamian Half Flight was born, so called because it was half the strength of a Royal Air Corps flight.

Petre quickly left for India to make advance arrangements, and it fell to White, who again abruptly abandoned the army in favour of the new air force, to pull Half Flight together. From some 300 eager volunteers assembled on the parade ground at Broadmeadows army base, he selected the mechanics and drivers for the mule transport. Half Flight was assembled and trained in haste, turning in their dungarees for tropical kit. Two repair shop lorries were built on heavy truck chassis to provide mobile workshops.

During the frantic preparations their volunteer cook provided the unit with some light relief. One day the camp learned that an 'injured aviator' lay recovering in the local hotel. Hastening to the hotel, his rescuers found their elderly chef, who had gone to town for treatment to a hand injury, regaling the locals with stories of how he had caught his hand in the propeller as he was throwing biscuits from the air to the troops. White later found him more than capable of dealing with the inevitable griping about military cooking.

After just two weeks under canvas — with time for a few joy rides for some of the new recruits — on 20 April 1915, five days before the Gallipoli landings, Half Flight sailed on the P&O liner *Morea* for Bombay. As White saw it, the little force was 'bound for glory or Kingdom Come'.

A week in Bombay gave the Australians an opportunity to spend three months' advance pay. 'The oppressive pre-monsoonal heat engendered thirsts that would not be quenched,' said White wryly. Indeed, the legendary Australian taste for beer almost caused White to miss the ship for Basra. Just as he had completed the paperwork and got the men on board White received a telegram from 'sweltering Basra' to bring a case of beer for the mess. When he returned to the wharf with the beer the ship had already sailed. He flagged down a native craft, catching up with the ship at the harbour mouth. 'Climbing the gangway at sea, with a case of beer ... seemed an unpardonable beginning for service, but was probably considered orthodox for Australians,' he quipped.

The trip through the Gulf of Oman and up the Persian Gulf to Basra gave White the opportunity to indulge his developing love of classical history and myth. As the barren coast of Persia slipped by he imagined the travails of Alexander the Great along this very coast. As the ship slipped into the palm tree–fringed waters of the Shatt al-Arab, the confluence of the fabled Tigris and Euphrates rivers, and steamed up to Basra, his mind turned to Sinbad's words in *The Arabian Nights*: 'We did land at Balsora to proceed to Baghdad.' White littered his letters home and later writings about Mesopotamia with such literary allusions.

For the Australians, Basra was indeed like something out of *The Arabian Nights*. In the bazaar helmeted soldiers in sunglasses mixed with Arabs in flowing robes and headdresses clasped with camel hair. Scribes with reed pens squatted on the ground writing love letters to the dictation of amorous illiterates. 'Slender canopied bellams, the gondolas of this eastern Venice, flit swiftly from point to point, ferrying veiled Arab women or gaily clad Chaldean girls along the palm fringed canals,' wrote White. 'Roads were then practically non-existent and the bellam served as the taxi for the natives.'

Half Flight laid out an aerodrome, or 'aircraft park' as it was called, in the grounds of the local cemetery, the highest ground available and the only dry land. There, protected by a surrounding mud dyke, they began assembling their three aircraft, two Maurice Farman 'Longhorns' and one 'Shorthorn'. Known as 'rumpeties' because of the noise they made when travelling over ground, these wood, wire and canvas biplanes were developed by the French Farman brothers, of bicycle and motor racing fame. They were propelled by a 70-horsepower rotary 'pusher' Renault engine mounted at the rear of a small cabin — the pilot and co-pilot sat up front. Two protruding, horn-like skids at the front gave the Longhorn its nickname, although some attributed it to the fact that the plane performed like a cow.

White would remember them as 'museum pieces of the sticks and wire period' of military aircraft. With a top speed of only about sixty miles per hour, the rumpety could be blown backwards in the hot, dry Mesopotamian wind known as the *shamal*, an unnerving experience for any pilot. 'Those wires sang like a jew's harp every time it touched sixty,' said White. Maurice Farmans, nevertheless, were early operational aircraft of Britain and France, and among the first in aerial combat.

The three aircraft were assembled and ready for action in four days. Museum pieces or not, the aircraft were a sensation with the Arabs as well as the Indian troops. For them, said White, aeroplanes seemed to 'possess the amazing and supernatural qualities of their mythical travelling carpets and magic steeds'.

'Will you give me a picture of the aeroplane, *sahib*?' an Indian *subadar* asked White when he landed from an early flight. 'Otherwise my relatives in India will not believe me when I tell them I have seen men fly.' After reflecting for a moment, he added, 'They should know better, for we have read how the same thing happened many thousands of years ago.'

Their local reception was not always marked by wonder and admiration, however. In some ways it was a precursor of what coalition forces would face some ninety years later in the Iraq War of the early twenty-first century: White was shot at from close range. One night a heavy beam was dropped on his head while he was trying to find a boatman to ferry him out to a supply ship. Small boys often passed their fingers menacingly across their throats as a warning of what the airmen faced.

Although attached temporarily to the Indian Army and merged into the Royal Flying Corps, with a mix of English, New Zealand and Indian flyers and aerial observers, Half Flight retained its Australian identity. They kept their own uniform, and always wore Australian shoulder badges.

If the heat and malaria were not bad enough, the ramshackle equipment was an even greater concern. As the journalist Fred Cutlack, official historian of the Australian Flying Corps during the war, wrote:

'The aeroplanes sent to Mesopotamia were quite unfitted for any sort of war service, least of all for war in such a climate. Their type was primitive. Machines were not provided in sufficient numbers; the supply base did not make proper allowance for casualties. Some machines were defective when they arrived, or were without necessary spare parts and instruments. Some were even second-hand. The engines were a constant source of trouble and anxiety.

'The machines were not fitted with machine-guns; there were none of the improved types to spare from the main fighting front in France. Such bombs as were dropped upon the enemy were, for a time, 2 lb infantry hand-bombs thrown out by hand; when 20 lb aeroplane bombs ultimately arrived, they were frequently found to have been damaged in transit. Bomb-racks supplied from England would not fit, and were unserviceable; these had to be repaired locally; and in some instances the only way in which the bombs could be dropped was through a hole cut in the floor of the cockpit.

'In general, the sole service to which these machines could be put was reconnaissance, and reconnaissance had to be performed in conditions of wind and heat such as no aeroplane designer had hitherto imagined.'

Inadequate or not, the rumpeties were readied just in time for the British push on Kurna, up the Tigris from Basra. Known as 'Townshend's regatta', after the British major-general who led the expedition, the men and supplies were floated upriver in more than 200 bellams, rowed by troops. In the bold move, Kurna was won and thousands of Turks captured.

This was the first military action involving the fledgling Australian Flying Corps, and Cutlack records that the aircraft 'caused consternation amongst the enemy on the river during the retreat'. Captain Petre made Half Flight's first reconnaissance on 31 May with Lieutenant W. Burn of New Zealand as his observer, returning with valuable intelligence on enemy movements.

But it was White's flight on June 2 with Major H. C. Reilly, a New Zealander who had transferred from the Indian Army to the RAF, that may be regarded as the first airborne military action by an Australian-born and -trained pilot. Their Shorthorn battled the dust-laden *shamal* for two hours before reaching Kurna, sixty miles from take-off. Through binoculars they observed the Turks in panicked retreat. Swooping low over paddle-steamers lined with Turkish troops they dropped several bombs, all of which missed their targets. They were later informed, however, that one steamer, thinking this a warning shot, pulled into the river bank to quietly surrender to a British ship that arrived subsequently.

Over the British flagship, HMS *Espiegle*, they dropped a message to Major-General Townshend, encased in a film tin with streamers attached. It revealed the extent of the Turkish retreat and gave him the location of the nearest enemy ships. The *Espiegle* soon caught and sank the Turkish gunboat *Marmaress*, and the town of Amara was taken the following day.

A lengthy report of White's day, in which he laid claim to being the first Australian in action, appeared in some Australian newspapers in June 1915, courtesy of a letter he had sent to his parents. Quite a few of White's letters home found their way into newspapers or *The Bulletin*. White wrote that after the action he went on board the *Espiegle* when it sailed to a captured Turkish position. Here Tommies and Indian troops rifled the stores left behind. 'There were tons of goods, but the day was so hot we couldn't be bothered carrying them away,' he wrote. 'I secured a water bottle, belt, ammunition, and some shell parts, also a document, which, I think, is a Turkish officer's commission, which I will have translated.'

White, who was adjutant of Half Flight as well as pilot, finished a long letter to his parents with a few comments about local conditions. 'I am pretty comfortable here, and have three clerks in my office, as well as two quartermaster-sergeants and their assistants. I only wish, though, that I knew when the campaign will end. We are at present about half-way to Baghdad, and meeting with little opposition.' The men were driven to distraction by the 'terrible' mosquitoes. 'As I write the table is absolutely covered with hundreds of mosquitoes. They were around the light, and I had some Keating's powder, which I sprinkled over them. The noise they made when flying around was just like the wind whistling loudly.'

As the campaign moved up the Tigris, and then the parallel Eurphrates, Half Flight moved up with the army, the aircraft sometimes loaded onto barges and shipped up to the new front. In Basra the heat was so intense that manual work was possible only in the early morning, late afternoon and night. The average temperature at the 'aircraft park' was 105 degrees Fahrenheit (40 degrees Celsius) in the shade.

Other aircraft began to arrive, including two Caudrons, four Martinsydes and four BE2c's. The troublesome 80-horsepower rotary engines in the Caudrons performed patchily in the desert dust, and would be the cause of their first casualties. White described these aircraft as 'mere toys more suitable for a flying school than for active service'.

The British turned their attention to the Euphrates for an attack on Nasiriyah. The two Caudrons were ordered up for reconnaissance, with Reilly and Treloar in one, Merz and the New Zealander Burn in the other. White reported that the engines 'behaved themselves' in the Nasiriyah fighting, but both aircraft came to grief on the return flight to Basra.

The pilots, Reilly and Merz, had agreed to keep each other in sight, but somehow they lost contact, and both were forced down through engine failure. Reilly fortunately landed near a camp of Arabs who had heard of the recent British victories and were impressed enough to be friendly. This was the real danger for the airmen — landing not among the Turks, but near one of the marauding local tribes.

Merz and Burn suffered just this fate. Their aircraft, like all those in service in Mesopotamia, had no machine gun, so they had no more than their pistols to defend themselves when attacked while frantically trying to repair the aircraft. They then fought a running battle for about five miles as they tried to reach friendly lines, killing one assailant and wounding five others. When one of the airmen was wounded his companion stood with him, and both died fighting. Their attackers then hacked the plane to matchwood, leaving only the engine in the desert. Such was the story told later by friendlier local Arabs.

White led a punitive expedition to a village where the murderers were believed to be hiding. No trace was found, but the houses of the local sheikh were burned in vengeance. White was devastated by the deaths, especially of Merz, his friend from flying school and a brilliant doctor who had worked only the night before in the sweltering, understaffed Nasiriyah hospital.

Merz was the first Australian Flying Corps casualty. 'In the rush mess hut at Basra we missed them sadly, and each wondered if when his own turn came he would die as nobly,' wrote White.

New misfortunes followed. As Townshend prepared for an attack on Kut after securing Amara on the Tigris, the Australian Treloar was also forced down behind enemy lines in a Caudron, accompanied by Captain B. S. Atkins of the Indian Army as observer. Roughed up by local tribesmen, they were taken prisoner by Turks and shipped off to Baghdad. White and Petre were ordered up with all available machines to the new front.

Floating their aircraft up the Tigris on barges one night, White's mechanics began singing 'Australia will be there', their voices floating across the water in the darkness. From the shore, British tommies called out, 'What regiment are you?'

'Australian Light Horse,' shouted back one of the mechanics, a typical Australian humourist.

'How many are you?' came back from the shore.

'About two thousand,' the mechanic fibbed, to cheers from the shore.

'Strangely enough, this simple leg-pull regarding the arrival of Australian cavalry, but much exaggerated, was noised throughout the army, and even appeared in the enemy press,' said White. 'How we wished that the Light Horse then being sacrificed as infantry on Gallipoli were with us!'

Townshend's brilliant victory at Kut lifted morale. Facing a stronger enemy across the river he made a feint cavalry attack from the right bank to persuade the enemy that this would be the focus of the main attack. The Turks duly moved troops across from strong positions, but during the night Townshend ferried almost the entire force back across the river, dispatching them in a wide encircling movement to attack the enemy's flank. The Turkish left flank was rolled up, and by the next evening the remnants of their army had fled.

White, meanwhile, was enjoying his own luck. The men had devised an accurate mapping device. It looked like a small garden rake with pegs along the handle. Holding the device to his forehead and focusing on a known object on the ground, an airman could accurately measure distances to enemy positions by moving his eye along the pegs. With his new observer, Captain Francis Yeats-Brown of the 17th Indian Cavalry (the famous Bengal Lancers), White was bringing back valuable information pinpointing Turkish positions.

It was hazardous work. Once, when he and Yeats-Brown were ordered to map enemy artillery positions near Ctesiphon, White floated his aeroplane towards earth as if it had been shot down, while his observer took measurements using the façade of the old Persian Palace of Chosroes as a marker. By the time Turkish gunners realised the deception they were off, climbing back into the sky.

The monocled, lisping Yeats-Brown was a genuine English eccentric. Born in Genoa, the son of a British diplomat, he grew up in India, where he developed a love for yoga and meditation. Colleagues in Mesopotamia called him 'the mahatma' owing to the hours he spent in contemplation, eyes fixed on his navel, or standing upside down holding his breath and chanting 'om'. He reputedly walked with fingers separated and extended so earth currents might flow through them more freely. Of slight, almost frail build and fair hair, Yeats-Brown had almost feminine good looks, with a very clear complexion, blue eyes and a pronounced aquiline nose. Cheerful, cultured and always immaculately dressed, he had a penchant for theatricality and the latest clothing fads. 'He combined the mental make-up of a philosophical dilettante with that of a very gallant gentleman,' said White. 'A monocle and a lisp gained him a good deal of banter, which he accepted so good-humouredly that his friends declared it essential to his manner.'

Yeats-Brown brought three polo ponies with him to Mesopotamia, which were later eaten by starving troops during the siege of Kut. He loved invention, once dropping a bomb from the plane with a parachute attached. His idea was that if it floated around for a while it would alarm the enemy.

With a colourful writing style, after the war Yeats-Brown became associate editor of *The Spectator* and wrote the novel *The Lives of a Bengal Lancer*, later made into an Oscar-winning film starring Gary Cooper. He was famous for epigrams such as 'sit loose in the saddle of fate', but his reputation suffered later in life when he swung to the political right, supporting fascist causes.

One episode with White certainly had Yeats-Brown loose in the saddle. On their return home from a mission over Ctesiphon one day, the engine on their Maurice Farman began to sputter. White put it into a dive, hoping the engine would pick up. It did. But just as White passed Yeats-Brown a 'praise-be-to-Allah' note it faltered again, forcing them to glide down to earth — unfortunately near mounted Turks.

'As the engine was still running feebly, I decided not to attempt repairs so close to the enemy, but to taxi until the engine stopped,' said White. 'The wind having given us a good start, Y-B stood up in the observer's seat armed with a rifle, on the alert for pursuers, and to keep a look-out for bad ground. As we drew away . . . he declared that the cloud of dust behind us was caused by pursuing cavalry. We hoped there were no racehorses among them.

'The ground over which we taxied was broken by old canals and rough patches of cracked earth where swamps had dried up in the tropical heat, and in places camel thorn grew thickly. By careful ruddering around the worst patches, and with occasional spurts of speed from the erratically running engine, the aeroplane rolled and bumped along at a rate that would not have disgraced many a motor car.'

The Turks at the cavalry encampment of Kutanich, into which White had occasionally dropped bombs when passing, must have watched with amazement the approach of the taxiing aircraft, with Yeats-Brown standing in his seat waving a rifle. Spying a narrow road at one side of the Kutanich ridge, White angled towards it.

'Opening the throttle to the full and hoping that the road was not closed by barbed wire or broken by a trench, or that the enemy were already waiting for us, we scurried along at our best pace and were soon safely on the other side, the Turks having evidently been too slow to seize the opportunity to send a party out to cut us off.'

The next camp, Aziziyeh, was home. Just as they approached it the engine righted itself, possibly from the jolting it had taken. White took off and flew into camp. They had taxied, just ahead of their pursuers, for an incredible 15 miles.

White's luck held through two further close calls. As Merz's death showed, the main danger for airmen was falling into the hands of the marsh Arab and Bedouin tribes now camped between the major antagonists, looking to take predatory advantage from the conflict. 'True sons of Ishmael — "their hand against every man"— these treacherous marauders hovered around the camps like jackals and spared neither Britisher, Indian nor hapless Turk who fell into their hands,' wrote White.

At camp in Aziziyeh the British liaison with the Arab tribes was Colonel Leachman, inscrutable to the airmen in his daily wanderings, although for White a man who demonstrated exceptional courage. But for his death at the hands of Arabs in 1920 White believed he might have rivalled the exploits of Lawrence of Arabia. One day Leachman poked his head into the airmen's tent, saying, 'I can't do anything with the tribe here,' indicating a spot on the map. 'They are hostile and are the people who are sniping our ships. I wonder if you could bomb them for me?'

At the end of the subsequent bombing mission, White decided to make one last run, but on this occasion his bomb carrier failed, with a bomb still lodged in the wire. Then his engine failed. Gliding down he saw only threatening-looking Arab camps. Then, at the last minute, a British outpost came into view. White landed directly in front of their trenches, only a few yards from the barbed wire. After hasty repairs he organised some Indian sepoys to hold the machine back so he could get up the revs for a short take-off.

Back at camp Leachman sent the airmen his congratulations. 'They have sent in their submission,' he said of the Arabs. 'One bomb went into the centre of the sheik's tent!' The airmen, said White, were as surprised as the sheik.

As the British forces prepared for their next push up the Tigris to Ctesiphon and then Baghdad, White was instructed to mount a rescue mission for a seaplane carrying the Chief of the General Staff in Mesopotamia, Major General C. V. Kemball, which was missing. He spotted the aircraft aground on a spit of sand in the Tigris, and saw Kemball and the pilot waving at him, but it was close to an Arab camp, and White feared he might already be too late.

Arab horsemen began shooting at him, one bullet piercing his propeller. White put the plane down on a narrow track in the sandhills about a thousand yards from the river. He pulled the aircraft around for a quick take-off and clambered out. Catching sight of a mounted party approaching he decided to try to bluff them. He began gesticulating wildly at the machine.

'I imagined that no Arab could conceive that a propeller could go on revolving with nobody to twirl it, so I acted a pantomime of walking away from the machine, pointing to the Arabs as if giving directions to somebody in the cockpit to keep an eye on them, and gazed at them through looped fingers as if regarding them through field glasses,' he said.

It worked. The Arabs held off. White set out for the riverbank, armed with two rifles. Men, women and children in an Arab camp peered at him as he ran to the stranded seaplane but did not try to stop him. Reaching the aircraft, he handed Major General Kemball a rifle and led the two back to his aircraft.

On return they found the plane surrounded not by the tribesmen but by a search party of Indian troops. The Arabs, said White, had 'hesitated to attack, no doubt fearing the phantom that had twirled the propeller'. The pilot of the seaplane stayed with the troops to salvage his own aircraft while White flew Kemball back to camp.

While White was lucky in most of his Mesopotamian escapades through 1915 — despite five engine failures in one month alone — another factor worked in his favour. The Turks had no flying corps, which gave the British freedom of the skies. 'One moderately modern aeroplane armed with a machine gun would have had little difficulty in disposing of the whole of the British air force,' said White.

As the big assault on Baghdad loomed, however, White's luck was about to run out.

3

'Rescued' by the Turks

Everyone was too polite to call it a suicide mission. Yet that is what it meant.

With likely headwinds, the mission was beyond the flight tank range of the Maurice Farman Longhorn, so extra fuel would need to be carried, and then pumped into the aircraft after a landing behind enemy lines. The aircraft carried no machine gun, and the two-man crew would have to rely on rifles if attacked. In recognition of the likely danger, volunteers were called for.

The mission — to cut Turkish telegraph lines west and north of Baghdad — was clearly important enough that the military command were willing to risk the loss of an aircraft and two crew. The plan was to isolate Baghdad so that the besieged Turks could not call for reinforcements when the British attacked. General Townshend's army had rolled up all before it and now, at Aziziyeh, stood at the gates of Baghdad. Rumour among the flight crews was that Townshend had advised against an advance on the capital but had been overruled.

The rumour was right. Townshend advised his superior, General Sir John Nixon, that although Baghdad was only some thirty miles away an attack with only one division was too risky. Better to consolidate at Kut, he cautioned. Nixon brushed these reservations aside, ordering Townshend to 'smash the Turk' at Ctesiphon and take Baghdad.

The strategic stakes were high. The original mission to protect British oil interests had expanded with Townshend's advance to the control of all of southern Mesopotamia. The timing was also crucial. After months of savage fighting and severe losses, the Allied force on Gallipoli was still bogged down in a small coastal enclave. It now faced an embarrassing withdrawal. Could the Anglo-Indian Mesopotamian force now give the Turks a bloody nose at the other end of their empire?

The Raj in India, backed by the War Committee in London, urged an advance on Baghdad. A combination of factors was at play. Restoring British prestige in the Muslim world was one. The Raj was also anxious to counter both German intrigues against India in Persia and Afghanistan, and Russian advances into the Middle East. General Nixon was given approval to advance, with two divisions of reinforcements from France promised later.

White and the other pilots had been hearing rumours of 'special stunt' missions as a prelude to the Baghdad advance. Low-altitude bombing of bridges and destruction of railway lines were mooted as possible tasks for the Flying Corps. When news filtered down that volunteers were required for an attack on the telegraph system deep behind enemy lines, White and Yeats-Brown conferred. Both were unmarried, and their Maurice Farman engine had been running well recently. They felt they had no reasonable excuse not to step forward.

'Yeats-Brown asked me if I thought we could do the feat, and as I thought so, because I could land in a small space, we volunteered for the job,' White wrote in his diaries. Both were apprehensive, however. 'We undeniably saw the possibility of two perfectly healthy officers and one antiquated aeroplane "going west" — for landing behind the enemy's lines for demolition work could hardly be called a before-breakfast constitutional, nor was it fashionable even during the latter stages of the war, when aeroplanes were faster and carried machine guns,' noted White.

The mission was almost certainly prompted by Townshend's worry that the Turks would fight tenaciously to hold Baghdad and call in reinforcements. It would certainly be dangerous, however. Major General Kemball, whom White had rescued when his plane ditched near the Tigris, told him later that the entire mission, with two landings, was a 'mistake'.

The main target, the western line from Baghdad through to Fallujah, was believed to carry six telegraph lines. Their fellow pilots were full of bright ideas on how to destroy it. Why not fly into the wires and break them, suggested one. What about tearing them down with a grappling line dragged behind the plane, suggested another. Very funny, indeed.

British telegraph officers told the pilots that the wires were too tough to be cut with wire cutters. A time bomb might have been the best solution, but none was available. Eventually it was decided that Yeats-Brown, as observer, would carry prepared explosives in the form of necklaces of guncotton. While White refuelled the aircraft, Yeats-Brown would shimmy up the nearest telegraph poles and blow up the wires. After destroying the western telegraph wires they would repeat the job north of Baghdad.

It sounded simple, but the logistics were daunting. It was at least sixty miles to the first point of attack, yet the lumbering Maurice Farmans had a range of only three hours' flight at about sixty miles an hour. As there was a strong possibility of headwinds slowing the aircraft, ground refuelling would be essential.

On the eve of the mission White and Yeats-Brown worked late. Army sappers equipped Yeats-Brown with the guncotton necklaces, assuring him they were 'sure uprooters of telegraph posts'. White stripped the plane of its bomb carrier and all superfluous weight to make way for extra fuel tins. After checking maps and rifles, his last tasks were to tell the CO how to dispose of his effects should he fail to return, and to scribble a note home to his brother Percy.

'Dear Perc [he wrote],

'Just a few lines in case anything should happen to me tomorrow. I have been detailed for a somewhat difficult risky task. With Capt. Yeats-Brown, my observer, I have to go beyond Baghdad to cut the two telegraph wires, which several miles apart run from

Baghdad to Constantinople. It is a long flight, and I will have to land in two different places to get off again. I have to carry extra tins of petrol and oil, and fill up as soon as I land.

'Yeats-Brown has the explosives and he will blow down some posts and short circuit the lines.

'The Turks have 13,000 troops in their various positions, but the real danger is from Arabs.

'Tomorrow is Friday the 13th. I have just been out on the aerodrome and tried the engine and find it alright. I am a bit superstitious, but really think that we will be successful.

'Should I not return, I have told Petre to sell up my clothing and send everything else home. I have about 2,000 rupees in Cox's Bank, which mother could apply for under my will.

'The idea of our trip is to cut off all communications with Constantinople while we attack the Turks at Ctesiphon and drive them back and take Baghdad.

'Well, Perc, hoping that I will be writing to you again in a few days, I will bid you "good-night" for I am leaving before dawn.

'Yours, Tom.'

Mechanics wheeled the Maurice Farman onto the airfield beside the Tigris River before dawn on the thirteenth. Yeats-Brown stowed the guncotton necklaces, wire cutters, a rifle, Very lights, provisions and the specially prepared map and then climbed gingerly aboard, feeling, as he said, 'highly charged with explosives and excitement'.

'Contact,' called Jimmy the mechanic after he had doped the engine with petrol and spun the propeller in the darkness.

'Contact,' responded White as the engine kicked in.

Half a dozen sepoys held the plane down to stop it tearing away as White throttled up to warm the engine. After a few seconds at full power to check that the revs were up, White adjusted his goggles and gave a hand signal, and the sepoys jumped clear. The plane trundled down the runway in a cloud of dust, its exhaust gases lighting up the darkness behind it in a ring if fire. The first rays of light were creeping over the horizon.

Yeats-Brown remembered feeling a chill of trepidation on take-off. In his pockets were the highly explosive pencils of fulminate of mercury to detonate the guncotton. 'The warmer the engine became, the colder I got, for the prelude to adventure is always a chilly business,' he would recall.

The heavy-laden plane rose slowly above the tent camp of the British army at Aziziyeh, all 'silver and still in the half light', as Yeats-Brown described it. Without waiting to gain altitude, White set the plane straight on course to economise on fuel, crossing to the right bank of the Tigris in the hope of avoiding being sighted by Turkish advance posts that might telegraph the plane's approach to their rear gunners. Below them on the Tigris they saw a double-decked paddle-steamer approaching the British camp from the south. The first ship to reach Aziziyeh in a fortnight, it would be carrying letters from home that both hoped would be waiting for them on their return — if they returned.

White and Yeats-Brown were in no doubt of the urgency of their mission. 'At all costs, we had been told, the telegraphic communications west and north of Baghdad must be cut that day,' recalled Yeats-Brown. 'Von der Goltz [the German commander] and a German battery of quick-firing guns were hasting [sic] down from Mosul to help their stricken ally, and reinforcements of the best Anatolian troops, magnificently equipped and organised by the Germans, were on their way from Gallipoli, whence they came flushed with the confidence of success.

'Our attack . . . was imminent. It was a matter of moments whether the Turkish reinforcements would arrive in time. Delay and confusion in the Turkish rear would help us greatly, and the moral and material advantage of cutting communications between Nur-ed-Din, the vacillating commander-in-chief defending Baghdad, and Von der Goltz, the veteran of victories, was obvious and unquestionable. But could we do it in an old Maurice Farman biplane?'

Could they indeed? They carried specially drawn maps — prepared for the eventuality of their falling into Turkish hands — tracing nothing more than the routes to the telegraph lines. They had also selected what appeared to be a blank piece of desert, two miles from the road between Baghdad and Fallujah, for their first landing and demolition job. 'That the map was wrong we did not know,' wrote Yeats-Brown.

At first everything went well. White piloted the biplane around the strongly fortified position of Seleucia, where a week earlier he and Yeats-Brown had hand-dropped half a dozen bombs on a Turkish steamer zigzagging its way along the Tigris. They did not sink it, but they managed to land a few bombs among disembarking Turkish cavalry nearby.

The two men indulged their classical and literary souls as they witnessed the beauty of the country below, now captured by the early sunlight. The dawn appeared bright with hope, restoring Yeats-Brown's mood to the extent that he began to sing from sheer exhilaration. 'The desert seemed barren no longer,' he wrote later. 'Transmuted by the sunrise those "miles and miles of nothing at all" became a limitless expanse where all the kingdoms of the world were spread out before our eyes.' The Tigris snaked its way to the east. In the west Yeats-Brown made out the occasional gleam from the gold domes of Khazimain, a city out of *The Arabian Nights*. White was momentarily entranced by the newly built redoubts and trenches that scarred the mounds of what was once the famous Greek republic of Seleucia, a relic of Alexander's day immortalised by its struggles with the Parthians.

The war quickly snapped them back to reality. As observer, Yeats-Brown felt his duty weighing heavily. The activity below was disquieting. Trains of carts were moving supplies across the Tigris. Feverish work was in progress on trenches and gun emplacements. 'Like ants in a burrow, men were dragging overhead cover into place,' he recorded. 'New support trenches were being built.' Occasionally, drivers of Turkish supply wagons would stop and shoot at the passing aircraft.

Yeats-Brown longed to be able to communicate this new information back to British lines. 'Our men would soon attack these trenches, relying largely on our photographs and information ...

When, a week later, there rose above the battle the souls of all the brave men dead at Ctesiphon, seeing then with clearer eyes than mine, I pray they forgave our shortcomings and remembered we did our best.'

Meanwhile they were driven on by the priority of their mission and the ominous flicker of their lowering fuel gauge, promising themselves a closer investigation of these Turkish reinforcements on the return flight.

Soon they caught sight of Baghdad, the object of the coming British attack. After the barrenness of the various military camps they had experienced in recent fighting up the Tigris it appeared, said White, like a wonderful city of enchantment. 'Seen from the air on this early November morn, with the sun gleaming on the gold cupolas and minarets of the mosques of Khazimain, with date plantations fringing the silver waters of the Tigris into hazy infinity, the historic city of the Caliphs appeared indescribably beautiful and fantastic as a dream city.'

There was little time for daydreaming. Swinging west of the city they caught sight of the real object of their dreams — the telegraph line. Sure enough, it was strung out not far from an unpaved road, but that road was not along some 'blank piece of desert', as expected. Even at this time of the morning it was swarming with troops marching towards the city, mingled with Arab cameleers heading for the Baghdad marketplace.

'We came low to observe better, and the camels craned their long necks upwards, burbling with surprise at this great new bird they had never seen,' said Yeats-Brown. 'The ships of the desert, it seemed to me, disliked the ship of the air as much as we disapproved of them.'

Clearly landing would be impossible here. Although the demolition was expected to take only a few minutes, 'even an Arab soldier can be trusted to hit an aeroplane and two airmen at point-blank range,' said Yeats-Brown, with the easy contempt for the Arab that was typical of the era. White followed the road westward, hoping to find another, more isolated landing place. More columns of cavalry, infantry and transports passed underneath. He contemplated returning to relay the information in case British intelligence was unaware of this stream of reinforcements. But they were determined to fulfil their mission. In any case, by now they had to land somewhere to refuel.

At last, about eight miles from the city, they spotted what appeared to be a barren patch of land where the telegraph line strayed from the road by some two hundred yards. It was a rectangular plot of recently cultivated land bounded by a canal on two sides and roads on the other two. Yeats-Brown later claimed that nearby mounds marked Nimrod's tomb, but classical scholars place the tomb of Nimrod, the legendary hunter warrior and a great-grandson of Noah, near Damascus.

Nimrod's or not, it was certainly to prove a tomb for White and Yeats-Brown's ambitions.

Passing notes to each other, they decided to land. Because of the narrowness of the ground, with mounds on each side near the road, it was impossible to land parallel to the wires. Coming in over a road White noticed a brightly uniformed Turkish horseman gazing up at the plane, and in the distance what appeared a disused building. 'His presence was disconcerting to say the least, as it indicated the possibility of others,' said White. 'Y-B was seated behind me arranging his guncotton charges, so stretching out a hand I jerked at his leg and pointed the man out.' But it was too late to reconsider as the plane landed only a second or two later.

The fates were to desert them from the moment of touchdown. A ground breeze had sprung up, blowing behind the aircraft and sweeping it along faster than White had anticipated towards the wires. The speed of the landing had cut White's room to turn as he approached the telegraph line. He faced the alternative of either running into the wires, certainly smashing up the front of the plane, or by a quick turn risk crashing into the canal. Choosing the latter option, White was beaten by the tail wind. As he turned, the lower left wing struck one of the telegraph posts, smashing the leading edge and a main strut.

White cursed the wind, and Yeats-Brown silently cursed White. But he knew this was no time for such indulgence, and donning sandshoes and the guncotton necklace he dropped to the ground and ran across to the nearest telegraph pole.

'With leaden heart, but light feet, I ran across to another telegraph post, leaving the pilot to ascertain whether by some miracle we might be able to bring the old 'bus to safety,' Yeats-Brown recalled. 'But even as I left him, I knew that there was no hope; the only thing that remained was to destroy the telegraph line and take our chances with the Arabs.'

Tying a necklace of guncotton around the pole, Yeats-Brown inserted a detonator, and then forced into the detonator one of the pencils of fulminate of mercury, to which a powder fuse was attached. Lighting the fuse he retreated a few yards as it sizzled. 'Looking around I saw that horsemen were galloping towards us from the four quarters of the desert.' They would be too late. Seconds later, after the first explosion, the post toppled over onto the sand.

Meanwhile, White faced a dilemma — shoot at the approaching horsemen, or try to repair the aircraft? They were still about 300 yards away but had already begun shooting as White jumped down to inspect the damage. Bullets kicked up the dust near his feet. 'Then the ground seemed literally to spawn Arabs,' he said. 'On both sides of us and on the road we could see them running towards us and hear them calling to each other, while the cavalryman [the rider they had spotted from the air] ... set off at full gallop down the road.'

A hasty inspection revealed extensive damage to the plane. The two outer struts that held the left wing together were hanging in the air. The ground was too rough to taxi across, and unless the wires could be temporarily tied down to the chassis, the plane could not be flown. But the advancing Arabs presented a more immediate threat. White clambered into the observer's seat and, kneeling down, took aim with the rifle and fired at the nearest man.

'He jumped and dropped beside the canal, though I do not think he was hit,' wrote White. Others had now reached the canal and began shooting at the crippled plane from the cover of mounds of sand. White got off a few more shots before deciding he should refill the fuel tanks. 'Bullets zipped past uncomfortably close, kicked up dust beneath, or whizzed through the machine.'

Suddenly the explosion of Yeats-Brown's first charge boomed out, bringing a telegraph pole to the ground in a cloud of dust and temporarily checking the advance of their attackers. Some horsemen even took fright and galloped off. When Yeats-Brown returned to the plane for a second charge he found White standing in the observer's seat 'treating' the Arabs to several bursts of fire 'to encourage the belief in our aggressive force'.

While White provided covering fire, Yeats-Brown raced to another telegraph pole. Bullets thudded into the sand around him as he fixed the demolition charge to the wires and insulators. 'The fire had increased in accuracy and intensity,' he recorded. 'So accurate indeed had it become that I guessed that the Arabs (who cannot hit a haystack) had been reinforced by regulars.'

Running back to the plane again, Yeats-Brown found that 'hot fire' was now being directed at the aircraft from ranges of between fifty and five hundred yards. White briefed him on their parlous position, and they decided to taxi away as far as possible in the hope of putting up another stand. White climbed into the machine, and, miraculously, the engine 'bit' on Yeats-Brown's first swing of the propeller. White throttled up as his co-pilot clambered aboard. The sight of the two airmen attempting to escape emboldened their attackers. Some now climbed out from behind their cover and started to charge the aircraft, while others increased their rate of fire.

Crack! The second charge exploded, scattering shards of insulator in all directions. Telegraph wires whipped through the air before wrapping themselves around the plane.

'Only then did I realise our utter hopelessness, with an unflyable plane, sixty miles from camp in enemy territory and on a piece of ground so circumscribed that we could not taxi away,' White later wrote. The second blast had again checked the enemy advance, but only momentarily.

'Do you see that fellow in blue?' asked White, pointing out a ferocious-looking individual brandishing a curved cutlass. 'I think he must be an officer. We had better give ourselves up to him when the time comes.'

White evidently believed that time was close. Leaving the engine running he stepped down from the plane. They were under orders that if taken they were not to destroy the aircraft, as the British expected that their own advance in a few days would enable its recapture.

Yeats-Brown, however, now had a rush of blood to the head and determined to try once more to fly the plane. 'I am not a pilot, and knew little of machines,' he conceded. 'But I was pig-headed and determined to have one more flip in the old 'bus. After disentangling the wires that had ripped round the king posts, I got into the pilot's seat and taxied away down wind.'

The situation was desperate. Yeats-Brown managed to swing the aircraft around as he taxied. But all his efforts could not get the plane to lift off the ground. Meanwhile a group of newly arrived mounted Turkish gendarmes began to chase the plane as the Arab irregulars descended on the lonely White. Yeats-Brown tried to swerve to avoid the galloping horsemen, but the crippled aircraft refused to respond to the controls. 'Then I pulled the stick back frantically in a last effort to rise above them,' he recalled. 'She gave a little hop, then floundered down in the middle of the cavalry.' Yeats-Brown was thrown clear.

By now White was surrounded by a hostile mob. 'The first man to approach me was a hideous black Arab with shaggy hair, who was stark naked but for two broad bandoliers of cartridges across his chest,' he recalled. 'He covered me from about ten yards with a large bore rifle that would have slain an elephant, and hardly expecting to be taken prisoner I put my hand in my jacket for my revolver to shoot him.'

Luckily for White, his adversary was distracted by the flailing aircraft and he took off towards it, perhaps in the hope of richer pickings. But now other tribesmen yelling '*Ingrazzi*' (English) quickly descended on him with clubbed rifles. White tried to duck, but a blow from a rifle caught him on the head, knocking off his pith helmet. Another whacked him with the petrol can that White had just discarded, while yet another struck him a stunning blow on the head with an adze-like chisel. The blow inflicted a three-inch cut, spraying blood over White's face and clothes, but it must have been blunt as it also raised an enormous lump on his head. Thankful that his hard head had saved him from being felled by the blow, White began wrestling with his attackers, who now appeared to be trying to strip off his clothes.

Meanwhile Yeats-Brown found himself surrounded by mounted Turkish gendarmes alongside the stricken plane. Surprisingly, the gendarmes levelled their rifles not at the co-pilot but at the plane. Yeats-Brown hesitated, holding his revolver behind his back and cocking it. One of the gendarmes, an older man, spurred his horse up to the crouching airman and held out his right hand in a friendly fashion. 'I grasped it in surprise, for the grip he gave me was a grip I knew, proving that even here in the desert men are sometimes brothers.' Yeats-Brown emptied the cartridges from his revolver and handed it to the gendarme. 'Not very heroic certainly — but then surrendering is a sorry business: the best that can be said for it is that it is sometimes common sense.'

Just as Yeats-Brown surrendered his revolver, 'the gentleman in blue', who White had previously taken to be a Turkish officer, appeared and, wielding his scimitar with both hands, struck him across the shoulderblade. The blow stunned Yeats-Brown, depriving him of all feeling. On recovering he found that his attacker was not a Turk at all, but an Arab smeared in some kind of paint. Whether he had purposely used the flat of the weapon or the sympathetic gendarme had deflected the blow, Yeats-Brown would never know. 'But of this much I am certain, that except for that kindly gendarme — to whom may Allah bring blessings — this story would not have been written,' he later wrote in his colourful 1919 account *Caught by the Turks*.

His captors soon tore off Yeats-Brown's uniform, stripping him down to shirt and shorts (miraculously he retained his monocle, then fixed in his eye — in fact, he kept it throughout his later imprisonment), while the kindly Turkish gendarme looked on with an air of resignation. Hustled back towards White, he found his pilot, bleeding profusely from a head wound, in the middle of a scrum of a hundred murderous, screaming tribesmen. 'I had a glimpse of the pilot, who is a very clever boxer, upholding British traditions with his fists . . .'

White would later speculate that he was receiving special attention on account of his shooting back at his assailants. His rubber-necked flying coat may also have given him the appearance of a soldier. The coat was evidently a prize worth fighting for, and White suffered more blows to the head and back as they tried to pull it over his head.

Yeats-Brown thought they were both about to be executed, the fate of Lieutenants Merz and Burn a few months earlier in a similar situation. He bitterly regretted having handed over his revolver. 'The memory of that moment is the most unpleasant in my life, and I cannot, try as I will, entirely dissociate myself from the horror of what I thought would happen.'

But the airmen quickly realised that they were now the object of a tug-of-war between the Turkish gendarmes and the Arabs. Suddenly, as Yeats-Brown noted, the scene had changed from prospective tragedy to farce. It seemed they were not going to be murdered — merely robbed. Binoculars and contents of pockets had already quickly disappeared.

'The Arabs were utter savages in different stages of nudity and variously armed, while the Turks, who were uniformed and well equipped, appeared to be a smart detachment of gendarmerie,' said White. 'Although in the minority, the Turks seemed desirous of taking us prisoners, and assuredly without them we would have received small mercy from the Arabs.'

The Turks appeared to be as afraid of the Arabs as the airmen were. What they had taken from the air to be a disused building was actually a small Turkish gendarmerie post, and amid much jostling the Turks tried to lead, or rather drag, the two men towards it. But the Arabs were not keen on surrendering their prizes. They ringed the party, dancing wildly and firing shots into the air. Heated disputes broke out between the tribesmen and the gendarmes. Several times the Arabs succeeded in dragging the airmen away, striking and spitting on them.

One party of Arabs broke away to attack the aircraft, firing repeatedly into the fuselage. Yeats-Brown, worried that the plane would be damaged beyond repair, tried to convey to the gendarmes the pointlessness of this activity, with the crew already captured. He succeeded only in giving the impression that a third airman remained on board, and a large party set off to investigate. The melee shifted this way and that. At one point Yeats-Brown tried to jump on a white mare whose Arab owner had momentarily released her. As he grabbed the reins and made to mount, the Arab whacked the horse on the spine, bringing the flyer to his knees. Once again, the old gendarme came to his aid. Addressing Yeats-Brown as 'Baba', he offered him a cigarette.

The tug-of-war continued, but the gendarmes finally managed to drag them to the building, locking out the shouting Arabs as they rushed the airmen through the gates. 'As the heavy doors were slammed on the howling throng we realised we were no longer free men,' White recalled. For his part, Yeats-Brown felt like he had been in a rugby scrum — with him as the ball. The gendarme at his side noticed his wristwatch and detached it with a meaningful smile. 'As the price of police protection I did not grudge it,' quipped Yeats-Brown. Pilfering was the least of their problems, however. A mob still surged at the gates, firing their guns into the air and setting off a deafening clamour. The Turks evidently feared the small outpost might be overpowered.

Asking what the Arabs wanted, the airmen were told their aim was to take the heads of the two captured airmen as trophies to the Turkish commander-in-chief in Baghdad. The gendarmes pointed out there would be far greater 'profit and pleasure' in taking them

Tommy White,
aged two, 1890

Moreland State School, 1898. Tommy, aged 10 (first left, front row)

Tommy, aged 13, as cadet bugler, Garrison Artillery, North Melbourne

The young army lieutenant

Mounted (right) and promoted to army captain

White (third from right) as army major

The great escapologist Harry Houdini's daring flying demonstrations in Australia in 1910 inspired Tom White to become a pilot.

Home of the Australian Flying Corps — a row of tents at Point Cook, 1914

One of Australia's first pilots, Flying Corps Captain T. W. White

After a less-than-perfect landing on one early flight, White hit the hangar.

White at the controls of the Bristol Boxkite, powered by a 50 hp Gnôme engine

A fragile Bleriot monoplane used in training at Point Cook

White at the controls of a BE2a, one of the first Air Corps planes

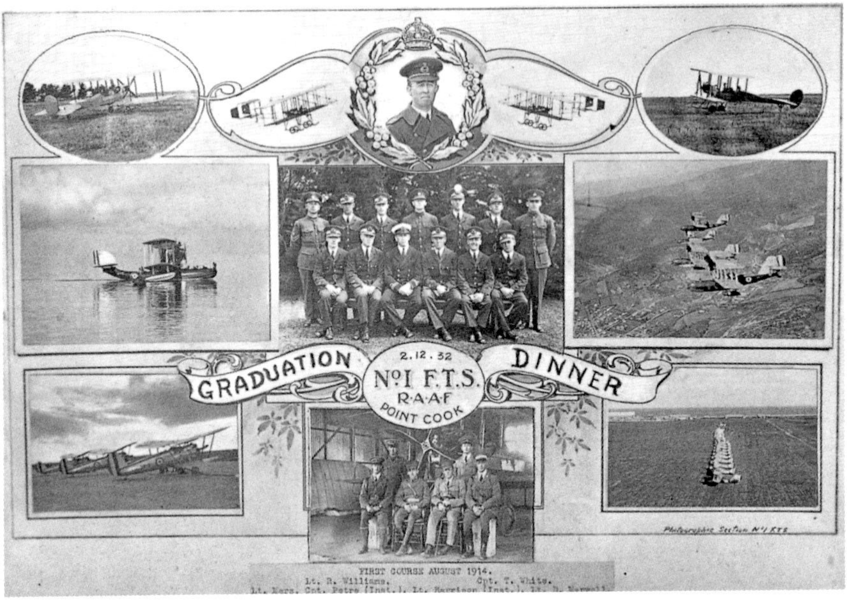

The postcard at centre bottom features the first Flying Corps pilot graduates. Back: Lt. Williams, Capt. White. Front: Lt. Merz, Capt. Petre (instructor), Lt. Harrison (instructor), Lt. Manwell.

Officers (White with cane, front right) and mechanics of the Australian Flying Corps, Point Cook, 1915

Half Flight, Point Cook, March 1915 (White in front row with cane; Lt. Merz on his right holds a kitten)

On the eve of war, the White family gather before Tom's departure.
Back: Tom, Charles Jnr and Percy. Front: Parents Emily and Charles, and Ada.

Half Flight in desert kit with topees, Bombay, May 1915 (White in front centre with cane).

there alive. 'We saved you from the Arabs,' Yeats-Brown understood them to be saying, 'and now you are safe until the war is over. You need do no more work.'

The airmen were escorted to a small room in the garrison, where their elderly benefactor offered them pomegranates and flaps of coarse bread from a saddlebag strung to the wall. They were too depressed to eat, and only later would learn from bitter experience never to refuse food. Meanwhile they reflected sadly on their fate. By now, thought Yeats-Brown, they should have been on their way home. Having reconnoitered the Turkish lines they would have been back for breakfast, bath and glory ... Instead they were beaten and captured, their aircraft wrecked in the desert. 'It's the thirteenth of the month,' groaned White.

Ever optimistic, Yeats-Brown believed their captivity would not last; they would surely fly again, but for a week or so they might have to accustom themselves to changed circumstances. He attempted to dress White's wounds, but with only brackish water and no bandages there was little he could do. Despite their gloom, the two discussed their options. Their best hope, they believed, was to be recaptured in Baghdad when the British took the city. They should make the most of their injuries so that they would not be forced to accompany the Turks in any retreat.

A Turkish colonel, or *Kaimakam*, the governor of the district, arrived to take charge of them. He noted their names, writing with a sharpened reed and drying the paper with sand. Speaking some French, he inquired if they had lost any valuables to the Arabs. They gave him a list, and after some of the Arabs who had been allowed to enter the garrison were searched, White's cigarette case was returned.

From the commandant they learned that news of their capture had been sent to Baghdad by gallopers, and their arrival was expected. By galloper, not by telegraph, Yeats-Brown noted to himself with pride. 'Whatever happens,' the commandant told them ominously, 'I myself will be responsible for your lives.' That might have sounded overdramatic, but when they were led out through the hostile mob at the gates to a waiting carriage it seemed only too apposite. White felt the crowd looked distinctly disappointed when it became apparent they would not be handed over.

Under an eight-man escort and with the commandant seated beside them, the carriage set off for Baghdad. White and Yeats-Brown were relieved to see the last of the Arabs, and felt the Turks were of the same view. In this area, they were told, the tribes respected no authority other than their own tribal sheikhs. Their sense of relief was short-lived, however. Three miles on, a lone Arab horseman rode up threateningly, causing great consternation among the guards. The horses were whipped to a gallop, and the reason quickly became obvious. Through the back flap of the wagon they glimpsed a line of horsemen strung out across the desert — in hot pursuit, firing their rifles into the air.

'They steadily gained upon us, firing as they galloped, or holding their rifles high in the air, until, overhauling us, they circled around till the carriage was brought to a standstill,' said White. It was like a scene from a Wild West film.

The sheikh glared in at the two airmen, White thought, as an animal eyed its prey, and summonsed the *Kaimakam* to descend from the wagon. As he stepped down, the colonel quietly asked the two airmen if they would fight. 'We readily agreed to do so, for we did not relish the possibility of falling into their hands again,' said White.

A long parley ensued, with much ostentatious gesturing by the Turkish guards. Some of them appeared to engage in mock combat with the Turks. White and Yeats-Brown learned later that the sheikh insisted that the two airmen were his prisoners, and must be handed over so he could take their heads to Baghdad for a reward from the Turks. Finally the colonel apparently struck a deal.

'Whether the *Kaimakam* promised that he would deliver the heads or pay the reward we were not able to ascertain, but accompanied by about twenty of the sheikh's cut-throats in addition to our guard we continued on our way,' said White.

With fortune again smiling on them, the two airmen, carrying their own heads, entered the fabled city of the caliphs.

4

Desert revenge

Baghdad, its gold cupolas and minarets shimmering in the morning sunlight, may have seemed like an eastern fantasy from the air, but from the ground White and Yeats-Brown found it less inviting. Indeed their reception was positively hostile. Some of the sheikh's men had ridden ahead to spread the news of their capture. With British forces on the city's doorstep, the appearance of the two captives quickly drew a hostile street mob armed with sticks and stones. As the prisoners' wagon trundled through the narrow streets of the Arab quarter elderly men cursed, women ululated, youths flourished knives and children threw mud and stones.

'No hated Tarquins could have received a more hostile reception,' said Yeats-Brown. 'We were both spat upon. A man with a heavy cudgel aimed a blow at my pilot which narrowly missed him, another with a long dagger stabbed through the back of the carriage and was dragged away with difficulty: I can still see his snarling face and hashish-haunted eyes.'

Again, the old Turkish noncommissioned officer came to their rescue. His small guard forced a way through the streets, pulling Arab protesters away from the prisoners.

White and Yeats-Brown tried their best to appear dignified, defiantly smoking cigarettes as the crowd buffeted their carriage. 'State arrival of British prisoners in Baghdad — what a scene it would have made for the cinematograph!' joked Yeats-Brown.

Drawing up before a barracks where rows of fezzed youths cheered their arrival from a balcony, the two airmen — exhausted, hatless, dishevelled and dirty — were ushered into a mirrored room decorated in faded gold and red. A bearded Turk seated on a divan rose to meet them. Claiming to be a war correspondent for the local newspaper, he requested an interview. What were their impressions? Indulging in irony, Yeats-Brown replied the Turks had given them quite enough impressions for one day, and words could not adequately express what they felt on their arrival in Baghdad.

'We chiefly want a bath,' he said.

In no mood to be interviewed, the two prisoners were escorted to the river's edge, again accompanied by the local mob. Before being ferried across to the governor's palace and hospital they bade goodbye to the old NCO who had saved their lives. He had helped brothers in distress, said Yeats-Brown. 'I grasped his hand in gratitude.'

In the hospital, doctors treated White's wounds, first shaving his head 'smooth as an egg' then swathing it in bandages down to his neck. That evening, as the two rested in a small whitewashed room, the Turkish commander, Hakki Bey, a tall and stern figure, visited accompanied by two or three doctors and a Turkish pilot. Hakki Bey carried a bottle of whisky, placing it on the table with great deliberation. They were to dine together, he announced. White and Yeats-Brown suspected there was more than traditional Turkish hospitality at play. With invasion imminent, Hakki Bey desperately needed information from his captives, and perhaps he thought whisky, conviviality and the camaraderie of a fellow pilot might loosen their tongues.

And talk they did. Having spent months in a 'dry' camp, this was no hardship. What Turkish intelligence staff would have made of the dinner conversation, however, was a matter of amused speculation for Yeats-Brown.

'We told them we had lost our way, then our engine had stopped, and we landed as near to some village as we could,' related Yeats-Brown. 'We knew nothing of an attack on Baghdad, we did not know General Townshend, but had certainly heard of him. We had heard a rumour that he had defeated the Turks at Es-sinn a month previously, and would like to know the truth of the matter. Eventually the bottle was exhausted, and so were our imaginations. We parted with the utmost cordiality and a firm intention of seeing as little of each other as possible in the future.'

White claimed he did not drink that night, but playing the game of 'babes in war' he congratulated the Turkish flying officer for guessing that faulty spark plugs had brought them down. Their captors were still puzzled about the flyers' mission deep behind enemy lines, but had not guessed their plan to destroy the telegraph lines. They wrongly supposed the explosions were bombs thrown by the two in self-defence. For days the two airmen declined invitations to cable home to their relatives that they were safe so as not to alert the Turks to the telegraph line damage, although their captors must have quickly twigged.

In the alley outside their first-floor room the two flyers noticed large earthenware storage pots, apparently water jars to be used in the forthcoming battle for Ctesiphon on the southern outskirts of Baghdad. Could this be a means of escape? Didn't Ali Baba and the forty thieves from *The Arabian Nights* hide themselves in such jars in this very city?

Any escape plans were quickly set aside after a further visit by Hakki Bey. Entering unexpectedly, he caught the two men looking out the window. That's dangerous, cautioned the commandant. You might fall on the bayonet of the sentry hidden from view in a recess directly below!

If escape was out of the question in a city where the two had no contacts, a visit to the Turkish baths in the hospital provided a strange and diverting consolation. White judged the Turkish baths a great institution. 'In the heated room, after sitting still till one begins to sweat, one is scrubbed, scraped and doused with hot water, then returned to the cooler room, and without being dried, swathed in many Turkish towels to cool off slowly.'

While this outing was agreeable, they found their interrogation less so. Each was questioned separately by Hakki Bey, still anxious to glean any details of the expected attack.

'The British will need an army of 200,000 men,' Hakki Bey asserted, hoping for a revealing response.

'Perhaps we have that number,' White replied.

'I know you have not,' responded Hakki Bey.

The commandant informed White that Yeats-Brown had told him quite a lot, an old interrogation trick that White recognised at once. Later in their room, Yeats-Brown remarked that the commandant had said White had told him nothing. White was privately gratified by this remark.

After refusing to answer further questions, White and Yeats-Brown were placed in solitary confinement for a week. For White, the time 'seemed unending', his only entertainment watching his sentry clean his rifle. Relief came via Raouf Bey, the Turkish journalist they had rebuffed on their arrival, who brought White two Walter Scott novels in English. In his last days of solitary White occupied himself reading *The Betrothed* and *The Monastery.*

As the expected British attack approached, the two airmen watched thousands of Arab conscripts being marched towards Ctesiphon. Shackled together by the wrist, they resembled biblical slaves. 'They were followed by weeping relatives,' Yeats-Brown observed. 'There was no pretence at heroism. They would have escaped if they could, but the Turks had taken care of that. They were tied together by fours, their right hand being lashed to a wooden yoke, while their left was employed in carrying a rifle. These unfortunate creatures were taken to a spot near the trenches and were then transferred, still securely tied together, to the worst dug and most exposed part of the line. Machine guns were then posted behind them to block all possible lines of retreat.'

On November 21 the two flyers heard the boom of the guns down the Tigris as the battle for Ctesiphon began. Evidence of the Turks' commitment to the battle was revealed when their Turkish sentries were relieved by Arabs armed with obsolete guns.

Then the wounded — both Turkish and Arab — began arriving at the barracks hospital. The flyers admired their stoicism in the face of a hospital system that generally neglected them. The Arab wounded were left to fend for themselves, relying, in Yeats-Brown's words, on 'charity and the providence of Allah'. Some of the Turkish soldiers showed remarkable fortitude. 'When a proclamation was read to the suffering in our hospital, announcing the success of the Turkish arms at Ctesiphon, the wounded seemed to forget their pain and the dying acquired a new lease of life,' he wrote. 'I actually saw a man with a mortal wound in the head, who a few minutes previously had been choking and literally at his last grasp, rally all his forces to utter thanks to God, and then die.'

The airmen never had any doubts that General Townshend would win at Ctesiphon then march into Baghdad, effecting their release. Were these hopes now to be dashed?

At six o'clock the next morning they were woken by a six-man guard and told they were leaving for Mosul in north Mesopotamia immediately. They tried every trick to delay departure, imagining British troops might arrive to rescue them at any moment. They dressed very slowly and 'lost' essential clothing. Yeats-Brown shaved twice, while White unwound lengths of unnecessary bandages from his head wound, which by then had almost healed. They sent Joseph, a Jewish youth who had brought them their meals, to the local market to buy bread, dates and a jar of water. White even paid a visit to the hospital barber.

One of the peculiarities of imprisonment in Turkey was that although captive officers were actually paid, they were expected to live off that pay. Turkey then debited the amount against an international account in Switzerland. The amount of their 'pay' varied depending on the mood of their commander or how many hands the money had to pass through. In Baghdad Hakki Bey told them that as officers their pay would be 10 liras a month, equal to ten pounds sterling. They received a month's pay in advance, enabling them to buy clothes and extra food.

Eventually their delaying pretexts ran out and the two flyers and their few belongings were hustled into waiting carriages. The kindly chief of the hospital, Sammi Bey, had made them a present of their quilts and mattresses. Hearing that Sammi Bey had personally paid for some of their hospital food, they wrote out 'cheques' to the Turkish Red Crescent for repayment.

A few miles out of town, the two looked back and saw shells bursting over the city. Their hopes rose. Was this a British artillery barrage ahead of an attack? White tried to persuade the guard to return to Baghdad, and was elated when suddenly the party wheeled around and headed back towards the city. Their hopes were soon dashed, however, when the carriages pulled up outside a private home. The guard commander had come back to collect some baggage and say goodbye to several pretty sisters.

The brief encounter with feminine company was some small consolation. 'They seemed the first real people I had seen in my captivity, femininity incarnate, human beings in a shadow-land of arabesques,' thought Yeats-Brown. 'I vowed that if Fate by a happy chance were to lead us back to Baghdad with roles reversed, so that they, not we were captives in the midst of foes, my first care would be to repay their kindly, though unspoken, sympathy.'

The journey to Mosul took eight days. They travelled in a Turkish *araba*, a basic flat carriage, with a mattress for the occupants to sit on and a small box seat for the driver. Sometimes a hood was attached. Hay feed buckets for the ponies were strung between its wheels. Drivers handled the ponies very cruelly, rousing them each day by shoving an iron skewer into their nostrils.

If White and Yeats-Brown were vexed by this mode of carriage — and of being constantly paraded before local dignitaries — they later learned they had travelled in the lap of luxury. In Mesopotamia in late 1915 European prisoners were a novelty, and warranted 'presentation' to each local official. Such meetings had their highs and lows.

White's diaries reveal one embarrassing dinner with a local magistrate in the town of Sawaki. 'A spoon is the full complement of the implements for feeding, and it is the custom to dine from the same dish, but we were not aware of this later fact until we had eaten the best part of the meat that was intended for us all,' he recorded. 'This could not have been too pleasing for the magistrate, who was a person that I should say dearly loved his meals and who ate with great gusto. As we could carry on practically no conversation, we went to bed in his magnificent room as soon as we concluded dinner.'

On another occasion White unknowingly broke local etiquette by declining to eat when the host picked up the best morsels of meat in his fingers and moved them around to the guest's side of the plate.

The customary meeting with the local dignitary, Yeats-Brown recorded, usually opened in a long, low room. The magistrate sat at his desk on which were set a saucer of ink, a dish of sand and some reed pens. A scribe stood beside the magistrate, handing him documents, which were scrutinised as though they were works of art. The magistrate would then scratch the document with a reed pen, sprinkle it with sand, and hand it back to the scribe. Meanwhile, he would conduct a conversation with the prisoners, or any of the ten or so other people usually in the room. 'They all made fragmentary remarks, one quoting a text from the Koran, another a French *bon mot*, and a third introducing some question of local politics,' he recalled. 'As the governor asked us questions and signed papers and kept up a running commentary with his friends, one felt exactly like Alice at the Mad Hatter's tea party.'

One such meeting, however, was quite threatening. At Samara the local governor was an oily, disagreeable member of the infamous Young Turks, the junta of officers who had seized power in Constantinople.

'Is it true that you dropped bombs on Baghdad?' he asked.

'Do you know that in another month the English will be driven into the Persian Gulf?'

Although White and Yeats-Brown ignored these provocations, they were startled by his claim that their commandant and a young English flying officer had been captured. When the Turk described the airman down to his fur coat, and said he had been killed by Arabs, their pulses raced. This was surely Captain E. J. Fulton, the nineteen-year-old who had taken a shine to Yeats-Brown. Only later did they find out the pilot was alive, although like them a prisoner after being shot down with their commandant, Major H. C. Reilly of the Indian Army.

On their daily journey one local custom really irked the two prisoners. Each morning they would be raised at dawn, although their guard would not be ready for hours, leaving the two waiting by the *araba* while their guards ate a leisurely breakfast. A rhyme kept passing through Yeats-Brown's head at such times:

> Slow pass the hours — ah, passing slow —
> My doom is worse than anything
> Conceived by Edgar Allan Poe.

One day, as they dozed in the *araba*, Yeats-Brown took his monocle from his pocket and fixed it in his eye. The guard in front of them gripped his rifle firmly and sat bolt upright, staring firmly ahead. He did not move until Yeats-Brown returned the monocle to his pocket. They learned later that the young guard believed he was being fixed with the evil eye.

At Tikrit, the birthplace of Saladin (and the scene of Saddam Hussein's capture after the 2003 Iraq War), they witnessed German archaeologists excavating ancient ruins. White thought the Arabs of Tikrit were the most warlike he had seen. At another town they saw Mesopotamia's first primitive oil refinery, where donkeys laden with tins carried away crude yellow petroleum distilled from a dozen antiquated boilers.

Occasionally there were breaks in the monotony of days parading before magistrates and nights spent in the open or in rough hovels. A chance meeting with some Turkish cavalry on their way to join the siege of Kut — General Townshend's inadequate forces had been driven back from Ctesiphon to Kut-el-Amara, where they were now surrounded — brought out some unusual camaraderie. Yeats-Brown, himself a former cavalry officer, waxed lyrical about the Turkish horsemen:

'They were a fine body of troops, a little under-mounted perhaps, but thoroughly businesslike. Their officers were most chivalrous cavaliers. Here in the desert, where luxuries were not to be had for money or for murder, they frequently gave us a handful of cigarettes, or a parcel of raisins, or else halted their squadron and asked us to share a meal. With these men one felt at ease. They were soldiers like ourselves. They did not ask awkward questions, and were told no lies.' Sitting in a circle drinking tea with the cavalrymen, Yeats-Brown was particularly drawn to one young officer who commented, 'Where there is no racing the people perish.'

One day a company of horsemen attacked the small convoy. The party had already noticed gruesome sights by the road, including beheaded Turkish gendarmes. This time the sergeant of the guard drove off the attackers with his rifle.

The sergeant had been educated in Baghdad, and although he knew no English he had picked up various nautical phrases from sailors on visiting steamers. Each morning he would greet the two airmen with 'Let her go! Haul in the slack! Hard aport', all delivered as if a single word.

Near Mosul the party stopped at the hot springs of Humman Ali, where they met (in the baths) a very old patriarch with a white beard who assured them of the beneficent properties of the water. Mosul, he told them, was heaven on earth. In Baghdad, too, they had been told that Mosul, site of the ancient capital of Nineveh and the tomb of Jonah, was a prison camp *par excellence*. So as they approached the domes and minarets through groves of dates and oranges both felt elated.

Their disillusionment was swift. Pulling up before a huge barracks, they were paraded before the commandant, Ibrahim Ghani Bey. With a large head, piercing eyes, a Prussian moustache and conspicuous top boots, his cruel appearance made an ominous impact.

First appearances proved correct. The scowling commandant who walked with a limp seemed to enjoy his reign of terror. 'He insulted the old, and struck the weak, and delighted in the tears of women and the cries of children,' said Yeats-Brown. 'This is not hyperbole. I have seen him stump through a crowd of Armenian widows and their offspring, and after striking some with a whip, he pushed down a woman into the gutter who held a baby to her breast. I have seen him pass down the ranks of Arab deserters, lashing one in the face, kicking another, and knocking down a third. I have seen him wipe his boots on the beard of an old Arab he had felled, and spur him in the face. I hope he has already been hanged [this was written in 1919] because only the hangman's cord could remove his atavistic cruelty.'

At this first meeting the commandant, through an interpreter, curtly inquired into the airmen's wellbeing and, assured it was satisfactory, had them removed to a dimly lit upstairs room. The two-storey barracks, more like a fort with heavy outside walls arranged around a quadrangle and with guards on the gates, looked to be escape proof.

Pushing their way past Arab prisoners lying on sheepskins they were moved into a small, even darker, cell-like room whose windows were boarded up. 'Death seemed in the air,' said Yeats-Brown. From the gloom, two figures emerged. They were Captain B. S. Atkins and the Australian Lieutenant W. H. Treloar, captured two months earlier. Both pilots were now physical wrecks, hardly recognisable in their rags. One had dysentery, the other fever. Both quickly disabused White and Yeats-Brown that treatment in Mosul would be better than in Baghdad.

Atkins and Treloar had suffered similar experiences to the new arrivals: shot down in their Caudron and too far behind the lines to glide to safety, they too had been attacked by Arab marauders and then 'rescued' by Turkish cavalry. Taken to Baghdad, they were put on photographic display alongside their plane, the proceeds going to the Red Crescent fund. Moved to Mosul, the two had been left to rot in their cell, their only relief an occasional outing to the Turkish baths.

Allocated an adjacent leaking, low-ceilinged cell, White and Yeats-Brown set about raising the spirits of their ill and dejected colleagues. They made playing cards from cigarette boxes, blacked in a chess board on a plank, composed outrageous limericks to recite and led the little group in singsongs — even the Turkish guards joined in.

There was no room to exercise except along the small verandah leading to the latrines, and that was often deep in human faeces as the toilets were also used by Turkish soldiers. Day and night they heard the screams of Arab prisoners below them as they endured the bastinado, an ancient form of torture in which the victim's legs are raised and the soles of the feet beaten. It is excruciatingly painful, the victim often unable to walk for days afterwards.

Once again the airmen witnessed the suffering of Arab 'conscripts'. Manacled together in two large cells beneath them, the Arabs were taken out only twice a day to the latrines. The stench from their cells was overpowering. One day in the quadrangle the airmen saw exactly how Ibrahim Ghani Bey treated these men. At a parade one old man was bent over, obviously ill. The commandant grabbed him by the beard, kicked him in the stomach, threw him to the ground and then stamped on his bent back until it was straightened out. They never saw the man again.

Another horror of the Mosul fort was quickly revealed. A large downstairs cell held Indian soldiers captured in the initial fighting in Mesopotamia. Some had belonged to the British consular guard in Baghdad. Held in frightful conditions with no exercise and little food, none survived the subsequent forced march to Turkey, as White later established. One Briton, Sergeant Blaker of the engineers' telegraph section, was among them. He had been captured by a Turkish raiding party and had been forced to run alongside the enemy cavalry on the journey to Baghdad. Blaker would have died in captivity had it not been for the food scraps smuggled to him by Atkins and Treloar.

Turkish treatment of officer and noncommissioned POWs was markedly different. The two were strictly separated, with little or no mixing allowed. Officers were paid and hence were able to buy extra food, and even permitted limited shopping and bathing opportunities. NCOs were herded together and ill-fed, and afforded almost no privileges.

White and Yeats-Brown complained to the commandant both about the treatment of the Indian sepoys, and about their own exercise restrictions. They also wanted to buy firewood and furniture for their cell. Ibrahim Ghani Bey told them they could visit the baths and bazaar once a week and buy what they wanted. As for the sepoys, the officers had only to apply in regard to any grievance and it would be fixed. Elated, the flyers passed the news to the sick men. 'They pitied us, asking if we were still so unsophisticated as to put any faith in a Turk's promise,' said White.

The men were right. Their conditions and physical state continued to deteriorate. The officers did get an occasional bath, but they never received proper pay to buy sufficient food or furniture. Further requests to see the commandant were ignored. The officers quickly learned three Turkish words, all starting with a *Y* — *yok*, *yassak* and *yarin*, meaning respectively 'no', 'forbidden' and 'tomorrow'.

Worse was to follow. Groups of desperate Indian and British prisoners began to arrive, captured at the siege of Kut, south of Baghdad, and force-marched in appalling conditions to Mosul. (Kut would hold out for months as the British mounted unsuccessful relief efforts.) With swollen and cut feet, these unfortunates staggered into the fort in appalling condition. Their stories were all similar. Stripped of clothing and fed little, they suffered from exposure and exhaustion. During the march men had been beaten, while those who dropped out were left to die.

White witnessed the arrival of a group of 249 POWs on 10 January 1916. 'As they tottered into the prison square they represented a pitiable sight,' he said. 'All were in rags, gaunt, dirty and unbelievably thin. A few who were too weak to walk were feebly clutching the donkeys to which they were tied, and the corpse of a sepoy bound face downward on a donkey brought up the rear of the wretched party.' One waved at White, who failed to recognise him. It was Air Mechanic Pass of the Royal Flying Corps, dressed in a ragged blanket, his skeletal frame covered in sores. Near to dropping out on the march, Pass was saved only when, passing through a swamp, he was able to wash his festered and swollen feet in the muddy water.

The whole party — all 249 of them — were hustled into a single cell. The airmen bribed the guards to bring some of the new prisoners to their rooms, where they fed them and gave them whatever money they had. But it was a forlorn endeavour. The survivors continued to die, leaving the officers to ponder the dilemma of which prisoners they might try to save with their limited resources.

The new arrivals dashed any hopes of an imminent British victory. After being driven back from Ctesiphon, the first British reverse in the Mesopotamian campaign, General Townshend's besieged forces were starving in Kut-el-Amara. Even now the Turks were rushing reinforcements to the siege.

White's diary of 9 January 1916 recorded a day of rejoicing among the Turks. Guards and other soldiers danced wildly in the courtyard. First the prisoners were told that Basra in southern Mesopotamia had been recaptured, but they did not believe it. Then it was rumoured that British battleships in the Dardanelles off Gallipoli had been sunk. Later they learned the real reason: Enver Pasha, one of the leaders of the Young Turk regime, had ordered two days of celebration to mark the British pullout from Gallipoli. With the Allied withdrawal from the peninsula in January 1916, both of the so-called sideshows in the Great War had turned into disasters.

The arrival of a second haggard group of prisoners prompted another confrontation with Ibrahim Ghani Bey. As the men staggered into the yard and fell to the ground, the airmen called down to Turkish soldiers there to help them, and promptly sent a message to the commandant. 'You carry them' was his reply. So the officers carried sick men on their backs. White helped British men and sepoys. One Tommy, racked with dysentery and reduced to a skeleton, remained optimistic. 'I've been prayin' all the way to reach 'ere, sir,' White recalled him saying weakly. 'I knew I'd recover in a decent hospital.' White dared not disillusion him. No sick prisoner had come out of the prison hospital alive.

The treatment of these men, and the subsequent barbarity meted out to the survivors of the Kut siege force-marched to Turkey, permanently embittered both White and Yeats-Brown towards the Turks. White estimated that the Kut survival rate was very low — possibly around only one in five of those captured. But a British government report at the end of the war claimed more than half survived, with some 4500 either dead or 'untraced'.

Both men wrote after the war that the view of the Turks as stubborn but clean fighters earned at Gallipoli had biased public opinion at home. Towards the end of 1917 the Turks established a parole camp where officers who gave an undertaking not to escape were well treated. Their letters home further compounded this false impression, the airmen believed. When White later toyed with titles for a book on his captivity, he settled on 'Guests of the Unspeakable', picking up on the description of the Turk used by former British prime minister William Gladstone.

Meanwhile, complaints to the commandant about the treatment of rank-and-file prisoners drew an ominous response. If they became too insistent they would be sent 'where there are no other prisoners' — solitary.

Prison life dragged on, made all the more desolate by the worsening war news. One bright spot, however, was the arrival of two other flying officers, Major Reilly of the Indian Army and Captain Fulton of the Royal Flying Corps. These were the airmen they had been told on the journey to Mosul had been killed by Arabs. 'He was alive, my friend in the fur coat,' Yeats-Brown rejoiced. 'The desert had delivered up its dead.'

With nine officers now in the small cells — including Lieutenant-Commander Goad, Captain H. G. Brodie and Lieutenant G. C. Flynn, all from the Indian Army — the prisoners were allocated two extra Arab servants in addition to Hamid, who had looked after the original group. 'Conditions have been slightly improved by their arrival ... and our squalid cells have been given a much needed sweep,' said White. The officers could bathe once every fortnight or so, and were occasionally allowed into the markets, although usually their food shopping was done by Hamid. The officers discovered only later that the servants charged them exorbitant mark-ups on their food purchases.

One day in the bazaar White bought a small notebook from a bootblack who sold mirrors and other trinkets to Turkish troops. Thus began his secret prison diary. With paper in short supply he wrote in minute script on pages measuring just nine and a half by three and a half centimetres. White squeezed about 360 words into a page, and hid the pages in his puttees (cloth wound around the lower leg to form legging) or in his headgear. In a bookshop in the bazaar he also found three English books, including a collection of Tennyson's poems, and these came to be well thumbed by the prisoners. On one outing to the baths they persuaded their guard to let them cross the Tigris to visit the ancient ruins of Nineveh, capital of the Assyrians, whose empire once stretched to Egypt.

Diversions were few, however. White's diary record of 25 December 1915 is a good snapshot:

'Christmas Day was not our merriest. For the past week we have not had a piastre between us, though Hamid has bought a little food on credit. The cold weather has set in, and, in strong contrast to Mesopotamia, there is little sun. Moreover it is raining heavily and the roof is leaking.

'Our pay is very much in arrears, in Atkins and Treloar's case over a month,' he continued. 'After much clamouring we have received a week's pay, so decided to celebrate. Hamid managed to purchase two bottles of alleged whisky and a goose, bringing the whisky, like a good Musselman, concealed in the folds of his capacious trousers. In taste and smell it was much like methylated spirits, but mixed with milk was drinkable.

'Treloar and I tried to roast the goose in ghee on a brushwood fire which we lit in the guardroom. Ghee is a rancid fat that is most disagreeable at first, and as our knowledge of cooking was rather rudimentary, we burnt the precious goose.'

Not surprisingly, thoughts turned to escape. Yeats-Brown was elated when one of the young guards muttered 'Jesus' to him and made the sign of the cross. But apparently this had more to do with another guard believing a spell was being cast by the monocle than with any sympathetic Christian overture. Hopes rose again when Yeats-Brown began to butter up a wall-eyed *chaoush* (sergeant), another horse fancier, who visited the prisoners as an interpreter and helped buy their food. After discussing the war with Ghaib Chaoush, as he was called, Yeats-Brown made him an offer: help us get to the Russian frontier and we will reward you handsomely.

'This is very sudden,' Ghaib responded. 'I could be killed if I am caught.'

At least Yeats-Brown knew he was willing. 'You won't get caught. With good horses and a guide like you we'll be across the Russian frontier in four days. It is worth a hundred pounds to you, over and above expenses, and a job for life.'

Negotiations continued over some time, involving at least one other British officer. Yeats-Brown gave Ghaib five pounds towards initial provisions. Ghaib claimed at least fifty pounds was necessary to buy three horses and two Mauser pistols.

Yeats-Brown dreamed of riding through forests to the Russian front. But in his later writings he was unclear of which other officer he conspired with to accompany him and Ghaib. Certainly it was not White, who unwittingly contributed to the collapse of the plan. For it seemed that other officers, including White, had given Ghaib another five pounds to buy food. When no food arrived, and Ghaib insisted he had not received the money, they complained to his superiors. The commandant arrested Ghaib, who, under the bastinado, spilled the beans on the escape plan. When confronted with this claim by the commandant, and a limping Ghaib, most of the prisoners quite genuinely denied it.

'The *Chaoush* says that you planned to escape from the back of the *hamam* [baths], and that you commissioned him to buy three horses,' alleged the commandant through an interpreter.

'Well, where are the horses?' responded Yeats-Brown, adding to the indignant protests of his fellow officers who knew nothing of any escape plan. 'Does anyone know anything about them? And where is the money? You can't buy three horses for five pounds.'

It was a telling point. Ibrahim Ghani Bey turned on Ghaib and spat in his face. 'Take him away,' he ordered the guards. As Ghaib was led away, one of the prisoners not in the know cried out: 'The commandant owes us an apology for this unfounded accusation!' Ibrahim Ghani Bey, obviously embarrassed, saluted sourly, and told the prisoners they would be permitted to visit the baths the following day.

Yeats-Brown later confessed he found this a dreadful moment, but he reasoned like this: If Ghaib had been 'playing the game' by his fellow conspirators, why did he talk to the Turks about the escape? If, however, he was a prison spy, then his punishment was not Yeats-Brown's fault. A fine rationalisation as far as it went, but the hapless Ghaib had been tortured to reveal the escape plot.

The incident was costly. All their guards (and likely Ghaib as well) were sent to the front, almost a certain death sentence. Their replacements were more vigilant.

If the vicious commander was embarrassed by being unable to prove the escape conspiracy, two other incidents probably forever damned the officers in his eyes.

One day the walkway outside their cell was cleaned down and fresh cement dumped over pools of filth. This unexpected event was soon explained by the arrival of a German medical officer. He told the prisoners he had noticed them one day on his way to the baths, but relations with the Turks were difficult, and he had been able to see them only after a great deal of difficulty. Did they have any complaints? He would make sure these were passed on to the German authorities.

Seeing that none of the accompanying Turks spoke English (and the German doctor did), White told him their treatment — and particularly that of the enlisted men — was nothing short of criminal. The men had been treated like cattle, and were dying from starvation, illness and cold. The doctor promised to do what he could. A day or so later five blankets arrived for the ill sepoys, apparently purchased by the doctor himself. White later speculated that the doctor was indirectly responsible for Ibrahim Ghani Bey's subsequent removal.

White and other prisoners reported many acts of kindness by German officers in Turkey. On one occasion in Mosul he was given a secondhand pipe by a German officer who had visited him while he was in solitary in Baghdad. White rationalised this friendly treatment from an enemy by the type of German officers sent to the eastern front, who tended to be men of 'culture and linguistic ability'. As well, he believed some Germans despised their Turkish allies as 'Barbarians who at the best had only a veneer of civilization'.

Another incident involving Yeats-Brown brought the commandant's cruelty to the attention of German diplomats. Out of the blue he was informed that the German consul wanted to see him. Yeats-Brown was escorted to Ibrahim Ghani Bey's office, where he found the consul, the commandant and various Mosul dignatories. Yeats-Brown was stunned by what then unfolded.

An old family friend then in Constantinople, Baron von Mumm, had sent him a present of 500 marks in gold, a very large sum. The baron had been a neighbour when Yeats-Brown's father was a British envoy in Italy. The gesture was typical of the old-world civility that existed between the English and German upper classes early in the war but was largely killed off by the later barbarity of trench warfare.

The money would be given to him the next day, and an aide from the German consul would accompany him to the bazaar to make any purchases he wished. As the conversation took place in

French, a language the commandant did not speak, Yeats-Brown seized the opportunity to pour out a stream of complaints of ill treatment to the consul. Embarrassed, the consul said he would return the next day.

Overnight, Yeats-Brown conferred with his companions and prepared three documents, which he presented the next day. The first thanked Baron von Mumm for his gift. A second was a proposal that the International Red Cross should immediately send a commission to Mosul to look to the interests of the prisoners. Men were being deprived of fresh air and food. Many suffered dysentery. Some had gone mad. A third listed the immediate needs of the men, including soap (they had been unable to wash for months), tins for drinking water and blankets.

Yeats-Brown's proposals stunned the meeting. 'The consul stared and the commandant glared, for the one hated fuss and the other hated me,' he recorded. The commandant summoned an interpreter, demanding that Yeats-Brown say if he had any cause for complaint. A curious three-cornered conversation ensued.

'The men must be moved to better quarters,' demanded Yeats-Brown. 'Until this is arranged nothing can be done.'

'He says nothing can be done,' explained the interpreter.

'Then of what does he complain?' responded the commandant.

'The very beasts in my country are better cared for,' Yeats-Brown continued. 'Our men are dying of hunger and cold.'

'He says the men are dying of cold,' said the interpreter.

'The weather is not my fault,' said the commandant. 'Perhaps it will be better tomorrow. Yes, *yarin*.'

The conversation was hopeless, but Yeats-Brown left the consul in no doubt that he now shared with Ibrahim Ghani Bey responsibility for the ill-treated Mosul prisoners. Yeats-Brown left all the money except five pounds with the consul to form a fund for the sick prisoners. (The money was later returned to him in England.)

Accompanied by a German diplomat dressed like a Bond Street commissionaire, Yeats-Brown in his dishevelled prison garb strolled the bazaar, with the diplomat carrying the prisoner's parcels.

Yeats-Brown used the occasion and his German diplomatic connection to sow disaffection about the commandant. To tobacconists, grocers, fruit sellers and bakers he retold the story: the commandant was an evil man whose hour had come. He found surprising agreement. 'It was a matter of minutes before rumours of his downfall were rife throughout the city,' he wrote.

About this time, the nine officers and some 250 men, mostly Indian, were ordered to be shifted west into Turkey. White believed the order came before the German consul's visit, but Yeats-Brown believed the two events were connected.

The journey would involve a 170-mile trek across current-day northern Iraq into Syria to the railhead at Ras-el-Ain. In line with the strict Turkish demarcation between officers and ranks, while the officers had *arabas*, the men would be forced to march. The commandant demanded six pounds from each officer to pay for the *arabas*, but they refused, instead handing the money to the men.

On 20 February 1916 the already weary group set out. Before departing, White and Treloar scribbled their names and some of the commandant's atrocities on the wall of their cell, adding an Australian flag and 'Advance Australia'. Other POWs who later passed through the prison reported finding the message still on the wall.

Ibrahim Ghani Bey, neatly dressed in fez and top boots, came to see them off. Yeats-Brown said the scowling commandant, legs astride, spat on the ground as they left. The hatred was mutual. 'As sure as there are beings whose actions have merited the hangman's rope, Ibrahim Ghani Bey deserves priority,' said White.

Two sequels to this mutual hatred were yet to be played out. Ibrahaim Ghani Bey lost his command. Yeats-Brown later claimed it happened after the complaints he raised at the meeting with the German consul reached authorities in Constantinople. 'I hope he was sent to some lingering and uncomfortable fate,' said Yeats-Brown.

The commandant also planned one final act of revenge — to have the troublesome officers murdered in the desert. But the hand of fate, in the most unlikely shape, reached out to save them.

5

'I'm a Yank. Can I do anything for you boys?'

On a hill outside Mosul, the POWs stopped and looked back at the city where White and Yeats-Brown had spent three months. There were no regrets at moving on — life could hardly be worse wherever they were headed. White pondered the fleeting nature of life. On the plain before him had once stood the Assyrian capital of Ninevah, now reduced to a few mounds of stones. It had also seen the victory of the Byzantine Emperor Heraclius against the Persians. His mind wandered:

> Lo, all our pomp and yesterday
> Is one with Ninevah and Tyre!

He was quickly brought back to reality. At a turn in the road, the officers on their six *arabas* parted company with the men on foot, already a pitiable sight. White wondered why they were separated, but it would be several years before he knew the sinister answer.

This stretch across modern-day northern Iraq into Syria to the railhead at Ras-el-Ain was dangerous territory — Yezidi country. They had heard that the Yezidi were then a primitive people, reputedly devil worshippers. Turkish convoys had been attacked by the Yezidi, who tried to capture their artillery. The British believed these attacks took place when the Turks were rushing reinforcements to the siege of Townshend's force at Kut. Along the dusty caravan route were many dead animals, and not far from the road they saw three Turkish corpses, stripped bare and partly eaten by jackals.

That night the party stopped at a small Arab village, where the officers were lodged in a filthy, lice-ridden mud hut in which, White wrote, the rats vied with cats for precedence. Still, anywhere was better than the cell in Mosul, and Yeats-Brown felt the desert winds clearing away 'the cobwebs of captivity'.

Late that night they heard their guards challenge some unexpected arrivals, who the officers hoped were the main column of POWs. But it was only three mounted Turkish officers, who were soon quartered in an adjoining hut. Later two of them looked in on the prisoners.

'Can I do anything for you boys?' asked one of them in a decided Yankee twang.

As the stunned prisoners stared back in blank surprise, the 'American' introduced his companion, a well-dressed young Turkish colonel, and then produced a small flask of brandy and handed it around. 'So, you're not a Turk?' ventured one of the prisoners.

'I'm no ***** Turk!' the visitor insisted. 'I'm a Yank. I'm really a Venezuelan, though I bin a stoodent at Boston University and a cow puncher in Arizona.' He handed them his card, which read:

Rafael de Nogales
Caracas

Into the POWs' rat-infested hut in the northern Mesopotamian desert had walked perhaps the most colourful soldier of fortune of the twentieth century.

Nogales claimed to be a descendant of Don Diego de Mendez — one of the first conquistadors — and an Indian princess. His nobleman grandfather Don Pedro de Inchauspe was a great advocate of South American independence from Spain. A shortish, thickset man, Nogales had roamed the world seeking adventure. He had fought with the Spanish against the United States in 1898, and with Japan against Russia in 1904–05. Other adventures took him to the Mexican borderlands to fight with the Mexican bandit revolutionary Pancho Villa, to Arizona to try his hand at cattle ranching, and to the goldfields of the Klondike, where he reportedly helped found the city of Fairbanks in Alaska. Now he was fighting for the Turks.

Nogales was no ordinary freebooter. Muna Lee, who later translated his book *Four Years Beneath the Crescent*, described him as a man who followed the knight-errant ideals of courage, chivalry and honour. How Lee squared this with Nogales' direction of part of the Turkish assault on the Armenian town of Van, where thousands were slaughtered, is not clear.

'I heard you boys had a rough passage in that gaol in Mosul,' Nogales told the amazed prisoners, 'and as I've bin a prisoner myself I'm going to see that while I travel with you the "dawgone" sheikhs of the villages where we stay get a rustle on in the way of prodoocin food for you.'

He would prove as good as his word. Nogales' arrival and his Good Samaritan gesture were no accidents, however, although it appeared that way at the time. Unbeknown to the POWs, Nogales had first noticed them one day in Mosul as they straggled back from the baths. He found it painful to see their reduced state. Their filthy barracks and obvious hunger contrasted sharply with the opulence of the German consulate where he was staying, with its dining table straining under the weight of champagne and caviar.

'When I saw these officers who endured their misfortune with so much dignity, I experienced that sentiment of universal brotherhood which every true soldier feels on seeing a comrade, even though an adversary, in the clutch of adversity; and I desired strongly to approach, to salute them and offer them some cigarettes,' he related in his 1926 account of his Turkish service. But the German consul, who had visited the barracks during the Yeats-Brown money gift episode that sparked the anger of the Turkish commandant, had restrained him.

Holstein was right. If Nogales was seen talking with British prisoners, the Turks would be suspicious. He might even be seen as a British agent. Nogales was in a precarious enough position in Mosul as it was.

When war broke out he had tried to sign up with the Belgians, sympathising with their underdog status despite his own German education. Rejected, he then tried to sign up with the French, but again got nowhere. Courted by the Turks and Germans during a visit to the Mediterranean, he finally joined the Turkish army.

While a great admirer of the Turkish soldier, Nogales was appalled by the barbarity of the Armenian massacres, which he laid directly at the door of the Young Turk junta. Probably the only Christian in the ranks of the Turkish military who witnessed the slaughter, he was certainly the only one who lived to tell the tale. It is estimated that at least 600,000 Armenians were killed during the war years as Turkey decided to rid itself of its Armenian population of about 1.8 million. Nogales' account of this barbarity does not make pretty reading. His book details one episode:

'It was not yet midday of June the 18th, 1915, when we drew rein before Sairt, whose narrow white houses indicated its Babylonian origin. Six minarets, one of them a leaning tower, stood out like needles of alabaster against the turquoise Mesopotamian sky. Herds of cattle and black buffalo were grazing peacefully over the surrounding plain, while a group of woolly dromedaries drowsed about a solitary spring. The momentary sensation of tranquility evoked in my troubled spirit was rudely shattered, however, by the atrocious spectacle afforded by a hill beside the highway.

'The ghastly slope was crowned by thousands of half-nude and still bleeding corpses, lying in heaps, or interlaced in death's final embrace. Fathers, brothers, sons and grandsons lay there as they had fallen under the bullets and yataghans of the assassins. From more than one slashed throat the life gushed out in mouthfuls of warm blood. Flocks of vultures were perched upon the mound, pecking at the eyes of dead and dying, whose rigid gaze seemed still to mirror the horrors of some unspeakable agony; while the scavenger dogs struck sharp teeth into the entrails of beings still palpitating with the breath of life.'

There was more, much more, of what Nogales called a 'bacchanal of barbarity'. At Van, scene of other massacres, Nogales stopped the Turkish commander aiming artillery at an American missionary building, surrounded by American flags. It was probably the incident that undermined his standing with the Young Turk leadership.

After leading the siege of Van, where he had tried vainly to save some Armenians, Nogales resigned his commission and headed for the Russian front. Turkish friends told him that the Young Turks had ordered his assassination on the road to prevent him revealing the crime of the massacres. Resolving to return to Constantinople, and thence to Germany, Nogales was passing through Mosul when he spotted the British prisoners.

The day before his departure, which coincided with that of the prisoners, Nogales received a visitor at the German consulate. A young man 'of highly distinguished bearing', on his way from Baghdad to Aleppo (in western Syria), presented himself and asked to accompany Nogales through the desert. He was on a mission that he would not divulge: the German consulate believed him to be a spy for the Turkish government. Nogales, however, found him a likeable and well-mannered young man, and agreed. The following morning he found his new travelling companion outside the consulate, dashingly dressed in the uniform of an officer of the volunteers, with a black felt shawl and gold embroidered cape, and mounted on a 'magnificent' horse.

On the way out of Mosul, the two were joined by a group of Turkish officers from the barracks, come to bid Nogales a friendly farewell. One was an aide to the prison commandant, Ibrahim Ghani Bey. As he said goodbye, the aide whispered in Nogales' ear that 'a certain group of English officers had also set out for Aleppo that morning, but the probabilities were that they would never reach their destination'. Nogales asked why not. 'Because there's a squadron of Circassian volunteers posted on the road with directions to see that they don't arrive,' the aide replied with a wink.

This was the commandant's revenge. Circassians — warlike Muslims from the northern Caucasus who had signed up with the Turks to win back their homeland from Russia — had been hired to assassinate the POW officers on the road.

'This news aroused in me the liveliest indignation and I resolved to prevent at all costs any such crime,' wrote Nogales. He hastened his march, and overtook the struggling group of Indian and British soldiers. Many of these, he said, clearly suffered from anaemia, fevers and typhus, 'and could barely drag themselves along on staves and crutches'.

He caught up with the officers after nightfall, and camped in the village. 'Two of them were gathering sticks for a fire, while their guard looked on with ironical and hate-laden glances which revealed to me clearly enough the imminent peril of the prisoners,' wrote Nogales. After meeting the officers, he joined the Turkish guards at their campfire. The guard captain was displeased when Nogales told him that from then on he would take personal charge of the convoy. Also at the campfire was a Circassian volunteer officer, who had mysteriously joined Nogales and his group on the road that morning. 'I suspected immediately that he was the leader of the Circassian guerillas about whom the Aide at Mosul had spoken to me,' he said.

Nogales called him to one side. 'They know all about this in the German consulate,' he told the Circassian. 'The consul has your names, so that in case the English officers are assassinated on the road, he will denounce you all and have you severely punished; because if any such crime were committed, the British government would certainly hold him responsible.'

By the next morning the Circassian had disappeared. When Nogales queried the guard captain, the man responded: 'What Circassian? There hasn't been any Circassians here!'

For Nogales, this brazen lie confirmed the plot.

For the prisoners, Nogales proved a godsend, riding ahead to arrange food each day, and directing the Turkish guard that the POWs were not to be molested. He had a word of caution for the prisoners, however. Yeats-Brown recalled him assuring them they would be safe as long as he was present, but adding: 'I tote a straight gun. Remember, no nonsense, though. I'm out to help you, but not to let you escape. If you try that, I shoot.'

Nogales was taking a risk in protecting the prisoners. He was no longer an officer in the Turkish army, and had no legitimate power to requisition food 'on government authority', as he did. 'But seeing the unhappy straits of those brave soldiers and gentlemen in the hands of scoundrels, I waived the technicalities with a contented conscience in obedience to an older law,' he said.

For the next six or seven days this strange convoy — prisoners, mercenary, mysterious government 'spy' and Turkish guards — wended its way across the danger zone controlled by rebel Bedouin tribes. Each day Nogales would find food, and each day he would remind the Turkish guards that the prisoners were not to be harmed.

While his self-invited companion may have been a spy — Nogales certainly believed he was — he proved to be almost as colourful a character as the South American soldier of fortune. Nogales learned later that he was actually a member of the royal family of Afghanistan on an intelligence mission for the Young Turk regime. Spy or not, the mystery man struck a chord with Yeats-Brown, who soon labelled him 'Boy Scout' for his kindness to the prisoners, including giving them brandy, raisins, sugar, tea and medicines. He wrote of Boy Scout in terms that modern readers might interpret as homosexually suggestive, but might have been no more than the flowery language of the times:

'He was unknown to me when I first saw him, dark-eyed and graceful, riding a white horse like a prince in a fairy book, and we spoke no common language, but somehow we understood each other ... At times a mere glance will proclaim a kindred spirit in a stranger: so it was between him and me: the war was far: we were more than brothers.'

While Boy Scout was a fervent Young Turk, in their discussions in fragments of French and Persian he and Yeats-Brown managed to avoid awkward issues like the Armenian atrocities. But Boy Scout guessed Yeats-Brown's anxiety to escape and one day told him: 'I shall fully understand if you try to get away, but you will forgive me, won't you, if I use my revolver.'

'Of course,' replied Yeats-Brown.

'Good,' Boy Scout laughed, 'because I am a dead shot!'

Fulton was violently ill with fever during this part of the journey. 'It was wonderful to see the tenderness with which his companions cared for him, depriving themselves of their coats to shelter him from the cold of those damp, unhealthful nights,' observed Nogales.

As the strange little convoy pressed on, solitary horsemen would often be seen on distant high ground. They would disappear as the convoy approached, only to reappear on the next rise. White believed Nogales was keen to provoke an open encounter with the Bedouins.

'We're like hunters in a forest,' Nogales told him. 'We see practically nothing while our quarry sees us all the time.'

Nogales intrigued White. As he rode alongside the *araba* he regaled the Australian with his many adventures, from fighting for the Spanish to acting as a lieutenant for Pancho Villa.

'Have you ever thought of writing the story of your life?' White asked him one day.

'I'd have every sheriff in Arizona after me if I did,' Nogales responded cryptically.

White quizzed Nogales on why he was fighting for the Turks. Prompted, White believed, by the fellowship of language and faith, the Venezuelan unburdened himself. He had been in Germany at the outbreak of war on a 'visit of political importance'. White interpreted this as Nogales lobbying Berlin to back South American independence, as Nogales was a supporter of the idea of a federation between Venezuela, Colombia and Ecuador. Whatever the reason, Nogales told him he had been appointed to General Von der Goltz's staff and sent to Turkey. 'But I have had enough of these *****,' White quoted him as telling the prisoners. 'I've seen more than is good for me. I saw some sights [in Van] that I shall never forget, and they know it and that I was the only Christian on their side.

'I'm going now to Constantinople and then to Germany, but I shall consider myself lucky if I get out of Turkey alive. They've twice attempted to do for me, but there are two things I never do ... I never leave this out of reach [slapping his Mauser pistol], and I never employ an interpreter.'

Nogales did go on to write a book of his experiences — two, in fact — in which he told a different story about fighting on the Turkish side. In these books, he details how he originally tried to sign up for the Belgians, and only after being rejected (or ignored) by the Belgians and the French was he wooed by the Germans and Turks.

For White, Nogales' later account of his Turkish service was both surprising and disappointing. Surprising because White and his fellow prisoners were unaware at the time of the assassination plot against them. Disappointing because of its revelations of Nogales' dubious role in the siege of Van and its massacres. Similarly, White was disappointed by Nogales' inexplicable inaction against Arabs whom he claimed to have seen mutilating and killing British wounded in the second battle of Gaza. Perhaps, mused White, in a character 'so cosmopolitan and inured to cruelty the best attributes could not survive'.

As the party neared Nisibin and the railhead at Ras-el-Ain their progress was slowed by heavy rain. White marvelled at a soaked Nogales riding on in the vanguard, bolt upright in the saddle and shrouded in a cloak with a comical tasselled hood, looking like a 'cowled Napoleon'. In the chill wind, the prisoners appreciated him passing them sips of his own blend of 'whisky' — Worcestershire sauce and water.

Some of the villages they passed through had been Armenian. After riding ahead, Nogales came back with depressing news. 'You couldn't find a man alive in any of those villages,' he said. 'They were mostly Armenian and the Turks cleaned them up. It is said that some Turks were poisoned there, though of course we don't know anything at all about that . . . anyhow, they're finished now and the women driven off and you'll be wise not to mention Armenians in Nisibin.'

In one village White noticed a little girl watching the prisoners from a side street. The girl gave the sign of the cross, and looked pleadingly at the men. Although closely watched, White was determined to show the girl that she had their sympathy. He rolled a cigarette, and placing it in a cigarette box with some money threw it towards the girl. 'The smiles of gratitude and appreciation from the child when she picked it up and the beams of satisfaction from her relatives were well worth the risk and expense,' he said.

They had hoped to reach Nisibin that night, but the heavy mud track delayed them. Exhausted and soaked, they squelched knee deep in mud into an Arab village. Fortunately, Nogales had arranged with the white-haired local sheikh for a veritable feast of spitted chicken, sour milk and eggs.

'You boys will excuse me now,' Nogales said as the prisoners sought to dry their clothes by a fire inside the sheikh's hut. 'Santa Claus here [indicating the sheikh] will entertain you 'til I return. I have an appointment with a lady in this city.'

The prisoners no doubt looked on enviously. As some consolation the sheikh provided them all with feather mattresses, and 'needless to mention we slept soundly,' wrote White.

In Nisibin, Nogales received some disturbing news. An Armenian telegrapher whom he had once protected slipped him details of several recent communications. One instructed two officers of the medical corps to spy on Nogales' conversations with the prisoners. Another said Nogales was not to be permitted to continue his journey to Constantinople. If he tried, he was to be arrested. Still another detailed Nogales' illegal ordering of food for the prisoners. The Young Turks had been keeping close tabs on him, and — as Nogales well knew — the Ottoman Turks ruled supreme in the art of espionage.

Returning to the former Christian church in Nisibin where the prisoners were billeted (White had unwittingly made his bed on the altar of a church where the Armenians claimed St James was buried), Nogales soon picked out the two new medical officers, who took an unusually close interest in his conversation. It was time to go on alone, for his presence was now imperilling the prisoners.

While Nogales was learning of the danger he was in, White, Yeats-Brown and Boy Scout visited the local bazaar. The prisoners tried to make a few purchases, but Boy Scout (his real name was Niet Bey) simply commandeered their provisions from the merchants.

That night, the last they spent with their South American benefactor, both Nogales and Boy Scout visited their quarters. The latter brought for diversion a collection of rare stamps and some autographed photographs of Enver Pasha, the Young Turk leader and minister for war. As Prince (as White had dubbed him) sang the praises of Enver Pasha ('greater than Napoleon'), Nogales bit his tongue. To speak out now would have been suicidal.

Before the convoy set out next day for the railhead, Nogales gathered his personal escort and quietly departed. Although the prisoners missed him, it was not the last they would see of the colourful adventurer. But at their next meeting their roles would be reversed, and it would be they who helped Nogales.

Ras-el-Ain, for many years a Roman outpost against the Persians and Parthians, was then the limit of the German-built Constantinople-to-Baghdad railway, although gaps remained in the Taurus Mountains in south-western Turkey. After the discomfort of the *arabas*, the relieved prisoners now bounced up and down on the upholstered seats of railway carriages, many of which appeared to be rolling stock captured by the Germans in Belgium and Russia. As the train trundled slowly towards Aleppo — rumoured to be their ultimate destination — Arab horsemen galloped by, shouting out racing challenges to the slow-moving iron horse and firing their rifles into the air. Crossing the Euphrates at the ancient town of Carchemish, once an important city of the late bronze age Hittite empire, the prisoners noted not only the splendid German bridge engineering but the feverish activity as the Turks loaded artillery and munitions onto rafts to be floated down to Baghdad.

Aleppo provided them with their first real escape opportunities, but on both occasions they were thwarted by Boy Scout, who seemed to possess an uncanny knack of appearing at the crucial moment.

The first occurred as they entered the city. Coming into Aleppo, Boy Scout told the prisoners they would be accommodated at the Hotel Victoria, which he talked up, said White, as a local equivalent to the Ritz or Waldorf Astoria. At the station they transferred to *arabas*, after Fulton had been dispatched to the local hospital, but one of their wagons soon became bogged. Meanwhile, the guard commander, who had become extremely drunk on arak, was nowhere to be seen. While the small contingent of guards were distracted by the efforts to extricate the bogged wagons, White and Treloar considered an escape bid. Certainly it was risky. They knew nobody in the city, and had little money or food. Yet the possibility of freedom was there. Suddenly Boy Scout appeared with half a dozen guards. The *arabas* were cleared from the mud, and the opportunity quickly evaporated.

As did the prospects of a hotel. The prisoners were taken instead to a barracks that reminded them depressingly of their hated quarters in Mosul. They were led to a rat-infested room where, White recorded, lice and vermin attacked them in massed battalions. 'And their bites seemed a penance for not having escaped when the opportunity offered.'

Next morning the prisoners had a pleasant surprise. The local commandant turned out to be a very generous one by the standard set in Mosul. He had no idea why they had been sent to Aleppo, he told them, and had not been informed of their arrival. This seemed to support Nogales' assassination story. The commandant said he would wire army headquarters to see what should be done with them, and in the meantime he would arrange better accommodation. True to his word, they were moved to the Hotel American, which to the prisoners' utter surprise had dining tables with real tablecloths and beds with bedclothes mercifully free of lice. They were in seventh heaven, and seeing little danger of being sued by their creditors, they immediately ordered a slap-up meal despite the high prices.

Yeats-Brown's mind raced. After a refreshing night's rest — between sheets and with breakfast served in bed — he dressed in haste. His idea was to order a carriage and drive to Mersina on the Mediterranean coast, where he believed he could charter a boat to Cyprus. He got no further than the hotel passage, where he found Boy Scout waiting. The guard commander was 'ill', he said, so Boy Scout had arranged the hotel accommodation, and he wanted Yeats-Brown and the others to lunch with him at 1 p.m.

'My face fell, but of course there was no help for it,' said Yeats-Brown. 'And of course Boy Scout's hospitality was princely indeed.'

That was an understatement. After a sumptuous meal, including Cypriot wines, coffee and cigarettes, the prisoners adjourned to Boy Scout's bedroom where he invited them to help themselves to an assorted array of English bully beef and slabs of chocolate, which he said was his share of the loot taken after the Allies withdrew from Gallipoli. It must have been an eerie feeling for them — eating food that had been left behind by their own troops. Still, they had learned from bitter experience to take whatever was offered.

Boy Scout also fitted them out with new clothing. 'He was ready, literally, to give us his last shirt,' said Yeats-Brown. 'After having fitted us out, he telephoned the hospital about the patient [Fulton]'. Shortly after visiting Fulton, Yeats-Brown himself fell ill. He was sitting at the window of their hotel when he began to shiver violently. Half an hour later he had a high fever, and that night he joined Fulton in hospital.

Five days later he reappeared at the hotel, looking to his companions like a shadow of his former self. 'His fever had been ignored, and after lying starved and unattended for two days he struggled out of bed to the office of the senior doctor, where, after saying what he thought of him and his methods, he fainted with weakness, but preferred to be brought back to the hotel rather than remain in the hospital any longer,' said White.

While unusually pleasant, life at the hotel was monotonous. The prisoners had the run of the place, but with guards at every exit they could not go outside. The local commandant had fixed their hotel rate at nineteen piastres a day, allowing them a shilling a day for soap, cigarettes and other necessities. Much of their time was spent sunbathing on the hotel roof, watching sunsets as they washed clothes. The Irishman Lieutenant Flynn had a good voice, and led the small group in nightly singsongs.

White interested himself in the ancient history of the area, and observed the local women. Passing through Kurdish territory on the way to Aleppo he had already noted the beauty of Kurdish women in their bright dresses. In Aleppo, the biggest city they had visited, where Abraham was said to have lived, White thought women's fashion rather out of date, but some dressed exceedingly smartly. 'Evidently they take their fashions from the American and German women of whom we have seen several in the town,' he wrote. Arab women, he noted, wore the usual black, head-to-toe *chador*, some even covering their face except for the eyes. 'It was amusing occasionally to watch Arab women gathered together like so many crows regarding Paris-fashioned women with mingled contempt and envy.'

Fulton returned to the hotel much weakened by his illness but free of fever, only to develop severe toothache. White had a similar problem, but watched in horror as the dapper Armenian dentist, wearing an astrakhan fez and boasting a row of gold teeth, yanked out Fulton's tooth without anaesthetic. White decided he needed only a filling. The dentist, said White, pressed some amalgam into the cavity and, excitedly announcing what he thought of the Turks, declared the job finished. Fortunately White had paid him only an instalment on his fee, for by the following morning, when the dentist arrived to claim full payment, his patient was in real pain. Their payment dispute escalated all the way to the commandant, who ruled that White should pay the fee. But White still refused, forcing the dentist to bring his drill and complete the job.

The following day the reason for the dentist's agitation over his unpaid fee became apparent. 'Puff-puff-Stamboul,' announced the guards, indicating they were to be moved on to Constantinople.

Immediately, it seemed. Within half an hour the prisoners were in the street, shoving and shouting with the hotel managers and guards about missing items. Then the guards demanded advance payment for the *arabas* to take them to the station. Suspecting it was only a habitual demand for *baksheesh,* the prisoners sat down on their bundles and refused to pay. Sure enough, with minutes to spare they were hustled onto the carriages. 'We were beginning to understand the Turk!' wrote White.

On the train the officers finally caught up with the enlisted men from Mosul — or those who were left. Of the 250 who had set out on the terrible march only about forty made it to Aleppo. Sergeant Blaker, the sole surviving Englishman (two other Britishers had made it to Aleppo but were too ill to continue), related the depressing story of the march. White recorded Blaker's account:

'The Turkish officer in charge of their party cared not the slightest for the welfare of his prisoners, riding off in the morning and disappearing till night. After the second day the Arab guard that had set out with them from Mosul, and whom we had bribed into being less callous than was usual, had been relieved by a Kurdish guard.

'The Kurds were cruel and heartless wretches who took delight in torturing the little band and seemed to think that their task was its extermination. Private X had died the second night when sleeping out in his scanty clothes without cover. Y had fallen from a donkey into a river and was found to be dead when pulled out. Z was left behind with a sepoy on a cart provided for the sepoys.

'The cart had broken down and the sepoy rejoined the column later with evidence of maltreatment, declaring that Z had been done to death by the guard because he was too weak to walk.

'W had gone mad, and so on and so on ... For many nights they slept in the open when the muddy ground froze beneath them or rain beat down on them in torrents. Dead were left behind at every halt.

'Their food, consisting of a handful of flour a day, which they had to cook as best they could, was totally inadequate, and for two days they received no food at all!

'They were repeatedly hit if they lagged behind, and Blaker himself had been struck in the back with a rifle butt and though dazed was fortunately strong enough to keep on his feet.'

The contrast with the treatment of the officers was stark. The officers had been fed — and protected by Nogales from the revenge of the Mosul commandant. If Nogales had extended his sense of chivalry to the enlisted men, many more lives might have been saved.

Over the next week they travelled around the Gulf of Alexandretta and through the Taurus Mountains to the plain of Anatolia. The journey was mostly by train, but where the railway was still being cut through high mountains, the prisoners marched.

The mountain scenery was stunning. They marched through the ravine of the famous Cilician Gates. 'Truly we were on classic ground!' White wrote in awe. 'Before us stood the Cilician Gates, the famous Pylae Ciliciae, through which Cyrus, Alexander, Barbarossa and a host of other conquerors had marched. Since the dawn of history, this pass had looked down upon the armies of the Hittites, the Assyrians, Persians, Greeks, Romans, Byzantines, Arabs, Crusaders, Tartars and Turks, as they passed between its portals, locking as they do the route to the orient. The great walls bear many evidences of ancient invaders, and high above the river bed Hittite and Roman tablets are cut into the rock face, one of them by Marcus Aurelius.'

But the nights were freezing, and the food sparse. The guards were usually officious, as the Turks feared the prisoners might try to escape and link up with bands of Armenians roaming the mountains. One night when they were unable to buy food, White recalled, a friendly German officer educated at Cambridge took them to a German cookshop, providing them with a 'never-to-be-forgotten' omelette.

At one railway station Yeats-Brown suffered an embarrassment that much amused his fellow officers. Still thin and weak from his illness, he decided to lie down and rest on some sacks. He was wearing a dark green and white cape not unlike the colour of the sacks. Some porters carrying baggage threw it on the pile. Yeats-Brown was too weak to cry out, but was eventually rescued by his companions.

Passing some German camps the prisoners marvelled at row upon row of German cars and transports. They were also impressed by the engineering of the new railway being forced through the snow-covered mountains, the one remaining obstacle in the dream of a Berlin-to-Baghdad railway. White described the work among the last peaks before the Anatolian plain as a 'continuous engineering masterpiece'. The railway was 'a succession of embankments, bridges and tunnels as mountain after mountain is pierced and swift flowing streams are crossed'.

The Turks conscripted many allied POWs, including Australians, to help finish the rail line through the mountains. Many of the crew of the *AE2* submarine ended up in malaria-infested camps such as Belemedik high in the Taurus Mountains. Some prisoners were put to work loading and unloading munitions between the gaps in the mountain railway, which finally opened just as the armistice was signed in 1918.

Captain Alan Bott, a British air officer who as a POW followed White through the Taurus Mountains a year later (and would join the Australian in his escape from Constantinople), was struck by the 'fantastic proposition' of thousands of Allied prisoners working in these mountains for a private German engineering company.

There was even an Australian paymaster-general, he noted — this was the highly entrepreneurial George Kerr.

Initially distressed by the idea of the prisoners helping load munitions for the enemy, Bott's anxiety turned to delight when he discovered what was happening to the munitions. Guns lost their breechblocks. Crated aircraft arrived in Turkey for assembly in an unusable state — records later revealed official complaints and demands that the original German packers be punished.

'Aeroplanes we attack mostly on the longerongs — those ribs 'uv wood that run dahn the length 'uv the body, ain't they?' Bott quoted one Tommy as telling him. 'English pilot 'oo passed dahn the line some months ergo giv' us the tip. No, it don't seem likely as those things over ther'll fly fer a long time.'

Reaching open country beyond the mountains, White saw another aspect of the railway — how the German financiers had conned the Turks. The Germans had tendered in sections based on mileage, and the Turks, seeing a bargain, clinched the contract. But the German businessmen evidently saw little profit in constructing the railway in a beeline, so the line meandered this way and that, accomplishing considerable mileage without actually reaching the mountains. In one section the line loops around a flat plain in almost a complete circle.

As the prisoners reached the flatlands the whisper went out: they were not going all the way to Constantinople; rather, their destination was to be a sinister-sounding place called Afion Kara Hissar, which translated literally as 'the black rock of opium'.

6

University of adversity

Life as a prisoner of war under the despotic Young Turk regime was a blind lottery. Prisoners reported treatment ranging from quixotic kindness through to neglect and barbaric cruelty. Survival often depended on money, something prisoners had in very short supply, and the whim and character of individual camp commandants.

There was little consistency. Perhaps due to traditional Turkish deference to rank and privilege, officers received very different treatment from enlisted men, being allowed a range of privileges that in many cases made prison life tolerable. Ordinary soldiers suffered much harsher treatment, although some officers were flung into solitary confinement in reprisal for the supposed ill-treatment of Turkish prisoners in British camps and for attempting to escape.

Turkey alone of the war's main antagonists refused to allow international bodies such as the Red Cross or representatives of neutral countries to inspect its POW camps, despite its Red Crescent having reciprocal rights. While British camps were open to inspection, Turkey's treatment of prisoners was hidden behind a veil of secrecy. The American embassy in Constantinople, under Henry Morgenthau and his counsellor Hoffman Philip, made constant representations about prisoner rights, but gained only one visit to a camp. After America entered the war the Dutch legation took on this role.

Officers' pay, on which they relied for survival, was irregular and subject to exchange rate manipulation and pilfering. Parcels from home were plundered by unscrupulous camp guards, and prisoners reported seeing British food tins obviously from their parcels on sale in local markets. Prisoners of war were robbed blind in charges for food. Turkish officers cornered the markets in beer and raki, a strong liquor distilled from raisins and flavoured with aniseed.

Some 16,500 Britons, Indians, Australians and New Zealanders were Turkish POWs. The bulk of these came from the Turkish victory in the siege of Kut-el-Amara, one of the greatest ever defeats of British arms. About 5,500 either died in captivity or were untraced, a depressingly high figure. While Enver Pasha proclaimed Kut captives would be 'honoured guests of the Turkish Government', their actual treatment was shocking. The forced march of these prisoners to Turkey was a modern horror story that makes sickening reading.

Afion Kara Hissar, Tom White's 'home' for almost two and a half years, was one of Turkey's main camps for officers from the start of the war. A small town on the main railway line high on the central Anatolian plain, Afion Kara Hissar was surrounded by fields of poppies and dominated by a huge black rock. Hence its literal name — opium black rock.

The climate here is extreme, with heavy snow and cold winds in winter, and searing heat in summer. Opium poppies, the town's cash crop, flowered in spring and summer, surrounding the town in a blaze of mauve and white. But the beauty was illusory.

Afion's mainly Armenian population had been forcibly removed — camp officials and officer prisoners now occupied the large Armenian houses in the village. White quickly observed that nearly all the Armenian men had vanished. The women and children who survived lived in desperate poverty and hardship. These women, wrote White, eked out a precarious existence by weaving cloth or working on the roads. 'Starving children and their mothers haunted the bazaars where they competed with the pariahs (beggars) for food,' he wrote.

At Afion, White experienced all the paradoxes of Turkish incarceration. It started badly. Turned out at the Afion railway station about midnight after their long journey, the prisoners were marched off — seemingly for hours — until they reached a small courtyard adjoining a mosque. As the group collapsed exhausted on their bundles, White noticed a group of Indians wailing around one of their companions lying inert on the ground. Sergeant Blaker told him that a guard had knocked the Sikh unconscious with his rifle butt for not leaving the train quickly enough. The same guards were responsible for beating the Indians at Pozanti. Blaker and one of the Indians had wrapped the beaten man in a blanket and dragged him from the station. White turned the injured man over. He suspected he was dead.

A Turkish naval officer approached, and in the face of authority the arrogant guards quickly turned servile. White seized the opportunity, complaining to the English-speaking officer about the brutal treatment of the Sikh, as well as previous beatings, and requesting that the guards responsible be punished. The officer promised an inquiry, and White was told later that one of the guards was actually punished. 'We were never sure if he received his deserts.' Fortunately the Sikh recovered.

Once again officers and men were separated. Installed in a newish house, the officers were surprised to learn that many other British prisoners were already at Afion. Indeed, that very afternoon they were visited by a group of fellow officers, who brought them food and cigarettes as welcoming gifts. 'In their ready-made civilian suits, clean and comparatively well fed, we could not but eye them with envy,' said White. Russian officer prisoners called to give each of the new arrivals a mattress.

There were British, French and Australian prisoners from Gallipoli, and Russians from the Caucasus front. The old hands quickly introduced the newcomers to raki, which the prisoners found a quick, numbing aid to forgetfulness. White and his companions relished exchanging stories of war and capture.

'It was good to meet fellow Australians again, and especially . . . men who had been in different campaigns,' White wrote in his diary. He swapped lucky escape stories with Captain Dacre Stoker, the Anglo-Irish captain of the little Australian submarine *AE2*, which had been the first sub to penetrate the dangerous narrows of the Dardanelles on the day of the first Gallipoli landings. Stoker scuttled the sub in the Sea of Marmora after being hit by Turkish fire while trying to disrupt enemy supply lines to Gallipoli. The crew survived and were imprisoned.

White was impressed by stories of Gallipoli, which he had not heard about in Mesopotamia. He wrote later of one officer POW who, badly wounded near Turkish lines, had been used as a rifle rest by Turkish soldiers before they discovered he was still alive.

In Afion White also met officers who would play central roles in his later escape, including Irish Lieutenant (later Sir) Robert Paul and Captain Alan Bott, of the Royal Flying Corps, and Russian officers such as Gabriel Zainchinkoff, Vladimir Vilkovsky and Konstantin Kambani.

In line with the Turkish deference to rank, White and his fellow officers were allocated lower ranked prisoners as servants, or batmen. White asked for an Australian, and Private 'Bluey' Mathews of the 9th Battalion arrived at his door. Mathews had been one of the first ashore at Gallipoli on April 25, and was later wounded in the big push of August. A bullet splintered the bone of his upper arm, from which Turkish doctors extracted some large pieces of bone without chloroform. These Mathews, a tough ex-boxer and shearer, kept in a bottle as a grim souvenir.

Just as White and the newcomers began to settle in, the entire officer corps were thrown into forced detention. It was their fourth day in Afion and they were on their way to visit some of the Gallipoli prisoners when they were stopped in the street by an excited Turkish officer, who counted their numbers several times.

At first the prisoners thought it might have been another problem with their sunbathing on the roof of the their house as they deloused clothes. Apparently they had been unwittingly 'entertaining' the wives of Turkish officers billeted nearby with their semi-nudity. But this time the problem was more serious: three officers had escaped, and the Turks were panicking. The prisoners were marched back to their new home, counted off again, told to pack and then marched with their batmen to a local square, where they found all Afion's officers and their servants assembled.

The scene was bizarre. Here were more than a hundred officers of different countries jumbled together, dressed in outlandish combinations of their national uniforms and local attire. Some were leading pet dogs. Others carried banjos, deck chairs, cooking utensils and items of furniture. The situation was far from amusing, however. The Turks were known to take vicious reprisals for escapes, a practice known by those left behind as 'strafing'.

The three escapees — Stoker of the *AE2*, and Lieutenant Commander Archibald Cochrane and Lieutenant Price of the English submarine *E7*, which had been trapped in a net in the Narrows of the Dardanelles — had climbed out a window the night before. They planned to trek the 200 kilometres to the Mediterranean coast, steal a boat and head for Cyprus.

Assembled at gunpoint in the square, all officers remaining in Afion were marched off in two lines, clutching whatever chattels they could carry. A huge Gurkha captain dressed in pyjama pants and a bowler hat led them in the never-ending marching song:

> We won't be bothered . . . about
> Wherever we go we'll always shout
> We're bothered if we'll be bothered about,
> We won't be bothered about [etc. etc.]

Eventually they were all crammed into an Armenian church near the huge black rock. Their servants occupied some of the galleries while distressed Armenian women and children, apparently ejected from the church, stood outside weeping. The prisoners were informed they would be closely confined until further notice.

Russian officers feared a massacre that night and formed watches to warn of the arrival of Turkish assassins. They led the singing of the various national anthems, including the 'Marseillaise' and 'God Save the King'. Finally they too fell asleep.

'The noise the 200 of us made in sleeping was remarkable,' Yeats-Brown recollected. 'The church was never silent through the night. Some cried out continually in their slumbers, others went through a pantomime of eating. Some moaned, others chuckled. One sleeper gave a hideous laugh at intervals. One could hear it deep down in his throat, and mark it gradually bubbling to his lips until he grew vocal like some horrible hyena.'

Given the traumas of these captured men, Yeats-Brown conceded that the wonder was they slept at all. After the assassination scare had subsided, the party settled down to a new life. Furniture arrived and was piled high, promenading walkways were cleared inside the small church, which measured about one hundred by thirty feet, and, after complaints, extra latrines were built.

The prisoners kept their spirits up. Some wandered from group to group exchanging stories, while others smoked, played cards and drank what raki they could get their hands on. Banjo players led singing groups, the entire assembly sometimes joining the chorus. Turkish sentries occasionally objected, brandishing their rifles from the church galleries. As Yeats-Brown understood it, their main worry appeared to be why the prisoners did not act like cowered Armenians rather than responding to their confinement with boisterous singing. Roll call was taken twice daily.

Yeats-Brown provides a colourful picture of how the assembled prisoners refused to be downhearted: 'See us then at midnight, seated at a table under the high altar. About fifty of us are celebrating somebody's birthday, and a demi-john of araq [raki] graces the festive board. We have sung every song we know, and many we don't. The chorus dies down, and the Master of Ceremonies, still in pyjamas and bowler hat, rises on his sound leg and standing (swaying slightly) at the head of the table, raps on it with his crutch for silence. "Silence for the prisoners band." The band begins. It consists of penny whistles, banjos, castanets, soup-bowls, knives and forks, and anything else within reach.'

By day three, the rowdy officers had mounted a play based on the escape of their three comrades. Produced by Lieutenant Scaife of the submarine *E7*, a former actor and stage manager at a London theatre, it featured the three men noisily escaping, furious prisoner head counts, a commandant under suspicion of taking *baksheesh*, and another prisoner questioned and convicted of helping the escapees.

'Vocal and instrumental items by the Russians concluded a programme that for a few hours carried us beyond the four walls of the church,' said White. 'In the strange surroundings, with the interior of the church dimly lit by flickering torch light, their sad music welling in unison from throats as rich in tone as organ pipes, sounded wild and melancholy and appropriate to the setting of a desecrated church with its flotsam of the eddies of war.'

A few weeks later the prisoners were asked to send the belongings of the three escapees to the local railway station, as they had been recaptured. Suspecting a ruse to steal the remains of the men's property, a receipt was requested, and sure enough, one came back from Captain Stoker.

Although robbed by bandits, the three men had made it to within sight of the coast. But a shepherd they approached for food turned them into police. Arrested, they were imprisoned in the dreaded cells of the ministry of war in Constantinople, where Stoker had already suffered solitary confinement as a Turkish reprisal for the alleged mistreatment of their POWs in British camps in Egypt. Price later died in captivity. Stoker survived, and Cochrane led one of only three successful Turkish escapes.

While the prisoners mocked the Afion commandant in their stage play, the Turkish authorities took the escape more seriously. The commandant was ordered to Constantinople to be court-martialled. His replacement, Bimbashi Musloum Bey, whom White described as a low-browed, baboon-like man with a 'fierce and bestial appearance', quickly earned the prisoners' enmity. Brute, swindler and degenerate were just three accusations levelled by White and others against the new commandant. Russian officers alleged they knew of him from before the war, when he had operated as a private executioner for Enver Pasha.

The prisoners soon received an insight into Musloum Bey's new style. In partnership with his chief aide, Kolassi, he cornered the local beer supply and set up a stall in the church. 'It was ludicrous and Gilbertian to watch our guardians — the booted Musloum and the dull and dignified Kolassi — seated at the table together (so that each might check the honesty of the other) selling stolen beer to whomsoever among their motley charges might allow his thirst to master his conscience,' said White.

Musloum Bey announced that any prisoner attempting to escape would be shot. Given that he had just arrived from a hardship posting in the Yemen — Siberia for the Turks — where he had been guarding Arab criminals, his message was to be believed. At the same time, he announced the arrival of new, more efficient guards.

The weeks wore on in the crowded church. The prisoners could spend the day staring up at the black rock nearby, a symbol of their captivity, but could do little else. The first anniversary of the April 25 Gallipoli landings was celebrated with a singsong, but White felt it rather a depressing show owing to news of the impending surrender at Kut-el-Amara after a five-month siege. At first, the prisoners did not believe the new commandant's boast that Kut had fallen. But the news was later confirmed in dispatches in *Hilal*, a French-language newspaper published in Constantinople. Although *Hilal*'s editorials were biased, prisoners found its news reporting from the various fronts reasonably accurate.

After six weeks in the crowded church the prisoners were at last moved back to houses in the town. British POWs found themselves in four new adjoining two-storey mud-constructed buildings between the railway station and the town centre. The compound had a walled rear garden and a guardhouse, and prisoners slept four to a room. The houses were so new they still lacked windows, toilets and kitchen equipment. Using anything they could lay their hands on — including old planks, packing cases and string — the prisoners built window frames, kitchen ovens, beds and tables.

The industriousness of some prisoners did not stop Musloum Bey from trying to exploit the move. The commandant offered to supply windows to the Russians, living in houses seized from fleeing Armenians, for 16 liras (18 pounds sterling). The Russians scraped the money together only to find the windows had been looted from another Armenian house, and fitted by one of Musloum Bey's guards masquerading for the day as a carpenter.

Extortion by Musloum and the guards knew no bounds. One military police corporal, Shukri Chaoush, levied local shopkeepers for the right to sell to the prisoners. White believed Musloum shared in these profits, for after prisoner complaints Shukri retired from the military, set himself up as a shopkeeper and continued to exploit the prisoners.

The involvement of other guards was confirmed after Shukri's new shop began displaying English groceries, tobacco and sweets obviously looted from parcels arriving for prisoners — all now on sale at fabulous prices. British prisoners boycotted the shop. When Russian prisoners were later transferred to a camp at Kutiah, the shop and some officer guards followed them. The avarice of the commander and guards often featured in camp plays, which were dangerous but satisfying parodies.

Life in camp quickly settled into what Yeats-Brown described as a 'long descent of wasted days'. Captain Alan Bott compared camp life to that of an English village, complete with the usual rumour mill and petty jealousies. There was one thing lacking, he noted — female company, although some officers climbed the walls to meet Armenian women whose desperate straits forced them into prostitution.

Daily routine was governed by whistles — for officers to return to their own quarters, and for lights out. Prisoners were allowed to write home only one four-line postcard in the first year; and both home-bound and in-coming letters were heavily censored. But the prisoners could still learn much news from their censored mail. Cryptic references in letters to 'dad has lost his bag' and 'poor dad has at last been bagged' told them, before reading any of *Hilal*'s doubtful reporting, that British forces (now strengthened under Major General F. S. Maude) had captured Baghdad in March 1917.

Prisoners devised a clever system for communicating with men in other camps such as Angora, Yozgad and Kastamuni. A prisoner transferring to another camp would be given envelopes from letters that had already arrived, and been cleared by the censor, to give to inmates of his new camp. Recipients could then write letters to the addressee using the already cleared envelopes. The system had to be used sparingly, for overuse would invite attention.

Life could be very boring in camp, however. Yeats-Brown later wrote up a diary of his daily routine: 'Monday. Up at 6 am. Skipped 200 times. Two eggs for breakfast, tried my new pekmes (a substitute for jam and sugar made from raisins). Read *Hilal*. Looked out places on my hidden map. Long argument about the use of cavalry in modern war. Walk in Garden. Mutton cutlets for lunch. Completed my new hammock. Argued about free trade. Played badminton in garden. Read philosophy with X and Y. Sakuska (Russian hors d'oeuvres of sardines, onions and anything edible) with A and B at 7.30. Watched Polly (a local woman) picking opium. Dinner at 8. Soup, eggs, suet; very satisfactory. Bridge and bed.'

Tuesday's entry was much the same, with the addition of an attack of mosquitoes, and so on. If this sounds surprisingly comfortable, the officers had applied their ingenuity to making prison life as bearable as possible. Dogs and gardening in the walled enclosure behind the houses were very popular. But gardening space clashed with exercise areas, which became an arena for spirited disputes. Pets accumulated at an alarming rate. A dog craze started with Lieutenant Robert Paul, Royal Flying Corps, who acquired a Persian greyhound. Poodles and virtually every shape and breed of dogs were soon adopted by other officers. The diversion seemed harmless enough until a poodle owned by one officer was found to be crawling with fleas.

Other than dogs, prisoners also acquired tortoises, rabbits and birds. Gambling on tortoise races was a popular pastime. One Russian, White claimed, was on friendly terms with a mouse. Pets even offered an instrument of prisoner retaliation against Musloum Bey. When the commandant loaned his pet parrot to the British prisoners to be taught English, the bird was given to the most profane prisoner, and managed to pick up some choice phrases.

Another example of Musloum Bey's rapaciousness was revealed with the death of Subadar Hazari Singh, who had been in charge of the guard at the British consulate in Baghdad. The British prisoners knew Singh had some money from pre-war savings and a few possessions, and when he died of a fever they were anxious that the Turks did not appropriate them. They wrote to Musloum Bey asking for the money so it could be sent to Singh's family. Fifty pounds was handed over, but Musloum Bey then asked if he could keep Singh's carpets!

The commandant also exhibited an obsessive interest in a number of the young, handsome officers, including the *AE2*'s Lieutenant Geoffrey Haggard. This behaviour horrified the internees, who protected would-be targets as best they could.

The American embassy in Constantinople actively supported the British prisoners, sending parcels of food, clothing and sports equipment. When a cricket ball arrived a guard muttered '*Bomba!*' and it was hastily taken outside and carefully pulled apart. Prisoners organised two opposing cricket teams, and the Turks gave permission for them to play — but initially insisted the teams play on separate grounds.

While cricket was popular among the British, 'boo-froo' was the main sport. The American embassy had sent four tennis racquets, but the prisoners had neither room for a court nor the necessary tennis balls. Then one officer made a net and turned some old socks into 'balls'. The prisoners enjoyed this version of badminton, which came to be known as 'boo-froo'.

Walks were occasionally permitted, and in summer the prisoners could stroll among the blazing poppy fields, watching the baggy-trousered peasant women cutting incisions around the seed pods so that the raw white fluid could ooze out before being harvested. In winter the snow-covered fields reminded many of them of winters at home in Europe.

For White, Afion was his 'university of adversity'. Determined not to waste his time, he took up classical studies and theatre, attended lectures and joined a debating group. He even wrote to education institutions back in Australia for guidance on the best books from which to study political economy. Ancient civilisations became a passion. Without referring to a book, he could accurately chart the rise and fall of Babylon and Ninevah, the Medes, Persians, Chaldeans and Assyrians. 'Yet he confessed that three years earlier, at a time when he was flying in Mesopotamia, he had no more interest in Babylon than in Nashville, Tennessee,' disclosed one later newspaper report, to which White agreed.

White even took up a little archaeology. He theorised that the great rock that dominated the town might be the site for a castle built by the Persian king Xerxes, as recorded by Xenophon. Once, when exploring the rock, he unearthed some broken pieces of pottery. White felt like he was plundering the grave of some departed soul.

Cultural pursuits were certainly not lacking among the innovative prisoners. Plays were produced so professionally that even Musloum Bey attended, bringing an interpreter, who White believed softened the language of some of the spoofs on the Turks. Wigs made from goat hair turned men into 'beautiful blondes' for the female roles. White himself took a hand in theatrical production. Back in Australia, *The Bulletin* magazine, given access to prisoners' letters home by their families, including White's, reported the following tongue-in-cheek item:

'Captain T.W. White, the first officer to gain his certificate at Australia's own Point Cook Flying School, has been prisoner in Turkey now for 11 months, and writes home an average of one letter per week. Abdul seems to treat his prisoners much better than his "cultured" ally, as the prisoners have plenty of books, run a debating society and have a theatre. A revue written and composed by Captain White — who is an old Bulletin contributor — was being staged when the last mail left, and was meeting with much success. For box-plan and prices of admission write to Captain White, Royal Flying Corps, Prisoner of War at Afion Kara Hissar, Turkey-in-Asia.'

The play, a two-act burlesque titled 'Hopeful Horace', featured the author himself as Horace. *The Bulletin*'s cheeky column led to another example of White's prison camp ingenuity. Harold Burston, the magazine's editor, opened his mail in March 1917 to find a two-page account from White in tiny handwriting recounting the cultural life in the camp. How did White get such a letter past the censors to a magazine editor? He addressed it simply to 'Ed Dighter' at 214 George Street, Sydney, which happened to be *The Bulletin*'s address.

Delighted to have a correspondent inside a prison camp, Burston wrote to White's family telling them of White's ruse. 'We have not written him, thinking perhaps that a letter from us may displace one from his own home if he is allowed to receive only a fixed number of letters,' said Burston. 'But will you please, when writing, let him know *The Bulletin* wishes him all sorts of good luck.'

A prodigious correspondent, White wrote regularly not only to *The Bulletin* and his family but also to the Red Cross in London, using his limited mail rights to supply them with details concerning the welfare of prisoners. White also wrote to Flora, his fiancée in Melbourne, whose picture he had displayed in his tent in Mesopotamia.

After his capture, Flora had written to the Defence Department that his mother had told her the news that he had disappeared and was presumably a prisoner. 'As I am engaged to Captain White I am naturally very anxious to hear further news and shall be very grateful if you will let me know when you receive any information as to his whereabouts and conditions,' she wrote.

The Defence Department replied somewhat pompously that any news would be sent to his father, C. J. White. With the war dragging on, Flora's position played on White's mind. He finally wrote to her cancelling their engagement. 'We might as well let things go as they are at present,' he told her. 'For after all . . . what's the use of being engaged when we are separated for such a long time and likely to be for much longer.'

Prison life could clearly be frustrating. White wrote to his brother Percy that he often felt 'fed up' idling his life away, and longed to get back into the family business. Concerns about the future of the business had escalated since his father died in September 1915. From Mesopotamia to Turkey, White had kept up a stream of solicitous letters to his mother, urging her not to worry about him, and relaying positive aspects of his situation.

Relieving the boredom was a constant part of camp life. The prisoners held New Year's Eve fancy dress balls in both 1916 and 1917, producing some sophisticated costumes. 'If some reveller in London had looked in on us at midnight he might easily have fancied himself at an Albert Hall dance,' said Yeats-Brown.

'He would certainly not have guessed that all the clothes and furniture and food were home-made, and that everyone in the room was a British officer. The self-confident flapper, for instance . . . was a major in the Flying Corps. And the girl at the bar, with big brown eyes, who would have offered him *araq* so charmingly was really a submarine officer of the Navy.'

The prisoners were a broad range of people who brought an array of talents from their former civilian lives. Lectures on everything from arctic exploration to life in Malaya proved popular, as did the debating group, until it was banned by the Turks, who feared it was being used to hatch escape plots. Some prisoners ran a weekly newspaper, *The Affioneer*, until it too was banned.

The debating group sparked an interest in current affairs that would dominate White's postwar life. In one debate he found himself leading the argument in favour of White Australia, a policy he and most of his generation firmly supported. To his horror, however, the opposition was led by a fellow Australian, and seconded by another. 'I was rather ashamed to think that my fellow countrymen would advocate a coloured Australia before this English audience,' he noted in his diary. 'I went over the history of the policy and explained its necessity, its popularity in Australia, and that our national existence would be threatened without such a law.'

Others dabbled in the plentiful local supply of opium. White tried chewing the poppy seeds often used by the guards, 'and did not altogether dislike them'. The flamboyant Yeats-Brown was more adventurous. Musloum Bey suspected Yeats-Brown and some other officers of plotting to escape. Those who would not give their sworn word that they would not escape faced solitary detention. Yeats-Brown conceived a scheme to convince Musloum Bey that he was just dreaming away his days in Afion by taking opium. In cahoots with a local Cypriot youth, he acquired all the opium paraphernalia, including the drug, bamboo pipes, a lamp and a bowl. At night he would meet the youth in a room of his home, strewn with carpets and cushions. There, the two would share pipes of opium.

Yeats-Brown claimed he was disappointed and disgusted by the experience. 'The beautiful dreams are a myth,' he said. 'So also is the deadly fascination of the drug. I loathed it more each time I tasted it.' Yet he persisted, claiming he felt he was doing something 'practical', instead of reading philosophy or playing chess like most of his colleagues.

Between sports, cultural affairs, raki and the occasional pipe of opium, the officers of Afion Kara Hissar ensured that their lives were bearable. White later defended this existence as 'no bed of roses', citing the fact that they had to pay for all their food, rent and water. As well, Musloum Bey was always capable of some new act of cruelty. One Russian officer, who raised his hand to defend himself from a sword in the commandant's hand, was given some two hundred strokes of the bastinado; about forty was the norm.

He was then thrown into an underground cell without food or water, and would surely have died there had some British prisoners not secretly lowered food to him through a manhole.

Still, compared with the smaller number of enlisted men — separately detained in much harsher conditions in the town and forbidden to communicate with their officers — life was relatively comfortable. Enlisted men were easy prey to Musloum Bey's cruelties. When Private McKay of the 9th Australian Battalion flattened a guard who had whipped him from behind, Musloum ordered him shot. Relenting under pressure from the officers, McKay was sent to another camp, but not before he was badly beaten.

If Afion POWs felt somewhat isolated from the main action, the arrival of men from Kut was a sobering reminder that the war around them was a horrific affair. By June 1916, officers arriving from the siege provided the first details of the surrender after their five-month ordeal. But officers had been given donkeys for the march, and it was not until groups of enlisted men began to stagger in through September that the true horror emerged.

According to initial British reports, some 13,000 officers and men were taken prisoner when Townshend surrendered, although later figures were as low as 10,000. Already weakened from the long siege, the men were force-marched to Baghdad. From there, batches of them were ordered to march west towards Turkey. With scant food and almost no medical supervision they were simply flung into the desert. It was almost as if it was hoped that the desert would swallow them.

For thousands, it did. Men in piteous condition were left dying by the roadside. A British Foreign Office report recorded that it was only when some British officers were later dispatched on the same route that some of the ill-treatment came to light. The report continued:

'The sights they saw at villages and halting places all along the road hardly bear telling. There were parties of men lying exhausted under any shelter they could find, in all stages of dysentery and starvation; some dying, some dead; half clothed, without boots, having sold everything they could to buy a little milk.

'Only here and there had an attendant of some kind been left to look after them; generally there was no one but the Arab villagers, who mercilessly robbed them, or the under-officer of the local police-post, who stared indifferently and protested that he had no authority to give help. The dead lay unburied, plundered and stripped of their last clothing.

'All across the desert, at one place after another, these sights were repeated; starving and dying men, in tens and twenties, lay in any scrap of shade or mud-hovel that might be allowed them and waited their end.'

One British estimate judged that 2,200 soldiers were never heard from again, with a further 2,600 of the Kut prisoners dying in captivity. The Foreign Office called it a crime of historic proportions; an Austrian observer described it as like a scene from Dante's *Inferno*.

White watched horrified as batches of skeletal men clad in rags fell into Afion in late September 1916. 'It was pitiable to watch [their] progress, staggering along like drunken men, stumbling and falling, being sometimes bravely helped to their feet by their comrades almost as feeble, then tottering along a few paces further before dropping again to earth,' he wrote. 'It was exasperating beyond measure not to be able to render any assistance to them.'

Twenty of the first arrivals died in the first week. Officers saw little processions of ragged men carrying the bodies of their comrades to the local Armenian cemetery. Although forbidden to communicate, the officers collected clothing, food and money for the Kut arrivals. White was particularly keen to find out what had happened to the nine Australians in the siege of Kut. Only two had survived. When one of them, Air Mechanic K. L. Hudson, arrived at Afion, White sent him clothes, tinned food and whatever money he could scrape together from the Australian contingent. Hudson was later put on a camp delivery detail, and one day in White's house the two, although not allowed to talk, held a 'conversation' with their backs to each other as if speaking to someone else. Hudson reported the following detail of one five-day march of sixty miles:

'The rations for this trip of sixty miles were six biscuits, two pounds of atta (coarse flour), one cake of bread, or two and a half lbs of whole barley. Many of the boys sold part of what clothes, boots and blankets they had to the Arab guards during the march. But it was a case of dire necessity . . . the guards had ample supplies and they also sold the fresh water they carried on their horse.

'During this march twenty-seven men dropped out to die through weakness caused by hunger and thirst. I know of three who went mad, and the guards knocked them out with rifle butts and then half buried them under the sand.'

The other Australian survivor, Flight Sergeant J. Sloss, gave White further insights into the march when he arrived at Afion the following year. At one stage Sloss had to tie his wrists to the back of a cart so that he would not drop out during the march. Dropping out meant death in the desert.

Like many others on the march, Sloss was put to work at Belemedik building tunnels through the Taurus Mountains for the Baghdad railway. Together with two Australian submariner prisoners he escaped, making it to the coast near Alexandretta, where, unable to steal a boat, they were forced to give themselves up because of lack of food.

Back in Pozanti camp, Sloss, a skilled engineer, was assigned to one of the repair workshops, where he quickly learned the prisoners' 'go slow' policy. Most of Sloss's efforts were devoted to secretly constructing a collapsible boat of canvas and iron for another escape attempt. Sloss, however, was sent to Afion before the attempt was made to sail the boat to Cyprus. His submariner colleagues did escape, but were again caught on the coast before launching the craft.

Flight Lieutenant Leonard Woolley of the RAF, shot down in Mesopotamia and later force-marched to Turkey, wrote a bitter poem summarising the feelings of those prisoners who were dragged across the desert and then put to work in the camps:

> Famished and spent across the waste, beastlike you drove us on,
> And clubbed to death the stragglers by the way.
> Our sick men in the lazar huts you left to die alone,
> And you robbed the very dying as they lay.
>
> Naked and starved we built your roads
> And tunnelled through your hills,
> And you flogged us when we fainted at work.
> Fevered beneath the sun we toiled, wrecked by winter chills.
> Till death released us, kindlier than the Turk.
>
> And the tunnels we drove for you, the roads that we have made,
> Shall be highways for the armies of your foe.
> We shall mock you in our graves, that in what we did as slaves
> We helped, we too, to work your overthrow.

At Afion, White was also plotting escape. He and Lieutenant Les Luscombe of the 14th Battalion AIF, captured at Gallipoli, would attempt a night flit through a boarded-up side door disguised as Turkish women. But Musloum Bey's fate intervened.

Following the visit to Afion of a Turkish Red Crescent official who took the prisoners' complaints seriously, Musloum Bey was arrested. The complaints included not only robbery of the pay for enlisted men working on roads, but acts of buggery on four of them. Senior British officers in the camp ordered all prisoners to be on their best behaviour during the inquiry so as not to influence the investigating commission in Musloum Bey's favour. Any escape attempts were to be put off for the time being. 'The best laid plans of mice and men ...' sighed White.

In the event, the commandant, who by then had become quite wealthy, was able to bribe his way out of these charges. However, by the time White finally left Afion in July 1918 Musloum Bey had been arrested again and replaced by a new commandant.

7

Escapades and a spook

Escape was a touchy subject among prisoners of war in Turkey. Some thought it every soldier's duty to escape. Others felt equally strongly that escape attempts resulted only in retribution for those left behind; better just to wait for peace.

The guards made it clear that reprisals — or 'strafing', as it was known — would follow any escape attempts, successful or not. Escape plans had to be kept a close secret, and not just from the Turks. Those planning escape found themselves pressured by their fellow officers who feared the repercussions. All Afion prisoners were confined for six weeks after the escape of Stoker, Cochrane and Price.

The Turks used informers among the camp orderlies to pick up information on escape plans. Prisoners doing physical exercise routines were regarded as suspect (perhaps seen as getting fit to run), and usually asked to give their word of honour not to escape.

These paroles divided the officers. White, an ardent escaper, believed officers who gave their word not to escape should face court martial after the war. Fortunately he himself was never asked, for refusal automatically meant a spell in solitary. Yeats-Brown was asked, and after refusing was transferred with a fellow officer to close confinement in a small, filthy house inhabited by innumerable vermin and lice.

The Turks held out another inducement to officers to give their parole — a camp without guards and better creature comforts. Gedos, near Afion, offered parolees greater freedom, and was the source of many a letter home extolling the virtues of Turkish camp life.

The guards also used surprise raids to uncover escape plans. White's secret diaries and documents secretly held by other officers, including maps, were threatened in one such raid. A shortage of pasteboard for cigarette packs had already made concealing the diaries more difficult. White was now hiding the slips of paper in the pith of his helmet and in the soles of his boots. He had carefully screwed out the rivets in the soles, enabling him to slide in the small diary pages. However, a snap raid almost caught him out.

Usually prisoners had time during such raids to hide potentially incriminating documents, but one day Musloum outwitted them. The officers were directed to assemble outside so that new orders could be read out. Once they were outside, guards were posted on all doors while others searched the houses from top to bottom.

White was lucky. He had walked out with the diaries in his pocket, and managed to hide them under a piece of timber in the courtyard. But the guards confiscated every scrap of paper found in the huts, including maps, letters and books. Bundled into sacks, these were stored in the outhouse between the prisoners' houses, with a guard mounted outside.

It was a crisis. Much of the material seized was incriminating, including not only escape ideas but damning criticism of the Turks. What could be done? Officers discussed burning down the out-house and its dangerous contents. Robert Paul was delegated to decide on a response. He made a list of the most incriminating material, then devised a plan.

With the guard at the front door of the outhouse, the only other entry was through a rear window covered by wire netting. This window faced prisoners' house number 4. The Paul plan required an officer to leave number 4 by the window that faced the outhouse, unravel the wire window covering, crawl through and retrieve the incriminating documents.

It was daring, but also very dangerous. The sentry had only to take a few steps from his post outside the outhouse, which measured about twelve feet square, to spot the intruder. The slightest noise on entry would betray him and provoke a ferocious response from Musloum.

So an elaborate subterfuge was hatched. A chain of lookouts was created to warn of any approach by Musloum and to monitor the movements of off-duty sentries. The guard on the outhouse was efficient, but known to have a weakness for dogs. As Paul quietly clambered out the back window of number 4 and set about unscrewing the wire from the outhouse screen, an officer led his Turkish poodle pup past the sentry, initiating a casual chat about dogs.

The sentry swallowed the bait. As other prisoners arrived to help stir the canine conversation, he revelled in the opportunity to air his knowledge of dogs. A spirited conversation of present and past dog breeds ensued, during which Paul made two visits to the outhouse, removing the most incriminating documents and leaving the remainder spilled on the floor.

Musloum pretended to ignore his defeat over the incident, although one officer who had torn up a notebook during the raid suffered 10 days' confinement. From then on, officers were permitted to possess no more than two loose pieces of paper, lectures were forbidden, and walks curtailed. Any notebook or diary was subject to censorship.

Another day, after White and Paul had been in the yards exercising with a dummy telegraph key, Musloum burst into their house. Apparently alerted by a guard who suspected the officers of having a secret wireless set, he rushed past a quiet chess party and proceeded to ransack the attic. While finding no wireless set, Musloum discovered a hoard of bread, rope and fezzes, stored in preparation for an escape bid by Paul and others.

Escapes were rarely successful. Situated in the central Anatolian plain, the main camps like Afion and Yozgad were hundreds of miles from the coast. Escapees were likely to be robbed by bandits or to run out of food before they reached the coast, and many returned of their own volition. At other times, peasants or shepherds they encountered would turn them in, as happened to Stoker, Cochrane and Price. The Turks offered tempting bounties to citizens to deliver escapees.

Some did succeed, however. Cochrane was later transferred to Yozgad, where he helped organise a mass break-out of more than twenty officers. All were recaptured, except his small party, which miraculously made it to the coast, where they stole a boat and sailed for Cyprus. Another group escaped from Kastamuni, making it to the Black Sea coast, from where they sailed to Russia and eventually back to England.

One of the officers in this escape, Colonel E. H. Keeling, later devised secret coded plans that he sent to imprisoned officers to help them escape. In Yozgad camp, Stoker opened an unexpected letter to find a coded message telling him to meet an agent on the coast whom he would recognise by the folded copy of *The Times* he carried under his arm! By 1918 escape had blossomed into a small industry. Some officers devised a wildly ambitious scheme for an RAAF bomber to land in their camp and airlift them to freedom.

Undoubtedly the most ingenious mind game played in any escape — and one in which White played a minor role — was that by the Welshman E. H. Jones and the Australian Cedric W. Hill at Yozgad. Spiritualism, mesmerism and seances were extremely fashionable in this era, with even writers like Arthur Conan Doyle, creator of Sherlock Holmes, captured by the craze.

It began when Jones's aunt sent him a postcard giving details of how to make a ouija board, which when set up with an upturned glass at the centre, supposedly enabled communication with departed spirits. Of course it was all fakery, with the moving finger of the player supposedly acting as a 'medium' to spell out words and messages from the spirit world. But Jones had the thespian knack of delivering a convincing performance, and although he took it up as no more than an amusing joke to pass the time, his fame quickly spread. Blindfolded, he managed to fool sceptics with his 'spook', as the medium he consulted was known, providing messages and war news. Jones's act gained a new dimension when he involved an Australian airman, Cedric Hill, a Queensland jackeroo and amateur conjurer.

The son of a Clydesdale stud manager from Cunningham's Gap in Queensland, Hill demonstrated early inventiveness, floating a homemade raft down a New Zealand river as a quicker means to get to his destination than the mountain roads. Later he built his own biplane glider. In Palestine as a pilot in the Royal Air Force, Hill devised a new bombing device that he used to hit a Turkish reservoir. When his plane was forced down by engine trouble he held off an Arab assault for six hours with a machine gun, a feat so impressive it was featured in the Turkish newspaper *Hilal*.

Jones's and Hill's amazing mind-reading tricks dazzled both prisoners and guards, with the blindfolded Jones, finger on a glass moving around the board, revealing all manner of 'secrets'. He deliberately played on Turkish superstition about spirits.

A Yozgad prisoner visiting Afion en route to the Gedos parolees' camp briefed the officers about the incredible partnership of Jones and Hill. So convincing had the pair become to fellow prisoners that the Yozgad visitor described himself as 'Secretary of the Spiritualistic Society' at the camp. His lengthy report on these wonders of spiritualism would eventually be passed on to bemused British authorities.

The visitor relayed stories of buckets of water that were miraculously overturned, windows that were supernaturally smashed, and amazing prophecies and mind-reading feats. To convince the sceptics, the visitor told of one Yozgad doubter, Colonel Coventry, who was converted when Jones's spook answered a question on a subject supposedly unknown to him.

'What was the question?' shouted Afion doubters.

'What won the Derby in 1862?' replied the visitor, telling how Coventry had written down this question on a piece of paper, and sealed it in an envelope in the presence of others. At the next seance it was answered by placing the sealed envelope on Jones's forehead.

'Why didn't you get the winner of the 1920 Derby as well?' asked White. His scepticism disgusted the faithful, who did not realise that Hill, Jones's accomplice, had unearthed the question and tipped off his partner.

Back in Yozgad, Jones and Hill decided to use spiritualism to help them escape. By now even the camp commandant, Kiazim Bey, and his underlings were coming under the power of the spook. Kiazim quite seriously asked Jones and Hill to consult the spook to find gold buried in the area by a rich Armenian before he was killed in the massacres.

They decided to implicate Kiazim in their escape, leaving evidence of his involvement to prevent any later strafing of fellow prisoners. The practical and resourceful Hill ingeniously constructed a camera partly out of old Cadbury cocoa boxes. The camera captured photographs of Kiazim unearthing some gold coins that Hill and Jones had hidden in the countryside. Naturally, the spook had directed the gullible Kiazim to the gold, being the first instalment of the Armenian's 'buried treasure'.

With Kiazim hooked, the two men were moved out of the camp by having themselves convicted of possessing telepathic knowledge of Turkish troop movements. Kiazim played along, resolving that the pair should spend all their time finding more of the treasure for him. The spook then revealed that another clue to the treasure lay on the Mediterranean coast, from where Jones and Hill planned to escape. But when the spook tried to ensnare Kiazim in a kidnap plan to get there, even the commandant's greed failed to lure him.

The obliging spirit then ensnared Kiazim in a new plan to send the pair of tricksters to a hospital in Constantinople. There, Jones and Hill planned to be declared insane so they could be repatriated to England under a new prisoner exchange program. They took phenacetin to slow their pulse, tore their clothes and smoked strong tobacco to turn their skin yellow. The spook dictated a message to Constantinople, which Kiazim signed. The pair were ordered to Haidar Pasha hospital in Constantinople, leaving their fellow officers with the pictorial proof implicating Kiazim, should it ever be needed. As a clincher of their 'madness', the two men feigned suicide attempts before departure, arranging to 'hang' themselves just as guards entered their room. Even in hospital they were visited by one of Kiazim's underlings, convinced to the last that the spook would eventually deliver riches.

At Afion, White had also reached the conclusion that his best chance of escape lay via Constantinople. The murderous trench warfare on the western front ground on, the 1917 Russian revolution freeing up German troops from the eastern front for their major spring offensive of 1918. From the vantage point of a Turkish prison camp in 1918, after almost two years' captivity the war seemed endless. 'Time ceased to be,' lamented White. Yeats-Brown agonised that the war could last another ten years.

Christmas 1917 was severe, with freezing conditions for weeks on end. White's diary entry of Christmas Day reflected the combination of depression and cold, as fuel stocks ran out:

'In order to get enough [wood] to cook our food we chopped out the ground floor of our house (where the cows are normally kept) and thus were able to carry on till we raised a loan and bought some at sixpence a pound. Some charcoal for the orderlies cost us one shilling and four pence per pound, and as we are unable to spare any for warmth for ourselves we tramp up and down in the snow until we are warm before turning in for bed.

'For a whole month the thermometer has only been once above zero and has fluctuated between six and fourteen degrees below. The chatties in which we keep our drinking water froze solid and cracked and water freezes in our glasses at meals.

'Nevertheless we decided at all costs to enjoy Christmas to the extent of a good dinner for the orderlies and ourselves. We bought a goose for ten shillings, getting it cheaper because it had a wing broken, but it died just as Moore (the orderly) brought it home. We could get no rebate on the dead goose and had to buy another for eighteen shillings. So we enjoyed our Christmas after all.'

After his escape plan with Luscombe was thwarted, White's thoughts turned to Russia. Was this a viable escape route if he could get to Constantinople? The presence of so many Russian officers offered an opportunity to learn the language, and White became a keen student. He made friends with Colonel Prince Constantine Avaloff, a cavalryman who had once been in the Czar's bodyguard. Another Russian, Gabriel Zainchinkoff, assured White after the Russian peace with Germany that he would return to Afion with false passports for him and Luscombe. The Turks had no intention of releasing the Russians, however. Vladimir Vilkovsky, another Afion inmate, became a valued intermediary later in Constantinople. But it was the Kambani brothers, formerly part-owners of a merchant steamer on the Black Sea, who gave White the original plan of escape via Russia.

White had quizzed Konstantin Kambani about life among the fishermen on the Black Sea coast, but the Russian quickly saw through the questioning. 'If you could reach Constantinople, Meester Wi-et,' Kambani said, 'perhaps you could escape to one of our ships which now trade between Odessa and Constantinople. A new prisoner told me there is a ship there now. And in the Café Maritza, which I knew before the war, there is a waiter called Theodore who may help you.'

Meester Wi-et was intrigued. But how to get to Constantinople? It was a dilemma many other officers wrestled with. Jones and Hill had accomplished it from Yozgad by feigning madness. Afion was about to experience an epidemic of *malade imaginaire*, as many officers descended into prison depression in the hope of a ticket to Constantinople.

May 1918 brought two developments in White's evolving escape plans. Seven new prisoners arrived from the Palestinian front, among them Captain Alan Bott of the Royal Flying Corps, later better known by his pen name 'Contact'. Bott, with heavily hooded eyes and a scared face from his Palestine crash, was an avid escaper who wanted to team up with White or others.

After the failure of the Allies' Gallipoli and Mesopotamia expeditions in 1915, new campaigns in Palestine and again in Mesopotamia in 1917–18 began to yield real success.

British forces under the command of Major General F. S. Maude recaptured Kut-el-Amara in February 1917, ten months after its surrender. Moving up the Tigris with new gunboats and armed river steamers, the British finally took Baghdad on March 11.

But it was in Palestine that the Allies had the first indication that their advances could 'roll up' the Turkish empire. British forces, including Australian and Indian contingents, reached the Palestine border in 1916 to fend off Turkish thrusts against the Suez Canal. The arrival in 1917 of General Sir Edmund Allenby — known as 'the Bull' — electrified the campaign. In October the Australian Desert Mounted Corps made its famous charge across the sands to capture Beersheba, while Allied forces took Ramleh and Jaffa, entering the holy city of Jerusalem in December.

T. E. Lawrence, of 'Lawrence of Arabia' fame, added a new dimension to this campaign, enlisting the aid of rebel Arabs against the Turks in a new form of guerrilla warfare. Whether Lawrence's Arabs or the Australian 10th Light Horse were first to enter Damascus in October 1918, ending the centuries-long Ottoman domination of Syria, is still a matter of historical contention.

Damascus, then still in Turkish hands, was the scene of Captain Alan Bott's second escape bid. Shot down on the Palestine front, Bott suffered a badly smashed leg and eye. He cursed his luck — he was just a few days away from leave in Cairo. While escaping from hospital, he further damaged his leg climbing the hospital wall, which forced him to return to his bed.

In Damascus he hatched a plan to escape with several Australians. They bribed a local Syrian, 'George', offering money and the promise of a lifetime job in Australia, to obtain horses and guide them to the Mediterranean coast. But George was arrested and confessed all. He was last seen under heavy guard on a train to

Aleppo. 'I ask pardon,' George pleaded pathetically of Bott. None was given then, but after the war Bott returned to Damascus in a vain bid to find George and pardon him.

On the train to Afion, Bott again tried to escape. He had the idea of stealing a German aircraft and flying it to British lines, but this bid was foiled by alert guards. On his first night in Afion, at a raki party thrown in his honour, Bott savoured the camaraderie of the camp, telling the strangely dressed prisoner next to him of his firm intention to escape. 'Not so loud,' the man whispered. It was Yeats-Brown, dressed in a military overcoat, Turkish slippers and monocle. 'You can't trust half these Russians. Come over to the corner.'

The smoke- and raki-filled room that night contained many of the characters who would figure in escapes and plots to bring down the Young Turks in intrigue-filled Constantinople in the dying months of the war. Apart from Yeats-Brown, there was White, Robert Paul, and the Russians Avaloff and Vilkovsky.

Yeats-Brown told Bott of the latest obsession — to get sent to a hospital in Constantinople. He himself had claimed nose trouble, and having gained the friendship of a local Turkish doctor, was being sent to the capital for 'treatment'.

Yeats-Brown's opium binge had helped him with the introduction to the local doctor. His run-down condition due to drugs, coupled with a few astonishing medical problems he culled from a French periodical in the doctor's waiting room, were sufficient to get him transferred. His opium use had led to his being viewed as an amiable invalid. If Bott could invent his own half plausible ailment, he might persuade the Turkish doctor to do the same for him, Yeats-Brown confided. Fortunately Bott did not have to resort to such subterfuge. He and the other recently arrived airmen were informed they were to be sent to Constantinople in any case, presumably for interrogation.

The second event in May 1918 that heightened White's anxiety to get to Constantinople was the rumour of an impending prisoner exchange. Overnight, prison ailments ran riot. Men began to limp, while old wounds that had healed were rebandaged. Prisoners began to claim deafness, memory loss and mental illness.

Contemplating what *malade imaginaire* he might adopt to get to Constantinople, White had a stroke of luck. At a rollcall outside 'Australia House' one night he was told by a guard that 'Vi-at Effendi' was to go before a Turkish prison medical officer for an inspection. White at first thought it was one of the two other 'Vi-ats' in the camp, but to his surprise found the initials were indeed his. Baffled by the purpose of this inspection, but determined to make the most of it, White decided to develop a 'tubercular' ankle.

A football injury sustained some time before had for some months left White on crutches.

The ankle had regrettably improved to the extent that White had won a recent hundred-yard dash, winning money and some raki from his fellow officers. Hoping that his recent brush with fame as a sprinter had not reached the Turkish medical officer, White resumed his crutches and began a campaign of strenuous skipping, applying bandages to the ankle, which began to show signs of the blue weal from a hot poultice wrongly applied after the football injury. A broken instep from an earlier football injury had also left some protruding bone, which White hoped would add to the effect.

Smoking copious cigarettes and taking quinine to give himself a haggard appearance, White practised his 'limp'. A French officer friend, Lieutenant de Vaisseau Bossy, who would accompany White to the examination as an interpreter to give him time to think over replies, warned him the meeting with two doctors would be tough. 'If you have only to pass the Ottoman Greek doctor, you will have no difficulty,' he said. Bossy had been under the Greek's care for malaria, and had found him sympathetic to the Allied cause, and always up with the latest war rumours. 'But the chief doctor is a Turk, and is ignorant as well as suspicious,' he warned.

Bossy argued White's case before the two doctors: the ankle wound had prevented any exercise; relatives in England had heard of the injury and no doubt were responsible for cabling for an examination; treatment for such a wound was just not available in Afion. Ordered to display the offending ankle, White gingerly unwrapped the bandages and winced appropriately as the doctors prodded it. He described sleepless nights and the discomfort of constant use of crutches. Both doctors appeared sceptical, until Bossy's sly wink to the Greek appeared to elicit some enthusiasm. But the Turk remained unconvinced, informing White the ankle was not serious enough to send him to Constantinople. White kept up the act, however, carefully rewinding the bandages and then hobbling on crutches until well out of sight in case the doctors used field glasses.

The following week White, still keeping up appearances, learned that his performance had succeeded after all. After much discussion and, apparently, observation as the airman limped back to camp, the Turkish doctor had finally agreed with the Greek's diagnosis. He was to be sent to Constantinople for treatment.

In the event, he had to wait more than a month, constantly hopping around on a walking stick and avoiding all games. White used this time to practise his Russian and talk over escape plans with Yeats-Brown and Paul, both of whom had also secured Constantinople passes with phony nose and ear ailments. He also spent time discussing underground networks in the capital with the Russian Kambani.

Finally the departure day arrived, and White was given orders to catch the evening train — with a guard, of course. But how to get on it? When the already overcrowded train pulled into the station the assembled crowd began pushing bags, clothing and sacks of flour through windows before clambering on board.

A railway official, trying to find a space for the two, wrenched at a compartment door. White abruptly realised that the bundles of old clothes he was standing on in the aisle in fact contained the body of a man lying at the door. In any case, the occupants of the compartment, a party of Turkish officers, refused White entry.

The official declared the situation hopeless and suggested they wait another day, but with his baggage aboard White simply had to find a place. Finally, two Jews in European dress offered standing space in their compartment. Forcing himself in, White was surprised to find a vacant seat and took it, knowing he might be told to move when the legitimate occupant returned. As White struggled to adjust to the heavy smell of tobacco and garlic, not to mention the unwelcome attention of fleas and lice, a man who spoke English appeared and asked him to guard the baggage beside him. White agreed, and waited out the hours until dawn.

Just before the train finally pulled out of the station, the English speaker returned to claim not just the bag, but his seat. While White looked on, a polite battle broke out between the English speaker and a Greek sitting next to White. Following a lot of gesticulation, the English speaker departed, presumably to find a place elsewhere. White slumped into the seat, exhausted.

Pandemonium reigned as the train pulled away at daybreak, with some would-be passengers forcibly ejected while others clung desperately to the carriage steps. But for White and his escape hopes, all roads now led to Constantinople.

8

Cuckoo's nest hospital

As White's train trundled towards the capital in July 1918, Constantinople was living up to its reputation as a city of intrigue.

It was high noon for the Young Turks, the junta of army officers who had overthrown Sultan Abdulhamid II in 1908, replacing him with his more pliant half-brother Mehmed. But the corruption and incompetence of the Young Turks, particularly its leaders Enver and Talat, had sown the seeds of their downfall, generating widespread popular unrest. War speculators drove up the prices of staples — butter was almost worth its weight in gold — and the Ottoman Empire continued to lose territories as the war progressed.

Rumours of plots and assassinations swept the city. Police spies were everywhere. British bombing raids from the island of Mudros in the Aegean both stirred up fear and encouraged underground opposition groups.

White's Greek travelling companion gave him his first insights into this den of intrigue. As the train wound slowly through Anatolia, White's pro-British neighbour bought him food and offered to lend him a substantial sum of money to help him escape. White declined the money, but lapped up the information.

The war news was bleak on all fronts. The Germans had launched a new push on Paris, while in the east, although the British had made gains in Palestine, Turkey had benefited from the withdrawal of Russia after the revolution. Turkish forces had overrun the Caucasus and occupied Baku on the Caspian Sea. The Young Turks had grand schemes of a renewed Turkish empire reaching into Central Asia.

White and his companion agreed that the end of the war was some time away yet. 'This conviction strengthened my resolve to escape,' recorded White, who found the two-day trip, punctuated by sightseeing and pleasant meals, very relaxing after prison camp. It was one of the ironies of Turkish POW life that despite the many cruelties suffered by some officers, prisoners were still allowed such luxuries.

In Constantinople, White regained his 'limp' during the walk from the railway station to Haidar Pasha hospital on the Asian side of the Bosphorus, part of a rambling barracks made famous by Florence Nightingale, who nursed wounded British soldiers there during the Crimean War in 1854–56.

On his first night he watched British aircraft bomb the city while a fellow patient, a conscripted Turkish Jew, pointed out the highlights of the city caught in the sweep of searchlights. While he found this exhilarating, disappointments followed.

British officers and his potential escape partners were mainly held at Gumush Suyu hospital over on the European side of the Bosphorus. The doctors at Haidar Pasha assessed his foot as not 'tubercular' after all.

'How can they make such a statement without having X-rayed it,' White protested.

'But we have no X-rays,' replied the doctors.

'Not here, but it is well known that there is a most complete apparatus at Gumush Suyu,' insisted White, having already ascertained this. 'Why should I not be sent there?'

He was. On a ferry crossing the Bosphorus the next day White was captured by the city's beauty. On the old Stamboul peninsula stretching down to the opening of the Golden Horn rose the domes and minarets of the ancient St Sophia cathedral, commissioned by the Emperor Justinian in the sixth century (now Aya Sophia

Museum), the Blue Mosque and the magnificent sprawling Topkapi Palace of the Sultan, famous for its harem. Facing Stamboul across the Galata Bridge was residential Pera. To the right the Bosphorus, with its pretty villas, kiosks and gardens, tapered away towards the Black Sea. Ferries plied the intersecting waters.

White's day-dreaming about these immortal landmarks was rudely interrupted when a ruffian tried to steal his kit, but a swift kick put an end to that.

At Gumush Suyu ('Silvery Waters'), White joined the growing band of POW malingerers flocking to Constantinople hospitals in the hope of being exchanged or devising escapes. Alan Bott, feigning 'melancholia, nervous fits and vertigo', had arrived, while Yeats-Brown (nose ailments) and Robert Paul (ear problems) had just passed through on their way to Psamatia hospital in western Constantinople.

Skylarking on his first day, White hid under the sheets pretending to be an Australian pilot shot down in the air raids, blowing cigarette smoke from under the bed linen at his fellow malingerers until they ripped off the sheets.

'Where is Hill?' White inquired, anxious to find his celebrated fellow Australian, for Hill and his spiritualism partner Jones were now the most famous tricksters of them all.

'That's him,' said one officer, pointing to a small figure crouched on a nearby bed whom White had mistaken for a demented Turk. 'Don't speak to him, he's quite mad. We've all tried to talk to him but he won't talk. He's got religious mania.'

White stared in amazement. 'I had never seen so woebegone an object,' he said. 'His unkempt hair grew almost to his shoulders and was lost in an untidy beard. His face was drawn and sunken, his jaw dropped, and his body thin and wasted. A small Bible lay open upon his drawn-up knees and with his pallid face resting in his skinny hands he alternately sobbed and moaned. Hill had not spoken, apart from praying, for months, and refused most food.

'What a consummate actor, I thought, with the admiration of the amateur malingerer for the master. I sat down to observe and admire a man whose fortitude and will power could carry him so far.'

White could not believe that a flyer praised even in the Turkish press for his six-hour struggle before capture could now be suffering 'religious mania'. He resolved to help Hill in any way he could. That night he lay awake late, creeping over to the bed of the also sleepless Hill at about 2 a.m.

'I took his hand and whispered close to his ear that I did not believe that he was mad, but that I could see he was very ill, and that as a fellow Australian I insisted on helping him,' said White. 'Mentioning also that I had a tin of butter, a tin of milk, sugar and a packet of cocoa in my kit, which I received the day I left Afion, I offered to feed him with these if he would allow me.'

White half expected an irrational answer, as except for praying Hill had not spoken for months. Instead he heard a very sane reply.

'I have been very ill with dysentery, and being neglected, am in a pretty bad way,' Hill whispered after a pause. 'I would be glad of a little of your food, but do not speak to me. We can correspond with notes that can be got rid of in the lavatory.'

That exchange began a covert routine that probably saved Hill's life. Next morning as Ibrahim the orderly tried unsuccessfully to feed Hill and clean up around him, White stood by, tapping his forehead. Ibrahim smiled and giggled knowingly.

Secretly Hill began to take food from White, who soon assumed the public mantle of someone who could somehow control the 'madman'. White doctored his food with opium and sugar. Within a few days the madman, who was actually genuinely ill with neglected dysentery, began to gain some colour in his cheeks.

The notes game enabled them to correspond. Whenever White saw Hill's gaze fixed on him he knew there was a screwed up note on the floor. 'For God's sake, make me have a bath,' Hill told him one day, having refused all bathing efforts by hospital staff in order to maintain his madman image. Picking up a stick and threatening Hill, White 'drove' him to the bath. Hospital staff and fellow patients assumed White had some power over the madman.

Another note begged White to get a larger print Bible from the Dutch legation. 'This one is blinding me,' he wrote. White tried to persuade him to give up his excessive mortification of the flesh and constant praying, suggesting Hill might really go out of his mind rather than just playing an elaborate hoax.

'I have made up my mind to persist to the end, if it kills me,' Hill wrote in a note. 'Maybe I am not so far from being mad already. Watch my eyes when I pray.' White did, and noticed Hill could not keep his eyes closed, with his eyelids persistently blinking and twitching.

Jones' act, meanwhile, was quite different. He maintained he had become a Turk, changing his name to Ahmed Hamdi Effendi and claiming he did not want to return to England. Imagining British plots to kill him, he wrote to Enver Pasha, the Turkish war minister and most notorious of the Young Turk gang, outrageously demanding protection. Again, both doctors and British patients were taken in. Jones tore up money he received in the mail, leaped into the hospital fish pond with his pipe in his mouth declaring he was on fire, and distributed aid parcels he received to Turkish patients. When British bombers appeared over the hospital at night, he would rush to the window, shouting, 'Give me a gun to defend myself, this is all a plot to kill me'.

Hill and Jones maintained their superb but gruelling performances for six months, fooling even the eminent Turkish psychiatrist Professor Mazhar Osman Bey. Doctors were planted as patients in neighbouring beds, but Jones and Hill survived even this scrutiny. They were finally exchanged and sent back to England just as the armistice was signed. Both admitted later there were times they thought of abandoning their act, but each was inspired by the other. Between them they pulled off one of the most consummate acts of malingering in medical history.

Yeats-Brown also found hospital in Constantinople a comic experience, almost like a picnic. He and Robert Paul invented a drink of half brandy and half sour milk so patients could stroll innocently around the hospital at their leisure with a creamy-looking medicine in their hand.

'The hospital at Haidar Pasha was the most delightfully casual place imaginable,' he wrote later. 'One wandered into one's ward in a Turkish nightshirt, and wandered out again at will, the only limits to peregrination being the boundaries of the hospital and one's own rather fantastic dress.

'Unless one asked for medicines or attendance, no one dreamed of doing anything at all in the way of treatment. The only attention the patients received was to be turned out of the hospital when they were either dead or restored to health.'

Rumour mongering and lies were a great source of fun. Yeats-Brown and Paul persuaded staff and visitors that the English bombers in air raids were really German designed, to show what would happen if their Turkish ally wavered. The rumour soon circulated back to the hospital.

'Nothing was too improbable to be true in Constantinople, and nothing indeed was too absurd to be possible,' Yeats-Brown wrote. 'Enver Pasha had made a monopoly in milk, and cornered [the market] in velvet. The new Sultan was intriguing for the downfall of the Young Turks. The funds of the Committee of Union and Progress [Young Turks] had been sent to Switzerland, where a Turkish pound purchased thirteen francs of Swiss security, or half its face value. Fortunes were won and lost on the meteoric fluctuations of paper money.'

As with Yeats-Brown and his nose problem and White with his 'injured' foot, Alan Bott was having difficulty making his false melancholia convincing. He admired Hill's ability to sit for twelve hours a day reading the Bible, not talking to anybody or joining in discussions. Even Jones's cheerful lunacy entertained and fooled him. 'If that were acting, we agreed, it was very wonderful acting,' he said.

Bott tried faking sleep walking. 'Wearing a night-shirt I walked woodenly into the passage, with arms outstretched and head upheld. The guard was dozing on a bench that faced the door.

He took not the least notice. Feeling hurt at such disregard, I turned and passed him again, this time taking care to nudge his knee. He rubbed his eye, shrilled an exclamation, and began running in the opposite direction. When he returned with the sergeant of the guard, a quarter of an hour later, I was in bed and apparently asleep.'

An ingenious fib, however, sufficed to keep him in hospital, at least for a while. He had gained a reputation as an English teacher, and when a doctor asked to be taught, saying he was a great admirer of British prime minister David Lloyd George, Bott let it slip that as a cousin of Lloyd George he would be glad to teach him. Soon hospital staff were lining up to be taught by the cousin of the famous Allied leader.

For the malingerers who would not possibly qualify for prisoner exchange, escape now became an urgent priority, for the alternative was to be sent back to prison camp. White and Bott, teaming up, pinned their hopes on a certain 'John Willie', a Bosnian aviator in an adjoining ward who wanted to get to America. Bott refined the plan with John Willie while strolling the hospital garden with books in hand, ostensibly giving him English lessons.

The idea was that the Bosnian, almost recovered from injuries suffered when shot down over Palestine, would return to his unit near Constantinople, steal an aeroplane and fly the three of them to Mudros. White and Bott would escape from hospital and hide in a wood near the aerodrome. The Bosnian would land the stolen aircraft, pick up the two escapees, and make the run to the island.

John Willie, however, was too talkative, and authorities got wind of the escape plot. The Bosnian disappeared from the hospital.

White and Bott fell back on their other plan to escape via Russia, stowing away on a Russian freighter in Constantinople harbour. That meant finding their contact Theodore, a Greek waiter at the Café Maritza in a narrow street in crowded Sirkedji in old Stamboul, across the Galata Bridge from Pera. White had heard about the Café Maritza — a mean but popular eating house, as he called it — from Russian prisoners at Afion. It quickly became a favoured haunt of the malingerers whenever they could wangle their way into town.

One Sunday shortly after his arrival in Constantinople, the guards gave White and two other prisoners permission to walk outside the hospital grounds under the supervision of guards, or *postas* as they known. After generous distribution of *baksheesh* among their *postas*, they walked through Pera, over the Galata Bridge and into the heady atmosphere of garlic and intrigue at the Maritza.

The small, blue-spectacled Theodore appeared quickly at their table. He spoke many languages, was a first-rate gossip and was always willing to act as a messenger — for a fee. Most important, the Allied officers believed he was trustworthy. Theodore always believed the Allies would win, and had reportedly refused offers to act as a Turkish spy.

After seating their guards at another table, he would sidle up to the officers' table and produce a menu. Bott described his technique:

'"Bon Jour! What would you like, gentlemen?" Then, running his finger down the list as if suggesting something to eat, he would continue: "I heard today that the Grand Vizor had quarrelled once more with the Sultan"; or, "Enver Pasha was shot at in Galata yesterday, and is wounded in the chest. It is said he will not recover". He never failed to produce at least one such rumour. Most often he would announce that Bulgaria (a German ally) was about to make a separate peace, which possibility was reported in Constantinople at least a dozen times before it actually happened.'

Theodore's fee for acting as a messenger was high — twenty piastres for each note delivered. Again, Bott describes his technique:

'"Theodore, my friend," one would say. "I want you to go to Pera for me."

'"Good! If you have not written the letter I will engage the guards while you prepare it."

'He strolled across to the guards table with the news that the British officers would be pleased to buy them whatever they wanted to eat; and the prisoner scribbled his note, a slip of paper resting on his lap and the body of Theodore screening him from the guards in the far corner. Later, the letter would be handed to the Greek waiter in the middle of the Turkish notes with which one paid the bill.

'If a reply were brought, Theodore delivered it under cover of a menu-card, always with a whispered reminder, "twenty piastres". During the last six months of the war he must have been the messenger for scores of communications.'

On that first day, White got straight down to business: 'Satisfied with his integrity as a conspirator, I threw all my cards on the table, and while examining the menu pointed enquiringly to a certain dish and quietly told him that we meant to escape to the *Batoum* [the ship mentioned by Russian friends in Afion] and would be glad of his help. He evinced not the slightest surprise but gesticulated as if in explanation of the menu and asked how he might be of assistance.'

By the time they departed the Maritza, Theodore had promised to make inquiries from the engineers of the *Batoum*, as well as to find them a hiding place in Constantinople. White's diaries contain the record of what he termed a Falstaffian feast while these arrangements were made:

Constantinople August 4 1918.

Omelette	25 piastres
Chop	28 "
Bread	18 "
Steak	28 "
Wine	30 "
Stewed apricots	20 "
Third share of postas's feed	37 "
Melon	15 "
	201 piastres
	(Thirty-one shillings, ten pence)

After completing their business for the day, White's party, complete with guard, visited his Greek friend from the rail journey to Constantinople, who bought them salads, coffee and cigarettes at restaurants along the Petits Champs. White admits the prisoners gorged themselves like small boys:

'Beneath shady planes and acacias and festoons of coloured lights, a moderately bad band discoursed immoderately ancient music, and as we watched the gay and well dressed heterogeneous throng, pretty unveiled Turkish women, attractive Greeks and Armenians, swaggering German, Turkish and Austrian officers in resplendent uniforms — we lived in a seventh heaven of transient freedom and content.'

Unfortunately they were spotted by police spies. The next day the authorities told them their truancy meant they would be turned out of the hospital immediately and sent to the higher security Psamatia.

White was determined to complete his escape plans. As the prisoners' walked to the Psamatia under escort he declared — right at the door of the Maritza — that his bad leg meant he could go no further without a rest. 'After a wordy argument with the most truculent of the guards we were permitted to enter,' he said.

Theodore quickly appeared at their table. As he pocketed his fee, he explained that while unable yet to find them a hiding place, he had talked to one of the *Batoum*'s engineers. They would provide shelter in return for an adequate bribe.

Hustled out of the Maritza by the guards, the prisoners chanced upon Prince Avaloff, the Russian colonel from Afion, in the street. After the Bolshevik peace the Turks had released many of the Russians and Georgians. Avaloff told them the latest news about the escape of Yeats-Brown and Robert Paul from Psamatia. The two had apparently separated after escaping the week before, with Paul setting out for the Bulgarian coast disguised as an Arab. Yeats-Brown was in hiding in Constantinople. Their guards dragged the prisoners from a beer hall where Avaloff tried to buy them drinks as they lapped up this news.

At Psamatia, however, security was quickly tightened following the escape. Prisoners were housed in a former Armenian theological college, with officers put in the various teachers' rooms and several hundred soldiers occupying the dirtier schoolrooms and outhouses. All were awaiting either transfer to an inland camp or exchange.

Once again the repercussions of escape attempts on the comfort of fellow prisoners left behind became an issue. As rumours spread of new escape bids, one British colonel told the officers: 'After the war I'll hang, draw and quartah the next fellow who clears off from Psamatia. A successful escape can't be done in Turkey, and it's futile to try.'

With news of Paul's recapture, the colonel's words carried the ring of truth. Yeats-Brown, however, was still at large — and in the most unlikely circumstances.

The pair had staged their daring escape on July 27, aiming to walk the five miles to a safe house arranged, through negotiations with Theodore, with Miss Whitaker, an English resident of Constantinople who risked her safety to aid prisoners. While fellow officers distracted the street sentries one evening, they climbed out a window, edging their way along a narrow ledge in full view of the sentries, had they bothered to look up. After scaling a wall they then crawled along rooftops to the next street, planning to drop down to the street and run.

To their distress, however, they found themselves directly opposite the local fire station, where a love-sick fireman was spending the night at the window waiting for his girlfriend. They lay there until dawn, when the fireman finally gave up his vigil and turned in, allowing them to slip down into the street. Disguised with dyed hair and fezzes, they made it to the safe house, the home of a Greek family. After a few days Paul donned Arab clothes and set off for the coast, accompanied by a young waiter from the Maritza. Every time police inspectors approached the house, Yeats-Brown had to crawl into the underground cistern. He quickly tired of this, so was quite amenable when one of the daughters of the household had a bright idea.

'You must be disguised as a girl,' she declared one day. 'I will buy you a wig at once.' Mademoiselle Josephine, a tall, somewhat eccentric German governess unfortunately suffering from consumption — hence the husky voice — was created.

The already eccentric Yeats-Brown loved his new role. 'After very careful shaving, I began to splash about confidently at my toilet table,' he said. 'There was Vesuvian black for the eyebrows, bistre for the eyelashes, rouge, carmine — more powder — more rouge — and at last I showed my satisfied face to Miss Whitaker, who gave a cry of horror, and flatly refused to be seen in my company.'

The resourceful Miss Whitaker quickly entered into the spirit of things, however, arranging new make-up and clothes for Mademoiselle Josephine. 'The dressing up was quite exciting,' admitted Yeats-Brown. 'Silk and lace and whalebone, especially a lot in front, was the basis on which I was built. Gloves I had always to wear, of course, and a veil was advisable, chiefly to tone down my blinding beauty to the eyes of passers-by.'

Mademoiselle Josephine became Miss Whitaker's constant companion, visiting restaurants and surviving surprise meetings with Turkish women. 'Never for a moment was there any suspicion of my identity,' he proudly declared.

Yeats-Brown revelled in his disguise, which afforded him at least limited movement around Constantinople. 'I learned how to walk in a ladylike fashion, and how to powder my nose in an engaging manner,' he said with no hint of embarrassment. "My arms and legs had to be kept under various restraints. A mincing gait was soon acquired, but I found sitting still more awkward. My knees evinced an almost ineradicable tendency to cross themselves or sprawl, while my gloved forearms, to the last, felt as unwieldy as a baboon's.'

Miss Whitaker found her companion new accommodation, and for a month Yeats-Brown maintained the disguise, even allowing a Russian colonel to kiss his hand in a restaurant as they conspired to help Yeats-Brown escape through the Caucasus. That plan fell through, and Yeats-Brown was finally forced to abandon his disguise so he could visit contacts in the docks and other low-life areas to arrange his escape.

Again Miss Whitaker came to his aid. She quickly found him a small fake moustache, spectacles, a secondhand suit, white waistcoat and watch chain, elastic-sided boots and a bowler hat. With more hair dye, Mademoiselle Josephine was transformed into an unemployed Hungarian mechanic.

The new disguise enabled him to mix more freely, and he lapped up the growing discontent in the capital with the corruption of the Young Turks and the intrigue to bring them down. The body of a Turkish officer involved in a coup plot was left in one of the main streets for days. Greek residents clapped in the streets during British air raids.

Five weeks after his escape, Yeats-Brown was arrested while meeting with other escapees in Theodore's own home. Theodore and his family were marched off with the escapees to the central gaol. Miss Whitaker, who was also under police surveillance, was lucky to escape. Yeats-Brown, fearing she could be traced through the hairdresser who had made his false moustache, tore it to pieces in his pocket while he was being questioned by police.

Transferred to the military prison, Yeats-Brown faced the military commander of Constantinople, the infamous Djevad Bey, who was fascinated by his fake passport. It contained a forgery of Djevad's own signature, which Yeats-Brown had suspected would not withstand much scrutiny.

'Who forged it?' Djevad Bey demanded.

'May I look?' Yeats-Brown responded. 'Is that really your signature?'

'It is indeed. With it you could easily have got out of the country.'

'What an idiot I was not to use it!' Yeats-Brown said, who later admitted he felt faint just thinking about the missed opportunity.

'You were!' Djevad Bey laughed. 'They would have passed you through the Customs on seeing this.'

Yeats-Brown endured a month of solitary, occasionally glimpsing his compatriot Paul in the corridors of the gaol. The two eventually teamed up again, acquiring fezzes and maps one day when allowed a visit into town. Not surprisingly, they also met the courageous Miss Whitaker on that visit. Later they simply walked out of gaol by mixing with a crowd in the square outside the prison.

No such opportunities were offered White and Bott, now in the more secure Psamatia. Time was running out. Unless they could convince Turkish doctors and a newly arrived British exchange board of their 'infirmities' they would be sent back to Afion.

As each prisoner lined up for his examination, Turkish guards tried to apply their system of patrilineal names. White became Char-les-Valter Viyett-Melbourne. A fellow prisoner whose name coincided with his father's became James Fulton-James Fulton. Another, whose Christian name was lost in the records and who was consequently questioned about his grandfather, became known as Stone-Stone-Stone.

When Char-les-Valter Viyett-Melbourne was called, to much amusement from his mates, White stumped upstairs for his examination as loudly as he could. He had cropped his hair short, revealing the scars of his Mesopotamian capture. But this time his act was not sufficiently convincing, and he was passed out for return to a camp.

Only two of the actually wounded officers and ten soldiers were marked down for exchange. For the rest, it was back to camp. But the group who intended to flit — White, Bott, Fulton and Stone — celebrated, laughing about their 'examination' in the privacy of their room.

They now had little time. After Yeats-Brown and Paul's escape, visits to Constantinople had been forbidden, so they were out of touch with Theodore and his negotiations with engineers from the *Batoum*. Luck was on their side, however, as quartered in an adjoining building was Vladimir Vilkovsky, the Ukrainian aviator from Afion. In the wake of the revolution in Russia, the Ukraine had emerged as a new republic, and Vilkovsky was angling to be attached to the planned embassy in Constantinople. He was the perfect go-between with Theodore, who had not yet been arrested.

The news from Theodore via Vilkovsky was good. They should try to escape during the week commencing August 24, making their way to a German beer garden, Zur Neuen Welt, in the Grand Rue in Galata. Here they should watch out for their contact, a Russian, who would take them to a secure house. He would be sitting at a table beyond the piano with a cigarette perched behind his left ear.

The *Batoum* would soon be ready to sail, and the ship's engineers, for a substantial payment, would take them on board as stowaways for the journey across the Black Sea to Odessa.

9

The rabbit

Escape preparations now became top priority. White and Bott cashed cheques written on scraps of paper with a Jewish messenger from the Dutch legation, which had assumed oversight of British POWs following America's entry into the war in 1917.

The 'lunatic' Hill, aware of the plotting, pressed forty-eight Turkish pounds on White as a loan, saying he should take the money before hospital attendants stole it. The escapees would also be robbed if recaptured, so they hid their money well. Buying a scruffy old pair of striped braces, White sewed some notes into the double webbing on either side, the dark stripes concealing his rough stitching. He hid more in the belt of his trousers. Bott also acquired a pair of suspenders into which he stitched money. Provisions — meat lozenges, chocolates and a few biscuits — were wrapped up in a couple of old handkerchiefs. Their only 'baggage' consisted of a small Russian–French dictionary, a watch, a pocket-book and a pipe, together with a map of Constantinople that White had torn from a guidebook in the library of Psamatia's old theological college.

But how to escape? Psamatia was now well guarded. After much discussion, they hit on a plan to elude their guards in the crowds at the busy Stamboul rail station when they went into town for dental treatment.

Captain Fulton and Lieutenant Stone had also resolved to escape but had no definite plans. White and Bott generously passed on their dubious aircraft escape plan. Although the Bosnian aviator had disappeared, a plane had recently stunted over their prison; it was not the type John Willie said he would fly, however.

'In no uncertain terms, we told them what we thought of the feckless "John Willie", and the risks they ran,' said White. 'Nevertheless, these determined youngsters, both of whom had celebrated their twenty-first birthday in captivity, decided to chance their luck.'

The day of their dental appointment arrived. White admitted that as the hours ticked by excitement had heightened his senses, particularly of the surrounding day-to-day noises. Fulton and Stone left first, having secured approval to see an optician. The commandant was furious when White and Bott then applied, but agreed when they showed they had prior dental appointments. He detailed an extra guard, however.

White had not shaved for several days, and had also grown a moustache. He wore an old brown suit and peaked cap, intending to don a concealed felt hat after escape, then shave his moustache and try to pass as a Georgian who had just been released under the new armistice following Russia's revolution.

Boarding the train at Psamatia station the four separated to avoid suspicion. They intended to head off in different directions at Stamboul station, but if any opportunity presented itself en route it was every man for himself. At Koum Kapu station, one stop from Stamboul, White considered leaping from the train onto the walls of a nearby ruin, but that meant climbing out a window in full view of armed guards.

'Miraculously, it seemed, soon after leaving Koum Kapu, the most astonishing piece of good fortune came to our aid and threw dust in the eyes of guards and police,' recorded White. 'Rounding a turn on an embankment, the train had just attained its maximum speed when, with a violent jolt and crash that tumbled passengers from their seats, we collided with some stationary trucks.'

Panic ensued. Women and children screamed. Some passengers, including officers and soldiers, made a rush for the doors, knocking others over. White bent to pacify a terrified woman, and saw the guards moving to seize the two prisoners.

'Now's our chance, I'm off,' he shouted to Bott.

'Right-oh, White! I'm with you.'

White pulled on his replacement hat and joined the mad scramble for the doorway. 'With elbows and feet I forced an ungentlemanly way through without once looking back,' he said. But disappointment awaited. Outside, passengers crowding onto a small viaduct prevented escape. White leapt into the next carriage, forcing his way along with a guard now in pursuit. Emerging onto the end of the viaduct, White jumped down onto the railway line, and then instead of running down the embankment to street level, leapt the ten to twelve feet to the street.

'So great was the din and confusion that the shouts of my pursuer were unheard, self-preservation being the dominant thought, though quite half the crowd belonged to either the military or police,' said White. 'The guard lost a dozen yards by running down the embankment instead of risking the jump.'

The lead gave White an edge on the big, athletic guard. He pushed his way through onlookers and people hurrying to the crash scene, with the yelling guard still in frantic pursuit. One Turk ran into the middle of the street to apprehend him. With no room to dodge, White ran at him, determined to knock him out of the way. But as he raised his fist the Turk drew aside, allowing White to dash past. Two others made half-hearted attempts to stop him, but White rushed on.

It was now a race through narrow streets. White took every turn, not daring to risk the guard taking a shot at him on a long street. His heart pounded. What if the next turn was a blind alley? But run and turn as he might, White could not shake the guard. Racing into a wide street, he saw a group of soldiers behind a fence. The chasing guard shouted to them, but none of the soldiers fired at the fleeing prisoner.

As the bigger, fitter guard gained on him, White knew he was losing the race. Several months of pretended lameness had not prepared him for this. The guard, he appreciated, would also be spurred by thoughts of his own punishment for failure. White thought of the irony of his leaving two liras for the guards back at the prison, knowing they would be punished.

As exhaustion set in, White began to slip and stumble on the cobbled streets, whereas the guard in his slippers ran on comfortably. White knew he had to find a hiding place. Turning a corner he spied an open door, decided to chance the consequences and rushed in. Two elderly women were washing clothes in the front room. White noticed immediately — and with great relief — that they were Greek. Frightened by his sudden, somewhat wild appearance, both women raised their hands as if to scream.

'Shush, Ingaleesh Zabot [English officer],' he whispered, putting his finger to his lips and hurrying through the room. He had only just got behind a door when he heard the pursuing guard rush past the house.

While continuing to wash clothes, one of the woman indicated to White a small cupboard beneath the stairs. Both expected the guard would soon return. White squeezed in beside a smelly garbage can.

'If any child should have seen him come in we are lost,' one woman said to the other in Turkish. White knew it was unfair of him to wait, and decided to leave as soon as he had regained his breath. Then inquisitive children began to enter the room, one sticking his eye right up against a crack in the cupboard door.

A young Greek woman dragged the child away, apologising. She asked if she could help. White asked for a drink of water, promising he would leave as he did not want to bring down trouble on the house. The woman, however, told him to stay as long as he wanted, and pressed him further on how she could help. White told her a disguise was necessary, as by now his description would have been relayed to all local police.

Together with the head of the household, who had in the meantime returned home, he ransacked an upstairs wardrobe, unearthing a fez and an old chesterfield coat, which he bought for twelve Turkish pounds, a reasonable price in the circumstances. White clipped his eyebrows and moustache, colouring the top of his head with boot polish to transform himself into 'the perfect picture of a nondescript Constantinopolitan', the small fez balanced on his head like a flowerpot.

The Greek and his wife were horrified to hear that White had been a prisoner for two years, and told him to stay at least until dark before venturing out, but White still had his rendezvous at the beer garden in mind.

'Perhaps some day we shall read of this in a book if you are successful,' said the woman. White thanked them, leaving some money for the old woman and the child. Later, in his 1928 book *Guests of the Unspeakable*, he wrote: 'If this should reach the eye of those unknown samaritans who risked so much for a desperate fugitive, may they realise his sincere and everlasting gratitude.'

It was arranged with the family that their young son would guide him to the Galata train. Checking that the street was clear, he strolled out in his new coat and fez, 'exulting in a consciousness of a new-found freedom'.

He almost came unstuck at the first hurdle. The boy dutifully led the way to the tram stop opposite a mosque, with White keeping a discreet distance behind. Thinking that all trams crossed the Golden Horn at Galata, White clambered aboard the first tram, only to see the boy shaking his head and waving his hands. He disembarked, as some Turkish officers at the tram stop began to pay attention. Unfortunately he then repeated the mistake, and this time the officers took a real interest. White tried to hide his faux pas by loitering nonchalantly, watching meat being grilled on a spit at a nearby shop.

Finally, after half an hour, the right tram arrived, and White climbed aboard after a signal from the boy, carefully allowing the officers to board first. Across the Galata Bridge the boy left him, flashing White a farewell smile of goodwill. Having memorised the Russian Vilkovsky's sketch of the location of the Zur Neuen Welt, White found the beer-hall without difficulty.

German and Austrian officers were drinking inside, sitting at tables near a piano. '*Biera!*' called White to a waiter, who returned with a mug of beer. He scanned the bar, sipping at his drink and nibbling the strips of salted dry fish the waiter had brought with it. None of the other drinkers had a cigarette stuffed behind his ear. To encourage some action, White placed a cigarette behind his own ear. Nobody responded. He ordered another beer — this one without the salty fish — as the Germans sank into boozy quarrelling.

To stay longer, White pretended to doze off, while covertly keeping an eye out for new customers. Eventually he decided to leave and return the following morning. But where to hide or sleep? He might be able to find where the *Batoum* was berthed. The walk to the waterfront, however, was frightening. 'More than once as I wended my way through the crowd of nondescript humanity that ebbed through the Rue de Galata, I suffered the interrogating and suspicious glances of passers by.' White decided to return their stares, knowing that if he looked anxious or uncertain it would attract interest.

Then, as he was passing some military policemen standing on a corner, one of them held out his arm and stopped him. 'Before he could speak, and noticing he held an unlighted cigarette, I proffered him my lighted one, nonchalantly looking up and down the street as if concerned only in the continuance of my walk, until a light was secured,' he said. 'With a mumbled thanks and gravely salaaming by touching heart and brow, he returned the cigarette. Salaaming in return, I proceeded on my way — rejoicing.' If White had been forced to speak, he would certainly have been discovered and arrested.

Along the street, another soldier drove him off the footpath. It was nothing personal; other pedestrians were being treated the same. White stopped to buy more cigarettes, waiting for the noise

Lt. Merz and Lt. Burn were killed after a forced desert landing in their Maurice Farnham Longhorn. The plane was later retrieved after being hacked to pieces by hostile tribesmen.

Five members of the Mesopotamia mess, Basra, 1915. From left: Capt. Petre; Capt. White; Lt. Christian, Indian Army; Lt. Merz; and (front) Wassif.

White (with head bandage) and Francis Yeats-Brown

A Tigris river taxi, Baghdad

One of the lucky few wounded survivors from Kut who found transport. Wounded POWs who were force-marched north died in their thousands.

Turkish soldiers in Mesopotamia

Turkish artillery in action

A Turkish *araba* (cart) of the type used to transport White and his fellow officers from Mosul to the railhead at Ras-el-Ain

A Chaldean Kalu, or priest, near Mosul. The Chaldean minority religion dates from Babylonian times, and once encompassed astrology and fortune-telling.

A public hanging in Mosul

White found one group who were even worse off than the POWs — Armenian women and children starving after being forced to flee their homes.

Rafael de Nogales. Their encounter with this eccentric soldier of fortune saved the lives of White and his fellow officers.

Kemal Atatürk, revered national hero and founder of modern Turkey, replaced the Young Turks and set Turkey on the path of reform and progress.

Less salubrious dwellings housed thousands of other ranks, including Australians, New Zealanders, British, French, Indians and Russians.

Australian officers at Afion. Back (from left): Lt. L. Luscombe, Lt. S. Jordan, Lt. W. Elston, Lt. Brown. Front (from left): Lt. C. Vautin, Capt. T. White, Lt. W. Treloar.

The incredible C. W. Hill, whose elaborate deceptions and mind games fooled his Turkish captors, along with many of his fellow prisoners. Photograph taken in 1930 after his return to Australia.

Four Afion prisoners (White second from right) in welcome winter coats provided by the Australian Red Cross

The boot in which White hid his prison diary. *Source:* Elizabeth Brenchley.

A caique on the Bosphorus, Constantinople

White in Turkish disguise while on the run in Constantinople

Francis Yeats-Brown as a German governess, on the run in Constantinople. *Source:* Yeats-Brown, *Caught by the Turks* (1919).

Capt. Alan Bott, White's co-conspirator and fellow escapee

White in disguise as the Russian Serge Davidoff, Odessa, 1918

ПАСПОРТНАЯ КНИЖКА.

бессрочная

Выдана Комиссаромъ Перваго Петроградскаго раiона

года

мѣсяца 23 дня

Цѣна книжки 15 копѣекъ.

A page from White's Davidoff passport

vastation in Odessa after the Bolsheviks blew up a huge Austrian ammunition store on the
ge of the city, 1918

Funeral procession for Bolsheviks killed in street fighting in Odessa

of a passing tram to hide his accent. The street vendor overcharged him, but White was unable to complain.

At a wharf near the Pera hill he watched people coming and going from the small boats used as water taxis along the Bosphorus, so he could learn the routine. As usual, there was much haggling about prices. Feigning deafness, White sought the price of a two-hour hire. The boatman held up some fingers, which he then lowered as White kept shaking his head.

With a price agreed, they set off, the boatman shouting a commentary on the sights. Eventually he gave up, and White relaxed and enjoyed the scenery.

'The music of a European band floated out to us as we pulled past, indolent guards staring vacantly down on us,' he recalled. 'The sun shone, other craft passed and re-passed. The city of Emperors and Sultans wore its finest raiment, and I felt at peace with it and all the world.'

Anchored ships were too far away to easily identify. White decided that if he could not find his contact at the beer garden the following day he would return to search out the *Batoum*. Making a sham appointment with the boatman — again to avoid suspicion — he began scouring the local streets for a meal and a place to sleep. His idea was to sleep in a local cemetery if he could not find accommodation.

It was Saturday night, and the streets were full of people. German officers strutted through the crowds. White even wandered past his old hospital, Gumush Suyu, where guards lounging outside, including the ward orderly Ibrahim, who had tolerated his control of the 'lunatic' Hill, failed to recognise him in his Turkish disguise. 'Truly, clothes maketh the man,' he chuckled to himself.

White found a third-rate eating house, complete with squeaking fiddles and mandolins, hoping its well-lubricated patrons would not be too inquisitive. He joined the applause and smiles for the band as he ate fish and olives, unsuccessfully inquiring from the waiter if he knew of any local lodging houses.

His Greek friend from the Afion train might be a help, and White set out for his hotel, but he was unable to find it. The cemetery looked the only option. On what he believed was the way, he decided to see a 'show' before retiring, giving him the cover of darkness for a few hours. Pushing into what he thought was a cinema, White found himself in a combined boot-polish and barber shop. Having found a cinema and bought a ticket, he realised he was the only person in the theatre, and the show did not start for another hour and a half.

He set out on the streets again, finding another cinema. An usher escorted him to a seat alongside three soldiers, with a row of military cadets sitting in front. But sitting in the darkness he enjoyed the entertainment, Anthony Hope's *Sophy of Kravonia* and German newsreels of the war.

Out in the streets again he could find neither his Greek friend's hotel nor the cemetery. As it grew late and the crowds dwindled, White worried that he would be stopped in the street. A woman he stopped to ask directions shrieked and ran off. Overhearing the Russian language he joined what he thought was a group of Georgian officers, to find to his horror that they were Bulgarians and very much on Turkey's side.

Becoming desperate, he decided to try what he thought might be a lodging house in a side street. He told a woman inside that he was a Georgian who had lost his passport and sought a room for the night.

'You look like a German spy, or deserter,' the suspicious woman replied in German. White maintained his new image, saying he wore a fez because he was a good Muslim. The woman then began speaking in Russian.

'Now you speak my native tongue I understand you better,' White responded. 'Can you let me have a room?'

The woman led him upstairs. Passing a room he saw two Turkish gendarmes drinking raki. Music and laughter rang out from other rooms. The presence of gendarmes almost prompted White to flee, but it would only have drawn attention to himself.

He paid the woman in advance, adding some *baksheesh*, locked his door and slept until morning. 'Not all the plagues invoked by Moses to annoy Pharoah could have kept me sleepless that night, having covered many miles by train, tram, boat and on foot, besides cramming into the day more incident than during a year at Afion,' he wrote later.

Leaving the house early to avoid his fellow guests, White arrived at the Zur Neuen Welt before it opened. He killed time in a local restaurant reading a newspaper. Reports on the train collision made no mention of the accompanying prisoner flit. But when a complaining customer sought his sympathy on the quality of the food, White quickly paid his bill and left to avoid drawing public attention.

'Outside I almost ran into the arms of a Naval chaoush who had belonged to our guard in Afion, but I might have been an inmate of the Sultan's harem, so unknown was I to him,' he said.

After window shopping to kill more time, he called into the beer garden, and sat sipping beer while watching the passing clientele. But again none had a cigarette behind his ear. He had almost given up hope when an elderly man wearing a battered panama hat entered and took a seat at a vacant table.

'Here was the man for whom I had waited so long! For, almost hidden by his hair and the turned-down rim of his hat, I saw a ragged cigarette.'

When White put a cigarette behind his own ear the new arrival became quite agitated. White wandered across to his table, ordered two drinks, and tried to calm the man down.

'I am one of the British officers you seek,' he assured him.

'But there were to be two,' the nervous man muttered.

'The other was caught, or you would already have met him.'

They agreed that White should follow the man to the hideout. 'We shook hands with many farewells as if our ways lay in different directions,' said White. Outside, he played follow-the-leader, keeping a discreet distance as he was led through the twisting streets. Eventually the battered panama stopped outside a dilapidated house with an iron door. The man unlocked the door with a giant key, and White followed him inside.

They were in what appeared in the gloom to be a disused carpenter's workshop. Wood shavings littered the floor, with rats rustling amongst them. A carpenter's bench and some planks were the only furniture. In one corner a rubbish shaft came down from above. An iron-shuttered window kept light out. The Russian go-between told him he would have to wait two or three days before boarding the *Batoum*, and that he would return that night with food. He left, locking the door behind him. In the darkness White could barely see, but some chinks in the wall and one missing brick enabled him to feel out the room, which measured about ten feet by fifteen feet. The inner walls were a thin wooden partition, with gaps between some planks through which he could see to the other side.

Later that day he heard a gate opening nearby, and someone walk into the room on the other side of the partition. He stamped upstairs to the room directly above White's head, threw his shoes on the floor and went to bed. A second person arrived. White heard an exchange in Turkish, and then the smell of a meal being cooked. He stayed quite still. Anybody with an eye to the cracks in the partition could see or hear him.

In the evening his Russian minder arrived, carrying a bag containing water, bread, white cheese and a melon. White had already given him the nickname of 'Lenin'.

'Who is the person upstairs,' White whispered.

'A Turkish officer,' replied Lenin. 'You will have to keep very quiet while he is indoors.' The other voice, said Lenin, belonged to the officer's orderly.

White showed him cracks in the partition where light from the orderly's lamp shone directly through. Lenin rearranged a few planks to cover them. Before departing he also clamped a plane to the end of the carpenter's bench as a pillow for White's 'bed'. Later a British air raid shook the neighborhood. Local guns fired in response, and his neighbour stomped angrily into the street.

Lenin returned the following morning on his way to work, carrying food in a tool bag. With the Turks already departed, they could converse normally. Lenin told him the Turkish officer and the orderly spent most of their days out. He also said he had met one of the *Batoum*'s engineers, who told him that a British officer had arrived on board. He would come ashore to hide with White and await the still uncertain date of sailing.

Later that morning White heard the rattle of dishes on the other side of the partition: it sounded like someone was washing and scraping tin plates. White recalled hearing the orderly talking in affectionate terms to someone while the officer was upstairs. While he had heard no response to the orderly's blandishments, he now feared he was being spied on. But peer as he might through the crack he could see nobody. Very cunning, he thought.

Deciding to smoke, he wrapped his coat around his head to hide the light, and rustled the floor shavings to imitate rats and disguise the sound of a match being struck. He spent a few hours studying his Russian dictionary in the poor light afforded by the missing brick in the wall. When Lenin returned he was accompanied by a man wearing a peaked cap and the coat of a Russian sailor: it was Bott.

He had an exciting story to tell — three close-call escapes. Like White he had leapt down the embankment after the train crash, but turned his ankle. The guards quickly pounced on him. Fulton and Stone also failed to escape. The recaptured group awaited the return of the guard chasing White, who finally rushed up cursing and invoking the wrath of Allah on all Englishmen. He threw his hat on the ground, shook his fist at Bott and shouted, 'English very bad!'

After another fruitless search for White, the guard angrily gesticulated to Bott that the guards themselves would now go to prison. 'Prison very bad, no food,' he said. Bott gave them a few pounds *baksheesh* as consolation, and gradually the guards and failed escapees cooked up a story: White didn't escape, he just disappeared in the melee of the crash.

They told this story at a local police station. Bott was searched, but he had disposed of all incriminating evidence, dropping a parcel of valuable cocoa into the lap of a delighted elderly woman only a few doors from the police station. Bott even went on to the dentist's surgery and suffered a filling in a perfectly good tooth to help maintain the story. Incredibly, he again lost his guard on the way, but ran into a blind alley. He returned to the furious guard, handing them some more money. 'They gasped,' said Bott, 'but a sense of humour dissolved anger into laughter.'

Back at Psamatia, the commandant was apoplectic with rage. Like the guards, he feared imprisonment. Bott embellished the story: White was queer in the head, and after the crash he probably just wandered off. The commandant seized on this, incorporating it in his official report, even pretending that White might return of his own free will.

Still, following these events the commandant ordered that all British prisoners were to leave for camps in central Anatolia the following day. That night Fulton and Stone tried to escape by climbing out a window, but a drainpipe broke, sending Fulton tumbling into the street. He quickly regained his feet and dashed back to bed as the guards sounded the alarm.

The following day the 'do-or-die-trio', as Bott called them, looked for any opportunity as the party of officers and men marched under guard through the streets to a landing point on the Bosphorus where they would catch a ferry across to the Asian side. Fulton tried unsuccessfully to hide in the little booth of a shop. Stone tried to slip away into a courtyard, but a guard dragged him back.

As the party assembled near the wharf, Bott gained approval to join two other prisoners being escorted to a nearby café. Walking into the café behind the others, he asked the plump waitress where he could hide. Without turning a hair, she opened a folding door that led to the kitchen and Bott hid behind it. Then, as the others left and the sound of the tooting ferry could be heard, the waitress said: 'They have gone and so must you. The Turks may come back any moment, and if they find you here I shall suffer more than you.'

'Goodbye, and a million thanks,' said Bott, leaving the café and swerving in the opposite direction from the wharf. Pretty soon he was rubbing shoulders with the street crowds. A glance behind revealed he was not being followed. Bott learned after the war that when the prisoners assembled on the wharf for the boat's departure and the Turks conducted a rollcall, his prisoner mates simply yelled 'present' when his name was called out.

Bott walked quickly to the beer-hall, where the Russian contact for the *Batoum* would be waiting from two o'clock to four each day. By the time he arrived it was 4.30. But he ordered a beer, and put a cigarette behind his ear. Nobody noticed, and no other drinker had a cigarette behind his ear.

'You seem hot,' said the corpulent German hostess. 'You must have been walking too fast.'

'No, I have merely been out in this atrocious sun,' Bott replied, nervous about his rusty German. When the hostess tried to settle in for a longer chat, Bott felt the tension of trying to answer her questions was more than he could stand. He looked at his watch: 5.25. Not much chance the Russian contact would come now. He paid his bill quickly, and left.

Out in the street, a policeman stopped him, holding out his hand. '*Vecika* [identity]?' he demanded. Bott, of course, had no *vecika*, but he had prepared himself for this eventuality. He handed the policeman a copy of a recent photograph actually taken in hospital, on which he had had written: 'Fritz Richter, Oberleutnant in der Fliegertruppen'. Bott protested loudly that he was a German officer in mufti, and the policeman would get himself into trouble for stopping a German flyer. 'Never was I more frightened than when uttering that bombast,' he said.

The rattled policeman consulted a passing Greek, who on reading the signature on the photograph, proclaimed Bott to be a 'Supreme Lieutenant of Flying Soldiers'. The policeman immediately sought Bott's pardon, saluted and handed him back the photograph.

Realising the danger on the streets, Bott headed quickly for the waterfront, hiring a rowing boat to find the *Batoum*. But search as he might along the Bosphorus, there was no Russian-flagged ship called the *Batoum*. Most ships were German, with a few flying a strange yellow and blue flag that Bott did not recognise.

Finally he got the boatman to row close to a German ship, calling out to the crew in German, 'Please tell me where I can find the Russian ship *Batoum*?'

There are no Russian ships now, they replied. What about those over there, said Bott, pointing to the yellow and blue flagged vessels. Ukrainian, was the reply.

Bott realised his mistake. The revolution had created a German-assisted republic called The Ukraine. He ordered the boatman to pull towards the ships, where he noticed that one was called *Nikolaieff*. The other must be the *Batoum*. He climbed the gangway, meeting a sailor.

'*Russky vapor Batoum*?' he inquired in his pidgin Russian.

'*Da*,' replied the sailor, ushering him down to the cabin of the chief engineer and main organiser of the *Batoum*'s extensive smuggling racket, Ivan Michaelovitch Titoff, a round-shouldered man with piggy eyes and a turned-up nose.

Titoff appraised the new arrival warily, running his finger down a list of English phrases, before finally asking, 'Seegnal?'

'Signal?'

'Yess, ceegarette seegnal.'

Remembering the German beer garden routine, Bott placed a cigarette behind his left ear. Titoff and the first mate, Ivan Balaef, broke into smiles and shook his hand.

Bott slept in the first mate's cabin that night, but the next day Titoff, who spoke no English or German, used the third mate Kuhlmann to tell Bott in German that it was too dangerous for him to stay aboard. He must go ashore dressed as a seaman and hide with White until the ship sailed in a week's time.

After rowing ashore, Bott, dressed in faded sailor's clothes with his civvies wrapped in newspaper, followed Lenin to White's hide-out.

'Glad to see you, old man,' said White coming towards him out of the gloom dressed in his shabby overcoat, with his fez sticking out of the pocket. 'I don't know which of us looks the more comic.'

The two settled down to wait out an agonising week for the *Batoum* to sail. When the Turkish officer and his orderly were home they had to maintain a death-like stillness, scarcely daring to whisper and certainly not to smoke. They slept side by side on the bench, with rolled-up coats as pillows. One night White woke to find Bott talking in his sleep. After that they slept in relays, with one keeping watch.

By day, several people rattled at the door. White warned Bott to be particularly careful after the Turkish soldier and orderly left each morning, as this was when someone, possibly the officer's wife, cleaned up. For three days, Bott listened to the daily scraping and cleaning sound, the noise coming right up to the partition. They alerted Lenin when he arrived one morning with food.

'We believe the Turkish officer's wife knows of us,' White told him. 'Every morning she comes to the partition and seems to be looking through it.'

Lenin grinned. 'The Turk has no wife,' he said. 'What you've been frightened of is his tame rabbit!'

To break the monotony Lenin partially opened the iron-shuttered window, covering the open space with boards. This gave them sufficient light to read. They spent hours sitting on bags of shavings beneath the partially shuttered window studying the Russian dictionary books.

'After hours of study, [when] our concentrative faculties became quite stale, the only alternative was to hope for success, and to live again in retrospect the extravagant happenings of the past few weeks,' said Bott. 'Most of the business usually associated with the crudest melodrama had been there, I reflected — spies, policemen, disguises, chases, female accomplices, and bluff. Decidedly it had been thrilling.'

Another thrill was to come — a face at the window. One morning, Bott noticed White suddenly stiffen as the two were clearing the bench. There was a noise as though someone was scrambling up the outside of the iron window.

'Look natural,' he whispered, 'There's no time to duck.'

Bott picked up a plank of wood. White started to measure another piece. Slowly a fez was rising above the top of the iron window. Then came a wrinkled forehead, bent nose and a pair of villainous eyes. The Turk must have levered himself up on the window ledge.

'Don't take any notice,' said White. They continued to act like workmen in a carpenter's shop. The face hovered for about two minutes, then they heard the sounds of a man walking away. Although the intruder had seen no more than two innocent-looking workmen and some pieces of fruit, White and Bott now expected the police to arrive at any moment.

When they told Lenin, he said he would consult the engineers on the *Batoum*. Maybe it was just an old customer, he said. But before he returned the next day the face had reappeared twice, each time accompanied by the scratching up the wall and the slowly rising fez. Lenin almost fainted when they told him. He was now sure the mystery face belonged to a police spy. If caught it might mean imprisonment for White and Bott, but it surely meant hanging for him. Pack immediately, he ordered. You're going to the ship.

The three left separately, mooching along on different sides of the street. Lenin was so nervous he twice led them into blind alleys. Two gendarmes stood guarding the wharf. Bott in his sailor's uniform saluted the chief engineer Titoff, waiting by a small boat. White sauntered up just as they were pulling away, hailed Bott like an old friend, and jumped in.

As they climbed the gangway White had his first glimpse of the dilapidated tramp steamer *Batoum* and its crew. They looked, he thought, 'as piratical a set of desperados as ever sailed beneath the "Jolly Roger" '.

That was to prove an understatement.

10

Lucky Friday the 13th

The *Batoum*, moored between old Stamboul and the Sultan's summer palace of Dolma Bagtche, may have looked like a rundown, thirty-year-old tramp steamer, but in the next thirty days, while White and Bott hid on board, it was to be transformed into a veritable Aladdin's cave of smuggled goods.

Prices were high in Constantinople, but in besieged Odessa they were up to four times higher still. Cocaine, opium, tobacco, leather, cognac, quinine and human stowaways were stashed in every nook and cranny of the ship. Almost the entire crew — except the doddery old captain, who was on his last voyage — were in on the game. The demand for cocaine to smuggle to Odessa was so high in Constantinople the week before the ship sailed that chemists in Pera and Galata would not sell it at under one hundred Turkish pounds a kilo. Yet in Odessa it would still bring four times as much.

The *Batoum* did not look like 'Smugglers Inc.' when the two escapees first boarded. Indeed, the old English-built steamer appeared more likely destined for a ship's graveyard: its decks were pitted with rust holes and its sides mottled with patched rust from years of neglect.

The ship had spent a quiet life trading in the Black Sea, later serving as a Russian transport to the Caucasus front. After the 1917 revolution she had gathered barnacles in Odessa until commandeered one night by drunken Bolsheviks bringing a swag of the city's stolen liquor on board and ordering the captain to sail to Novorissik. After Odessa's occupation by Austro-German troops and the creation of a new Ukrainian republic, the *Batoum* was engaged in the limited trade allowed with Turkey.

White and Bott quickly found the cabin of the third mate, Andreas Kuhlmann, a stockily built young Latvian. Not much larger than a telephone booth, it contained a bunk with a locker underneath, a low seat surmounting a drawer and a ship's wash-basin. When the door was open it filled the room. If closed, the room became hot and stuffy, with little air penetrating the small porthole.

Kuhlmann was asleep when the pair arrived, but quickly awoke and warmly welcomed them. He was to prove an important ally in the struggle ahead with the rapacious Titoff.

'In case you are followed, I shall go to deck,' he said. 'Should any boat come alongside I shall rap three times on the deck immediately overhead, upon which one of you must hide in the locker and the other in the drawer beneath the seat.' Seeing the disbelief on their faces, Kuhlmann added, 'It is not as difficult as you suppose,' laughing as he left them.

Savouring the light of day after a week in darkness, White and Bott were starting to relax when three unmistakable raps on metal rang out. Bott, the shorter of the two, pulled open the drawer and squeezed in, doubling up his legs and trying to ignore the filthy sheet. The door of the bed locker was nailed up, so White lifted up the mattress, removed some wooden slats and climbed in from above. The locker was about two and a half feet high by two feet wide.

'With much squirming and wriggling I pulled some clothes over my head in case the mattress was removed from the bunk,' he wrote. 'The heat and stench were almost unbearable, for sailors on Russian freighters do not change their own nor their bed linen too frequently, nor without good cause.'

They stayed hidden for about an hour and a half, listening for the turn of the door handle and cursing all Turks and Russians. It eventually became so unbearable that after a muffled exchange they both climbed out, perspiring heavily. No sooner were they convinced it had been a false alarm than the three-rap signal rang out again. They jumped back into their hiding places. This time they waited only a short time before climbing out again. Two more alarms followed, with the pair scurrying to their cupboards each time.

By now they were becoming quite blasé about the warning signal. Staring out the porthole for clues, White discovered the cause of the problem — the rapping signal was caused by the gangway striking the ship's side with the wash of passing vessels.

'After the tame rabbit prank, we should have been prepared for Fate's practical joking,' he thought. But there was no practical joking that night when they met Ivan Michaelovitch Titoff over a few drinks. Titoff was head of the smuggling syndicate, and the real master of the vessel.

'He was a thief, a mean blackguard, a cunning liar, a cringing coward, a rat and an altogether despicable cheat,' said Bott. 'Otherwise, he was not a bad sort of fellow.'

Impressions of Titoff began to sour at the first meeting. Before their escape, they had organised with Vilkovsky for a parcel of food and tobacco — items they could not carry but would need — to be sent to the ship. They were initially delighted when Titoff handed over the package. But far from containing the biscuits, butter, tobacco and other small luxuries they had packed, it had only a few ounces of rice, two small pieces of chocolate and four dried apricots.

When White asked about the rest, Titoff solemnly declared that was all he had received. Titoff was more interested in their money. Four hundred pounds was the agreed fare for the two of them to be smuggled to Odessa. Had they brought the money? he inquired, rubbing his thumb and forefinger together like someone counting notes. Money was becoming a worry for White, but he told Titoff they would pay some of the passage when the ship sailed and the remainder when it reached Odessa.

Titoff shifted to another money issue: they were to pay him four pounds a day for their food until the ship sailed. When he left the cabin briefly White peeked into his cupboard, finding a tin of English biscuits unobtainable in Constantinople. White was convinced they really belonged to him.

'We decided to say nothing for the present and to have our reckoning later, but the discovery confirmed our suspicions as to his character,' he said.

The two escapees soon became known identities around the ship, as they walked the deck at night dressed in striped sailor's skivvies. Only the octogenarian captain seemed unaware of them. They passed him in corridors, but he seemed to take them to be crew members.

The wonder was that over their month on board word of their presence did not reach the myriad police spies in Constantinople. The crew were often ashore drinking, and brought women back to the ship. Yet the news did not leak. This may have been due to the crew's anxiety about their own smuggling rackets. They did not relish police attention. The Bolshevik stokers specialised in smuggled vodka; the engineers in cocaine. Titoff had a hand and likely a cut in every scheme. He terrorised the crew, and the junior officers lived in fear of him.

White and Bott quickly saw through Titoff's grasping nature. Other crew members they regarded as honest rogues, prepared to lend a hand to friends — or British escapees — although all were keen to make money from smuggling. Even White and Bott were caught up in the contraband obsession. In partnership with Kuhlmann they invested in a consignment of leather. White hoped the expected profits would defray their costs. At their request, Kuhlmann also bought them two revolvers, which they believed might be needed if relations with Titoff or the Bolsheviks on board turned sour.

Apart from Kuhlmann, Feodor Mozny and Josef Korotky, the second and third engineers, showed great kindness to the stowaways. They told them how Titoff was robbing them over the cost of daily food, which he obtained free from the kitchen. Josef's wife, who accompanied her husband on the voyage, washed the escapees' one pair of underwear each. Josef briefed them on how, after arriving in Odessa, they could travel by boat, rail and foot to the Allied forces then fighting the Bolsheviks in Siberia.

Some of the Bolsheviks on board, however, were threatening. One of the hard-drinking stokers had been a Bolshevik commissar, and was Titoff's main conspirator on the ship. When drunk, he terrorised the stokehold. Another fireman, a former sailor of the Tsar's Black Sea fleet, happily related how he and others had murdered their officers. He personally had shot two on his ship.

An incident on the Russian cruiser *Almaz* chilled White and Bott. As the stokers related it, the crew mutinied, shelling Odessa without doing much damage because the gunners were drunk. Some four hundred captured officers and prominent Odessa citizens were brought on board the flagship, where they were subject to mock trials by the revolutionaries. Sentences of 'hot baths' or 'cold baths' were ordered and carried out. A 'hot bath' meant being pushed into the ship's furnace, while a 'cold bath' meant being thrown overboard with weights attached.

One crewman, 'Bolshevik Bill', became their protector, however. White was helping a work party making a pretence of painting the rusty deck when a red-headed Russian — larger, said White, than a gigantic Scottish Highlander — offered him some figs, likely stolen from the cargo. White accepted, and the giant produced a Russian–French grammar book. Would White teach him French? Viewing this giant as a valuable potential ally on the ship, White agreed.

While Bolshevik Bill was a happy student, his intellect was limited. His French consisted largely of two favourite phrases — '*parlez-vous francais*?' and '*un peu*'. The latter was his favourite, repeated many times with wide grins when he had had a few drinks. He became a friend, offering to accompany the two escapees in Russia. No Bolsheviks would molest them while he was in their company, he said.

When White first heard of the Black Sea fleet's slaughter of their officers while playing cards with the *Batoum* crew, he declared straightaway that it had been wrong. Officers should have been granted a fair trial, not simply slaughtered. Bolshevik Bill agreed, adding that of course it would not have happened to British officers, who fraternised with their men rather than bullying them as Russian officers did.

The wait for the *Batoum*'s departure dragged out. In a week, they were told. Then another week. Extension after extension followed, as the monotony of shipboard hiding dragged on. Ramadan, Turkish and even Jewish public holidays stretched out the waiting. Cargo began to arrive, bales of tobacco, figs and raisins being unloaded from small boats as the ship swung at anchor.

At first the two escapees stayed in Kuhlmann's cramped cabin, but with the captain's cabin just across the corridor, this became untenable. Many ship visitors called on him, and the possibility of bumping into customs or police in the corridor was high.

Titoff took them to a small cabin off the bridge, previously used by the wireless operator when the *Batoum* was a Russian military transport. Much of the radio equipment remained, but the Germans prohibited Black Sea merchant ships from using radio. Titoff ripped apart the remaining equipment, searching for the platinum points on the transmitter, planning to sell them. He seemed disgusted that an earlier thief had already removed them.

This cabin became their home for the next twelve days. They took turns to sleep in the solitary bunk made up of old sails and lifebuoys, and during the day they studied Russian. Often they were forced to crouch down under the windowsill to avoid being spotted by ship visitors.

The panoramic view provided some compensation. They were only fifty yards from the Sultan's sprawling summer palace, and down the Bosphorus old Stamboul with its minarets and domed roofs glistened in the sunlight. Their hiding place also gave them front-row seats when British air raids lit up the night sky. Although they exercised on the deck each night, both men were becoming weaker and thinner as the weeks of cramped conditions began to take a toll.

Never-ending delays began to wear down their finances, too. They arranged with Titoff to take cheques to the Maritza and hand them to Theodore, who would cash them with their contact at the Dutch legation who worked in the section dealing with British prisoner relief — White always referred to this contact, an interned British citizen, as 'Mr S'. But two days after Titoff had delivered a sealed envelope to Theodore and was supposed to have picked up the cash at a meeting with Mr S's delivery agent in the Taxime Gardens, they had heard nothing. In their isolation, White and Bott were convinced Titoff had swindled them. They sent Titoff a note asking for an explanation.

In Kuhlmann's presence, Titoff swore that he had handed the cheques to Theodore, but that nobody had showed up at the Taxime Gardens to pass him the money. When he went back to the Maritza a waiter told him that Theodore had been arrested.

'What kind of fools do you take us for?' demanded White, with his and Bott's pistols close at hand.

Titoff loudly protested his innocence.

'I'm going to the Maritza to see for myself,' White declared. A risky trip, but they were becoming desperate. With their funds running down, they now did not have enough to pay for their voyage. They agonised over the three hundred Turkish pounds for which they had written out cheques. Had Theodore robbed them? Had Theodore and Titoff joined up to rob them? And if Theodore had been arrested, could the money be traced back to Mr S, exposing him to prison or execution?

Just as White was about to leave the ship, dressed in his Chesterfield overcoat, Bott's felt hat and a fake moustache, a crewman brought on board a new copy of *Hilal*. It contained a small news story on the arrest of three British officers, caught hiding in the home of one Theodore Yanni, a waiter.

The newspaper report appeared to confirm Titoff's story, but not to go to the restaurant would signal their faith in Titoff. As well, they urgently needed to know what had happened to their money.

The three officers were likely Yeats-Brown, Fulton and Stone, the last two having again jumped a train on the return to prison camp. Through Theodore they were in the process of arranging to join White and Bott on the *Batoum*'s voyage to Russia. Now the four were in the infamous ministry of war prison known as 'the black hole of Constantinople'.

White and Bott could see it from their hiding place on the bridge of the *Batoum*. 'Knowing the horrors of the special punishment cells, we shuddered with sympathy for the strangely mixed party [including Theodore's family],' wrote Bott. 'Theodore himself, we supposed, would be hanged out of hand.'

White set out, accompanied by Kuhlmann and Titoff. The Maritza was crawling with police, sprawled at tables and wearing pistol holsters. 'The dim low-roofed interior seemed to reek of suspicion,' said White. 'The police appeared to be gathered together in anticipation of further developments or perhaps to congratulate themselves upon their success.'

As White sat down, an officer of the gendarmie took a seat right behind him, within earshot of his table. White spoke Russian to the waiter, who sent along another who could speak the language. White recognised him as a friend of Theodore's. Ordering a bottle of Smyrna beer, White whispered an inquiry about Theodore.

'He has fallen with the three British officers,' came the whispered response. 'I pray you not to talk of it.' White's aim was to get Theodore's address so he could visit the house and see if he could find the money.

'What is the address,' he persisted. 'I am a British officer myself, you need have no fear . . .'

The agitated waiter became so frightened he scurried off, and would not come near White's table again. Sipping his beer, White noticed an obvious police spy in plain clothes lurking close by, suspiciously eyeing the escapee as he ostentatiously washed his hands at a basin at the back of the room. White knew that the longer he loitered at the Maritza, the more he exposed himself to a long stay in solitary in 'the black hole of Constantinople'. Quickly finishing his beer he left, finding Kuhlmann and Titoff at the corner. Titoff was pleased that White had corroborated his story, but refused point-blank to join White's risky new mission — a visit to Mr S to get to the bottom of the mystery of the lost money.

Entering the Dutch legation, even the daring White could see the excessive risk he was taking. Here he was, dressed in an unsuitable disguise as a local, with a Turkish police guard whom White recognised from prison days staring suspiciously at him. White scanned the walls as if in search of a name, then left.

Outside, Kuhlmann was greatly relieved that White had got in and out without being arrested. 'And in that coat, too,' he chuckled. 'I swear there is not another like it in Turkey.'

Back on the *Batoum*, White and Bott considered their position. They had to either find out what had happened to the cheques or arrange for new ones to be cashed. A visit to Mr S was imperative.

The next day Bott set out, dressed as a Russian sailor and again accompanied by Kuhlmann. Mr S, who administered British Red Cross funds for prisoners from his office in the prisoners of war section of the Dutch legation, was absent for the day. Bott went again the next afternoon, this time using heavy make-up to disguise the facial scars that were a legacy of his plane crash, fearing that one of the police guards might recognise such distinctive marks.

Mr S, he learned, was on the first floor of a nearby Dutch legation annex. Waiting in the corridor, he and Kuhlmann became very nervous at the appearance of a Jewish attendant, Levi, whom Bott knew well from his hospital days. 'Only then did I realise the foolhardiness of the visit,' Bott conceded. When two Russians in the office started to question the pair — assuming naturally that Bott was a Russian sailor — they hurriedly left.

With Titoff becoming agitated about the pair's finances, White decided to give it one last try, this time disguised as an American missionary. Several American missions and schools remained in

Turkey despite Washington's entry into the war. White figured some Americans would have stayed on, as the US was not formally at war with Turkey. Borrowing Bott's old suit and hat, White prepared to set out as Henry O'Neill from an American mission at Tarsus. But there was one added hitch. It was Friday the 13th of September, White's notoriously unlucky day. 'The Fates did not seem propitious,' he noted.

'White shook hands and left me, after a reminder that if he were captured my clothes would go to prison with him,' said Bott. 'He was far from cheerful, for it was Friday the 13th and he remembered that his capture in Mesopotamia had taken place on Friday the 13th of September 1915.'

This time, however, the fates would turn out differently. Leaving Kuhlmann at the corner, White approached the Turkish guard at the annex front door.

'Shrugging my shoulders at the superstition, I attempted to walk past His Magnificence,' said White.

'What do you want?' roared the guard in Turkish.

'I want to see Mr S,' replied White, also in Turkish.

'What name?'

'Henry O'Neill of Tarsus. I am an American and an old friend of his. If you let him know I am here he will come right down to see me.'

'Wait and I shall inquire,' said the guard, turning on his heel. White lit a cigarette, anxiously pondering his disguise and the fates. But he also calculated that on such a hot day the lazy guard would not run upstairs to make inquiries. After standing around a corner for a few seconds, the guard returned, saying, 'That's quite alright. Go upstairs.'

Bluff had got him past the ground-floor guard, but upstairs he still had to face Levi, whose presence had frightened off Bott, and also Mr S, whom he had never met. Levi had brought letters and parcels to the hospital, and had met White several times.

Upstairs, White spoke English in asking to see Mr S, but confessed to being Russian when asked by a secretary. Levi, overhearing this, and obviously trying to remember where he had seen White before, told him he spoke English like an Englishman. Slapping him on the back in a friendly way, White said confidently, 'Of course I am English.'

The penny must have dropped for Levi, as he said to White, 'Did you come by yourself?'

'No, my guard is downstairs,' White replied.

Levi accepted this, as it was not unusual for prisoners to bribe guards to remain outside while they searched for parcels. Fortunately, the secretary then told White that Mr S would now see him.

Speaking in a low voice, White quickly told the grey-haired Mr S who he was, adding that he would leave immediately if the diplomat did not want to talk to him. Showing no concern at all, Mr S ushered him into a private room, where he expressed delight at the double disguises White had pulled to get past the guards at the legation. White pressed him about the money.

'I had no chance of sending you the money for the cheques,' Mr S told him. A clerk went to the Maritza with orders to give the money discreetly to Titoff, but it was the day that Theodore and the others were arrested, and a Turkish police spy was watching Titoff. Later, when the clerk followed Titoff as he strolled in the Taxime Gardens, the Turkish spy followed him, and the clerk had no opportunity to complete his mission.

'I've had some sleepless nights,' Mr S confided to White, indicating the risks he was taking to help prisoners. 'I think I've been watched since [the three prisoners] were taken with Theodore. I know your friend Titoff is watched. If Theodore should blab under pressure my head will be as near the noose as his.'

Miss Whitaker was also in danger, he said, as she had helped Yeats-Brown, Fulton and Stone, and only narrowly escaped arrest herself. She was on her way to Theodore's house when the police raided it.

'Yeats-Brown stayed too long in Constantinople,' he said. 'The police want you badly. If you are caught in this city I want to be able to say that I have not helped you,' he added, offering to send the money to the *Batoum* shortly before it sailed. In parting, he also gave White the name and address of a Russian friend in Odessa who might help the escapees.

White's Friday the 13th luck had really turned around. He now had money for the voyage and contacts in Odessa. Elated, he bounded down the stairway so fast he ended up in the basement. Back on the *Batoum*, he burst into the wireless room where Bott was hiding, shouting, 'I've seen S, and the money's not lost.'

The scheming Titoff, however, had other views. Anxious about his own neck since the arrest of Theodore, and using their lack of ready money as an excuse, he now wanted White and Bott off the ship. In typical cowardly fashion, he detailed one of his assistants to order the escapees to leave in two days' time.

'We will resist being put ashore,' White told the second mate, revolvers again at hand. The prisoners gave the messenger a real stinger for Titoff: if they were captured ashore they would tell police Titoff and some of the *Batoum* crew had sheltered them. As Bott sarcastically put it, if they did leave the ship it would be to give themselves up to police, with the request that their dear friend and colleague Ivan Michaelovitch Titoff should join them in prison. Titoff quickly dropped his threat. Indeed, after Kuhlmann, Josef and Feodor offered to take them to Russia for no fee he said those were his sentiments as well.

But they were still not safe on the ship. Police raids in search of a notorious woman thief whom the boatswain was hiding on board intensified. Strolling the deck one night, they were approached by the first mate, Balaef, a Titoff conspirator. The crew were celebrating Balaef's birthday with much vodka and music, and he told them a new plan had been devised for their security. When a police boat was sighted leaving the shore, White and Bott were to dive overboard, swim to the stern and cling to the propeller blades until police had left the ship.

The horrified prisoners refused point-blank. Currents swirling down the Bosphorus past the *Batoum* would surely carry them away. After five police raids in a week, however, they were forced to ask Titoff for a safer hideaway. The wireless room on the bridge was exposed, and unless the two remained lying on the floor they could be seen by ship visitors from the main deck.

An alternative hiding place was offered, although one only slightly more palatable than clinging to the propellers. With a police boat approaching one day, White and Bott were taken to the ballast tanks, in the very bowels of the ship below the propeller shaft. Feodor led them down the dark tunnel housing the propeller shaft. Lifting boards from the floor, Feodor exposed a cast-iron lid, telling the escapees there were about thirty small compartments inside connected by narrow manholes. He advised them to crawl to the furthest one in case police flashed lights inside.

The two men climbed into the black cavity. As the lid was screwed down behind them, they crawled through the manholes from compartment to compartment, easing their way along through mud and slime.

It was a horrendous place. Each compartment measured about two feet square by eight feet long. They stank of years of filth. There was no light in the compartments, and the air was fetid. Standing up was impossible. The only thing to do was to lie down or squat in the shallow water. As if these conditions were not appalling enough, White and Bott contemplated the nightmare of the ballast tanks being accidentally — or even deliberately — flooded by the flip of a lever while they were inside.

After half an hour of such chilling thoughts they heard heavy footsteps in the tunnel above them, and then the noise of the manhole being unscrewed. Feodor's voice rang out through the compartments: 'Signor.' It was the all-clear signal, and they climbed out, relieved to be out of the steel coffins.

Six times in the week before sailing the ballast tanks became their hiding place during police and customs visits. Their emaciation had the benefit of enabling them to slide more easily from compartment to compartment. They took small mattresses, which although sodden with bilge water at least provided some comfort. Their hopes were lifted, however, by the news that Titoff had bought coal for the forthcoming voyage. Naturally Titoff had struck a deal on the purchase. He ordered one hundred tons, with the coal dealer delivering only ninety but presenting a bill for the full hundred to the Turkish merchant. Titoff and the coal dealer then split the difference. In the final days before departure all remaining cargo — legitimate and smuggled — came on board.

The day before sailing White and Bott were surprised to see a small boat pull alongside and Vladimir Vilkovsky, their Ukrainian friend from Afion and Psamatia, alight. Now a free man, Vilkovsky was still angling for a job in the new Ukrainian delegation in Constantinople. He had heard from Mr S that money needed to be taken to White and Bott aboard the *Batoum* and volunteered for the task.

The escapees were anxious to ask him one question: had he delivered to Titoff that package of goods they had left with him at Psamatia before escaping? Of course he had. Titoff was so embarrassed at this confirmation of his fraud that he rushed off, returning with half a can of condensed milk he said he had forgotten. Vilkovsky told them that if he didn't land the job at the Ukrainian delegation, he would stow away on another Ukrainian ship that had just arrived. 'In that case I shall see you soon in Odessa,' he said.

That night White and Bott slept uneasily with revolvers ready and the new money in their clothing. White heard the knob turn quietly before the door to their cabin opened. 'Who's there?' he shouted, cocking his revolver and pointing it at the door. The intruder fled. Throughout the night they could hear the crew carousing on their final night in port. Later they heard of knife fights by drunken firemen and greasers.

At 6.30 a.m. White and Bott trudged to their ballast tank hideaway, taking revolvers, money, water, bread and cheese. With the expected final police searches, they were prepared for a full day in the dark. They lay on the wet sacking, their revolvers and food on their chests to keep them dry. The air was so stale they allowed themselves only one cigarette each.

The ship echoed with noises, but there was no movement. Except for the bilge water. Alarmingly, they began to notice it rising.

'The horrible suspicion that some ill-wisher might let water into the tanks took hold of us at first,' recorded White. 'Two feet of water in those iron coffins would have drowned us and there could be no escape.' They scratched lines in the mud to time the rise. Striking matches, they saw that it was too gradual to affect them.

Sounds of police launches scraping alongside the hull were followed by the footsteps of police searching the nearby engine room. Eventually, about 11.30, came the rhythmic swish of the engines followed by a grinding sound as the anchor was raised.

'Put it there, old man,' said White, thrusting his hand through the hole to Bott's compartment. 'We're leaving Turkey at last.'

Not yet. Although they calculated that by nightfall they would be safely out of Turkish waters the engines stopped after only two hours, and they heard the sound of the anchor splashing back into the water. What had happened now?

After an exhausting fourteen hours in the wet darkness they heard the all-clear signal of 'Signor'. The *Batoum* had reached the mouth of the Bosphorus, but the Turkish merchant who had chartered it had forgotten some departure papers. More likely, thought White and Bott, he had forgotten to bribe some official. The captain anchored the ship while the merchant returned to Constantinople. Several police remained on board, spending the night drinking with crew.

After a few hours' sleep on the floor of Feodor's cabin, White and Bott returned to their steel purgatory. Six hours later, after again monitoring the engine and anchor noises, they heard the much-welcomed 'Signor' from Feodor.

'Fineesh Turkey,' he added as they clambered out with stiff and aching bones. White and Bott were delighted to see the coast of Turkey finally disappearing behind the ship. Only then did they discover the extent of the *Batoum* crew's smuggling. People suddenly appeared from every cupboard and hiding place — about twenty of them, all delighted to be out in the open at last.

Especially one woman. The captain might have appeared an enfeebled old man, but even he managed to smuggle aboard a passport-less woman, hiding her in a deep locker in the chartroom off the bridge. She had been there two days when she got the shock of her life.

Katrina, the kitchenhand, had smuggled aboard her Turkish boyfriend, an army deserter. Unaware of the captain's lady, Katrina also selected the chartroom locker as the place to hide her lover. She unscrewed the top, stuffed the Turk inside — right alongside the woman — and screwed down the lid.

Inside, cheek by jowl, the two stared at each other in the close darkness. Their screams were muffled, and they could barely move in the cramped cupboard, much less escape. The woman became so agitated she fainted. The Turkish deserter dozed off. With the *Batoum* in open waters, the captain was first to release his lady friend. Stuffing his arm inside the locker, he jumped back in horror when he pulled out instead a smelly Turk with coal-blackened face and untrimmed beard.

Once in the fresh air, the poor young woman revived. The entire ship chuckled. 'I should imagine that never again will she become a stowaway,' said Bott wryly.

The voyage across the Black Sea proved to be no pleasure cruise. One bejewelled stowaway was blackmailed several times by drunken stokers. Unless she gave them her jewels they would betray her to the port authorities in Odessa. She had no choice. Others suffered the same fate. White and Bott were fortunate to be carrying revolvers.

On the second night out the stokers stole a case of liquor from the cargo and drank themselves stupid. Between alcohol, blackmail and chasing the women they had brought on board, they were much too busy to stoke the furnaces. The ship gradually lost way, until it was almost dead in the water. Josef armed himself with White's revolver and spent the night as an engine stoker until the inebriated men returned the next day.

By the fourth day the *Batoum* should have been in sight of land. But the horizon was empty in all directions. At the urging of the impatient Turkish merchant, anxious to get to Odessa with his cargo, the captain took a sounding. Finding the ship in shallow water, he admitted he was lost.

Balaef, the first mate, took a new sounding, calculating that the *Batoum* had drifted so far east it was actually headed for the Crimea. The captain handed over to Balaef. On his last voyage before retirement, and with his young lady friend on board, he obviously had other things than sailing on his mind.

That night, as the lights of Odessa twinkled before them, White and Bott arranged a tense settlement with Titoff. Although Titoff had schemed to take all the money and then divide it himself between his accomplices, the two escapees pre-empted him by calling in their friends Kuhlmann, Josef and Feodor first. They proposed handing them the money for distribution, deducting from Titoff's share what he had overcharged them for food and stolen from their prison food package. The trio were nervous, afraid of Titoff's revenge. But fortified with a few vodkas — and arranging in advance to accompany the escapees ashore — they called in Titoff. White told him of the new plan.

'Titoff was beside himself with rage,' said White. 'But he saw much meaning and no sympathy in the revolver I put on the table, and the row of smiling faces that confronted him.'

White handed the wad of notes to Josef for distribution. 'There is nothing more to be settled,' he told Titoff. 'Here we are among friends. Now leave us.'

Titoff walked to the door, but turned as he stepped out, telling Josef, 'I shall have business with you later.' Josef, who intended to leave the ship in Odessa, scoffed and poured himself another vodka as he handed Titoff his allotted share.

A scowling Titoff watched from the ship's rail as Kuhlmann and Josef rowed the escapees towards the dock. White and Bott had discarded their seaman's gear, and packed their revolvers, toothbrushes, razors and some bread that they had kept hanging by a string from the ceiling to protect it from cockroaches. The only farewell wave was from 'Bolshevik Bill'.

Approaching a wharf, they noticed Austrian soldiers on guard, protecting nearby buildings behind sandbags and barbed wire. An officer peered at them through field glasses, apparently ordering men to intercept them. White directed Kuhlmann to row around a point, where they joined a stream of boats coming ashore at another landing from a coastal steamer. At the landing stage they strode past a group of Austrian sentries, the ship's uniforms of Kuhlmann and Josef giving them plausible cover.

The escapees hoped they had at last found freedom. Instead they were to find themselves trapped by the nightmare of the Bolshevik Revolution.

11

Out of the frying pan . . .

'We soon realised that the problem of leaving Russia was almost as difficult as that of reaching it.' This was White's sobering conclusion shortly after arriving in Odessa. For the two escapees, it was very much a case of out of the Turkish frying pan, into the Russian fire.

Initially they were optimistic: Odessa would surely be a good jumping-off point for the Allied detachments in Siberia or Archangel in far northern Russia. Or perhaps to Bulgaria, which was threatening to swap sides. But the city was like a powder keg, and they were now trapped inside it.

Odessa was traditionally a charming mix of western and Byzantine influences, its wide curved harbour embraced by long causeways stretching out into the Black Sea. Known as 'the pearl of the Black Sea', the city sits on an escarpment and is famous as a holiday destination. But its myriad small sailing craft — the 'white-winged boats of Odessa' — were stained by blood in 1905 when Odessa witnessed the naval insurrection on the battleship *Potemkin*. Russian film-maker Sergei Eisenstein used the great stairway leading down to the quay to brilliant effect in his silent epic *The Battleship Potemkin*, shot only seven years after White and Bott were in the city.

When the two fugitives arrived aboard the *Batoum* in September 1918, Odessa had experienced only one terrifying burst of the

Bolshevik violence. Worse was to come, but in the meantime the city, occupied by German and Austrian forces at the request of the Ukrainian nationalists, was a haven for hundreds of thousands fleeing the savagery of Lenin's proletarian revolution.

Ukrainian nationalists moved quickly after the events of October 1917, seeing the revolution as a means of gaining their longed-for independence from Russia. When they declared the Ukraine an autonomous republic, the Bolsheviks responded by creating a Ukrainian soviet government, briefly occupying Odessa. White described that occupation, as told to him by locals:

'The mutiny of the Black Sea fleet [in Sevastopol] and the massacre of officers was followed by an orgy of shooting and violence in Odessa.

'The Committees of Soldiers and Workmen resolved themselves into so-called Committees of Public Safety, and under the pretext of searching for arms to prevent a counter-revolution, they robbed householders of every conceivable weapon of offence and defence, looting and killing to their heart's content. Resistance or attempts at concealment of arms or valuables was sufficient pretext to shoot their owners.'

Some residents did resist. One band of officers and Cossacks took on a Bolshevik machine-gun emplacement. Some sixty Bolsheviks were killed before the small group of officers withdrew from the city. Another group of eight Ukrainian officers barricaded themselves with machine guns in the railway station. Having held off the Bolsheviks, and despite the guns of the fleet trained on them, the officers eventually escaped.

By the time White and Bott arrived, Odessa was a pocket of comparative calm as the revolution raged across Russia. But to keep that calm some 20,000 Austrian and 11,000 German troops had to suppress a simmering Bolshevik underground just itching to break out again.

Hiring a four-wheeled droshky, they rode through wide tree-lined boulevards to the address Mr S had given them, the flat of Professor Constaninoff, a former Russian teacher in Constantinople.

The professor was not at home, but his mother and sister greeted them as if the arrival of such refugees was an everyday occurrence.

In fact, it was. Only three days earlier, the women told them, two Ukrainian officers of the Russian Imperial Army arrived in similar circumstances, having escaped Moscow with false credentials and made their way through Bolshevik territory to Odessa. These officers were now in the flat below, and only too happy to swap experiences with the two Allied airmen. Detained by Bolshevik forces, they had escaped only because their fake passports carried the imprint of the Bolshevik authorities. Now they were home, they didn't need the passports. Why don't you take them? they offered the airmen.

Once again fate had intervened. The passports were invaluable for survival in the city, enabling them to walk the streets in comparative safety and draw rations from the occupation authorities. White's passport made him Serge Feodorvitch Davidoff, a native of Turkestan with a nineteen-year-old wife called Anastasia. Bott was Evgeni Nestorovitch von Genko, a German-speaking Latvian from Riga.

'Once we had learned our names [we had] a sense of safety that was hardly exceeded by the comforting knowledge that we possessed firearms,' wrote White.

Some British subjects remained in Odessa after the first Bolshevik uprising and the subsequent Austro-German occupation. They were virtual prisoners, required to register with the authorities and report regularly. The Constantinoffs knew one of them, a tanner named Hatton. The revolution had left Hatton in reduced circumstances, but he was still generous enough to offer the escapees shelter in his home.

After prison camp, hospital beds and shipboard ballast tank 'coffins', home comforts delighted them. 'The ordinary comforts of a civilised household savoured of the luxuries of a palace to our starved souls after long years of the simple life, and we bounced up and down on the upholstered divan in Hatton's flat like two-year-olds, and felt inspired to write panegyrics on table linen and easy chairs,' recalled White.

Life in Odessa, however, was still a gamble, and to travel outside it into Bolshevik-held country was virtually impossible. The Austrians had artillery trained down the main streets, and their troops patrolled day and night. Any civilian carrying a firearm could be shot on sight. Austrian sentries suffered sniper attacks every night.

Bolshevik terrorism combined with old-fashioned thievery to threaten residents. White reported an instance of a man killed for his boots. Warehouses were regularly robbed, the produce quickly turning up in street markets. Bolsheviks blew up a huge ammunition dump just outside the city. In another attack two hundred Austrian soldiers were killed when their barracks were set alight. White saw how lightly human life was regarded in the explosive atmosphere of Odessa when he visited the site of the ammunition dump some days after the explosion. 'Austrian sentries, disregarding Hatton and me, opened fire at about twenty-five yards on a party of peasant women collecting cartridge cases, and sent them screaming from the scene,' he reported.

With Russia in chaos, the fugitives agonised over where to go from Odessa. They contemplated crossing Russia to link up with a British force that had landed near Archangel on the Arctic northern coast. But refugees flocking to Odessa told of absolute turmoil in the countryside, with erratic train schedules at best. Another possibility was east to Baku on the Caspian Sea, where another British force had landed. Together with some of the crew of the *Batoum* they had even mapped out the journey, before receiving news that the Turks had captured Baku when overrunning the Caucasus.

Their best option seemed to be to join the anti-Bolshevik forces then operating in southern Russia. Known as the Volunteer Army, it boasted leaders such as Generals Mikhail Alexeiev and Anton Denikin. Their agents actively recruited in Odessa, while czarist officers on leave openly wore their imperial uniforms in the streets.

Denikin at the time was making overtures to the Allies, and his local agent was delighted at the prospect of recruiting two British flyers (White was regarded as British). The plan was that White and Bott would fly missions for Denikin's army, and also help to organise his flying corps. Later the Volunteer Army would help them get to Siberia to link up with Allied forces.

In retrospect it seems a crazy plan: flying against the Red Army on the promise of assistance to get thousands of miles across Russia to Siberia, and possible escape home. Such were the desperate times, however, that the two were inclined to accept. Once again fate intervened. Bott was laid low with jaundice — the result, believed White, of lying for days in the wet ballast tanks of the *Batoum*. Fighting with the anti-Bolshevik forces was put off for the moment, and White passed the time waiting for his comrade's recovery by working in Hatton's tannery.

Hatton introduced him to the workforce — largely repentant Bolsheviks or former czarist officers — as a refugee from Petrograd. White's Russian was still limited, but he managed to cope with the situation. 'As I trimmed hides brought from the smokeroom or tacked others upon boards, I had to call upon my imagination to answer questions fired at me regarding the price of boots, cost of food and clothes and the latest doings of the Bolsheviks, and in fact how the world wagged in a city I had never seen.'

Although the fugitives were trying to stay low, Bott's jaundice brought them some unwanted attention. The male bathing fashion in Odessa at the time was to swim naked. To wear a swimming costume would be conspicuous. At a beach one day, White, Bott and Hatton disrobed and strode across the beach below the public gardens towards the water. Jaundice, however, had left Bott's skin a deep shade of saffron.

'The spectacle of a yellow man in all his nakedness drew many sightseers, including Austrian soldiers,' recalled Bott. 'I dressed under cover of a rock, and lost no time in leaving the gardens.'

On another occasion their fake passports gave them a false sense of security. The two were running short of funds, and spent much time sitting under the trees along the terraced boulevard overlooking the harbour. One day, White suggested they visit the local free museum. Bott thought it too risky, but White prevailed. On entering, one sentry took their coats, while another asked them to sign the visitors' book. Both signed with their aliases. But the museum was crowded with German officers. 'We decided, once we had regained our hats and the street, that we would avoid such places in future, even though they had the attraction of being free,' White remarked.

Out of fairness to their host Hatton, who had to report to the police regularly and would have been imprisoned if it had become known he was harbouring two British fugitives, the pair decided to find new digs. Through Hatton and the Constantinoffs they met Vladimir Franzovitch, a Ukrainian lieutenant of artillery who had fared badly in the revolution and now lived in a small flat in the Bolshevik quarter.

'He lived in daily fear of being assassinated, and out of the goodness of his heart, and because we owned pistols, he was glad to have our company,' wrote White. 'His quarters consisted of two small but tidy rooms, in one of which the three of us slept on camp beds, the other being occupied by his mistress.'

The old janitor of the flats used their passports to secure daily rations of tea and bread for Evegni Nestorovitch von Genko and Serge Feodorovitch Davidoff from the Austrian Commissariat. As a former noncommissioned officer in the Czar's Imperial Guard and a fervent anti-Bolshevik, the janitor was completely trustworthy.

The city was not without its bright side for the down-at-heel escapees. Although they sought to keep a low profile, they also needed to meet people to find a way of escaping across Russia. Hatton introduced them to another Englishman called Waite, who had lived in Russia for years and knew many officers in the Odessa mercantile marine. Through Waite they came into contact with the legendary Pat O'Flaherty.

Renowned for his eccentric lifestyle, O'Flaherty became their contact around the city's bars and restaurants. An employee of the Eastern Telegraph Company, he was a great friend of Louis Demy, captain of the steamer *Nikolaieff*, who later assisted the pair in escaping Odessa.

'I met Pat yesterday,' Waite told them one day. 'He said he would like to meet you. He was carrying a carpet under his arm, and when I asked him if he was trying to sell it, he said he had turned Muslim and always carried a prayer carpet now.'

The carpet story was an appropriate introduction to the madcap, heavy-drinking O'Flaherty, an Irishman who had been kicked out of the army many years previously for striking an officer. Pat's favourite prank was to introduce the two fugitives to his various café friends in many different guises, and expect them to instantly fill the new roles.

'On one occasion we were Jewish cinema showmen who had come to Russia to evade conscription in England,' recalled White. 'Later we were travellers for a Coventry firm of motor car manufacturers and could quote for automobiles complete in every detail except for tyres. Anon we were traders in furs, and introducing Bott as M. Califatti to an unctuous English-speaking Jew who joined our group, he described in minute detail a valuable coat made from four skins which Bott was anxious to sell at a great reduction as it was slightly moth-eaten.'

The potential buyer offered a thousand rubles for the mythical coat, provided it was quality astrakhan and in four skins. 'White and I remained speechless with astonishment, embarrassment, and the desire to grin,' said Bott.

After one night with Pat at a new restaurant opening, White and Bott, having just managed to stop the inebriated Irishman from leaping amongst a tempting pile of crockery, led him back to his lodgings. Shielding the singing O'Flaherty from a German army patrol, they accepted his invitation to stay the night.

'The stove and walls of his apartment were riddled with bullet-holes,' White recounted. 'On enquiring the origin we learned that there had been no romantic indoor battle, but that a Russian friend and kindred spirit when drunk had the playful habit of indulging in target practice with his revolver before retiring.'

The restaurant crowd gave White and Bott an insight into the devil-may-care life of carpetbagger traders who won and lost paper fortunes in Odessa as the Bolsheviks encircled the city. Odessa's Austro-German garrison gave it the atmosphere of the last refuge for Russia's bourgeoisie, who were the main target of Bolshevik fanaticism. They flocked in hundreds of thousands to the city, swelling the population from 600,000 to 1.5 million.

'The middle classes — professional men, merchants, traders and speculators — knew they living on the edge of a volcano, and tried to drown the knowledge in revelry,' wrote Bott. 'Each evening, parties costing thousands of roubles were given in the restaurants. Wine and vodka, as aids to forgetfulness of the fear that hovered over every feast, were well worth their hundred roubles a bottle.'

Bott likened the frenzied speculation to an orgy, but it forced up prices and created scarcity for the poor. He was trenchant about speculators. 'All day long Franconi's and Robinart's, the two principal cafes of Odessa, were infested by swarms of swarthy Jews who wandered from table to table, selling and reselling and piling up enormous fortunes in paper roubles,' he observed. 'And elsewhere in the city hundreds of thousands of Russians were in little more than rags, many thousands of them half-dead from want of nourishment.'

Vilkovsky's arrival as a stowaway on another steamship from Constantinople revived the plan to join the anti-Bolshevik forces in southern Russia. Vilkovsky had strong connections with the Volunteer Army, and undertook to make the arrangements. One day he arrived at their flat with the news that a party of ex-czarist officers was leaving by train that night for Novorissisk to join the Volunteer Army. White and Bott could join them. Unfortunately, this coincided with a booking the pair had made for the Odessa opera, planned as a celebration for having cashed a cheque with the Dutch consul.

'We debated whether we would forego the opera ... The opera won, and we enjoyed an incomparable rendering of Boris Godunof at the world-renowned Opera House,' wrote White. 'Next day we learned that trains might not run for weeks to Novorissisk . . .'

This was another lucky escape for the aviators. Denikin went on to capture much of the Ukraine but was defeated by the Red Army at Orel in 1919. Then, reversing the airmen's own trail, he escaped to Constantinople before going into exile in France.

Inevitably, White and Bott were drawn into the Ukrainian struggle for independence. Vladimir Franzovitch used the flat as an office to organise supplies for the embryonic Ukrainian army. He also took them to meetings with ex-czarist Ukrainian officers who were determined to put up a fight should the communists rise up again. They built a small fort on the outskirts of the city, inviting the pair to join in its defence. They were also invited to help man a gunboat.

'We agreed to go where we would be of most use, provided we were still in Odessa,' said White.

Another lucky escape. They heard later that when French and Greek forces arrived after the war they found the bodies of officers in a fort outside town, where they had attempted to hold off the communists after the withdrawal of the Austro-German army.

Then came their most important break. The Austrian authorities agreed that the hospital ship *Euphrat* could sail to Varna in Bulgaria to bring back released Ukrainian prisoners. Rumours swept Odessa of a Bulgarian armistice as an Allied force rolled into the area. Could they smuggle themselves aboard the *Euphrat* and get to Allied lines? It certainly beat leaving Russia by leapfrogging to Siberia via the anti-Bolshevik forces.

Through their friend Louis Demy they visited the shipping office, waiting outside while Demy arranged with the captain for them to be slipped on board. They saw Demy pointing them out to the captain as he sealed the deal.

The ship would not sail for at least ten days, however, and as if on cue both White and Bott came down with influenza, then raging through southern Russia. They could not stay in Vladimir Franzovitch's flat by day, so they passed the time sitting in the sunshine in the city parks, dosing themselves with aspirin. Street bulletin boards cheered them with the news that the Allies were obviously winning the war. The glum looks of the occupying Austrian and German troops acted as an excellent tonic to supplement their aspirin.

It did the same for local Bolsheviks, who boisterously sang revolutionary songs in the neighbourhood. White was chilled by the revolutionary song 'Yahblotchkaw', about the slaughter of officers on the cruiser *Almaz*, an incident he first heard about on the *Batoum*.

Rumours swept the city of an imminent Bolshevik rising to drive out the occupying force. Among the thousands of refugees who fled to Odessa were many Bolsheviks who had reportedly brought arms with them. Former czarist officers and soldiers staged anti-Bolshevik street rallies, but only about five hundred of them signed up to fight. The Austrians raided the office of the Soviet consul, uncovering the names of many infiltrators. Arrests and executions followed. The Austrians mounted artillery on all major streets as the city braced for an uprising. Anyone found with a weapon was shot.

Vilkovsky and Franzovitch became quite depressed. 'From tomorrow I shall cease to shave and wear collars,' Vilkovsky declared. Franzovitch, who had fought in Russia's 1905 war with Japan, saw nothing but doom in the communists' hatred of the middle classes and their plans to nationalise industry. White was amazed that Franzovitch showed no personal hatred towards the communists who would later kill him. Franzovitch simply grieved for their ignorance, imploring White and Bott to drum up support for the anti-Bolshevik forces when they reached home.

'And as a patriot he died,' White recorded later. 'Since the armistice we have heard that Vladimir Franzovitch met his death while gallantly fighting for his country's honour ...'

As the Bulgarian armistice was signed and the Allies advanced on both the western and Palestine fronts, rumours grew apace. According to one, a French force was marching from Bulgaria to

Odessa. Another had it that the British fleet had forced the Dardanelles. 'Crowds assembled daily on the Puskinskaya Boulevard searching the horizon for the ships of their deliverers,' wrote White. The mood of the crowd was one of desperation. They had witnessed the horrors of the Bolsheviks once already. 'There was an expression of terror in the faces of the unarmed citizens and the defenceless women that can only be realised by those who have been in a similar situation.'

The Austrians stepped up their street patrols as a cover for an anticipated withdrawal. Some troops sympathised with the Bolsheviks, while others joined the scramble to make money before the end. Walking down a street one night White was stopped by an Austrian sentry. 'Rightly guessing that he would have something to sell I asked him what price he wanted,' said White. 'With a grin he produced a large box of the vilest cigarettes I have ever smoked, which I gladly purchased for twice their value.'

In their final days in Odessa the aviators tried to assemble as much information as they could about the Austro-German forces and the Bolsheviks to pass to Allied intelligence. They compiled notes on the number and location of the occupying force, their ammunition dumps and stores, as well as information on the communists.

After farewelling Hatton, Vladimir Franzovitch and other friends, one night they accompanied Louis Demy and Pat O'Flaherty to the docks. Austrian sentries guarded the wharf where the *Euphrat* was berthed. Hiding in the shadows, they waited until sentries were busy supervising the boarding of a group of returning Bulgarians, then slipped up another gangway. Demy found a crewman who led them to an unused cabin, where they farewelled their friends.

'Next morning, through the porthole, we saw Odessa of the fine streets and crescent harbour blur into the distance,' wrote White. 'We could only vainly conjecture its fate.'

Fate was not kind to Odessa. A French fleet bombarded the town before the arrival of a combined French, Serbian, Polish and

Greek force. A second Soviet government was created in April 1919, only to be overthrown by General Denikin later that year. The communists finally recaptured the city in February 1920. Large parts of this beautiful city were destroyed in this cycle of war between occupying forces and Bolsheviks.

Ukrainians would not see independence until the Soviet Union collapsed in the early 1990s.

The Odessa interlude left Tom White with a lifelong hatred of communists. Even socialists he described as 'Bolsheviks with a shave'. He long advocated that communist supporters should be sent to Russia to see the system in action for themselves.

In one respect White was remarkably prescient. Bolshevism, he said, had to be fought, 'and fought to the finish if the world is not to slip back into savagery'. As early as 1919 he called for a *cordon sanitaire* to isolate Russia and dissipate her resources. There would be forty-five years of cold war following the Second World War before Russian communism finally collapsed.

12

'You're the Greek caterer's sons, aren't you?'

Arriving in the Bulgarian Black Sea port of Varna, White and Bott were confronted with a stunning sight — two khaki-clad armed British soldiers on patrol in the street.

'In our scarecrow clothes and [with] paper parcels of belongings, we stood and watched them with mixed feelings — the finest symbol of freedom that we had seen,' said White.

Freedom now beckoned, but it would take some painful incidents before it was finally achieved. The voyage on the *Euphrat* had been much less exciting than that on the *Batoum*, but it nonetheless included a cast of mysterious passengers.

Ukrainian partisans in Odessa had told them that among their shipmates would be a general from Denikin's staff en route to Salonika in the Aegean Sea to seek Allied military and financial help for the anti-Bolshevik forces. They found him sitting quietly in the second-class dining room, wearing clothes almost as ragged as their own. The general was travelling under the guise of an engineer's mate, accompanied by the 'engineer', a former commander in the Russian imperial navy.

Another passenger was a former Russian navy lieutenant who had been spying at the big dockyards at Sevastopol, the navy's main Black Sea port. He had details to give the British about the ships, submarines and men now at Germany's disposal.

At Varna, the passengers were herded into quarantine owing to the huge influenza and cholera outbreak in southern Russia. The two escapees and the anti-Bolshevik emissaries hid. They then lowered a boat and headed to shore, where White and Bott parted company with the Russians as they made for the French naval detachment that had come overland immediately Bulgaria agreed to an armistice.

At the Hotel London, where the British advance guard had made their headquarters, they handed their reports on the situation in Odessa to an intelligence officer. Later they were taken to the mess of ten officers, who with fifty men of the Durham Light Infantry formed the new British garrison.

Some of the officers doubted that this emaciated pair of shabby if colourfully dressed refugees were actually British officers. White wore a strange, oversized yellow waistcoat with green checks given to him by a friend of O'Flaherty's. Both carried their worldly belongings in newspaper parcels. White and Bott demonstrated their bona fides with a string of military cusses and a few renditions of the chorus of 'Good-bye-ee'. No new clothes were available, but they were given two blankets.

British officers told them of an Allied column headed for Constantinople and another on the way to southern Russia. Like old war horses, both immediately applied to return to duty. White's military ardour had not been dampened by three years in captivity. Lack of uniforms was one obvious handicap. Brigadier General Ross, commander of the garrison, told them their best option was to get to Salonika headquarters in Greece and reapply there.

On the train they still carried their newspaper-wrapped belongings and looked, thought White, like a couple of Australian swagmen. Bulgarian officers on the train wanted to evict them from first class. In Sofia the cabmen at the station refused to pick them up. At British headquarters an orderly announced them as two tramps who 'said' they were British. Intelligence officers tried not to laugh at White's checked waistcoat.

Even the car and driver provided for the road trip to Salonika did not give them the dignity they longed to recover. At one checkpoint near a British column a sentry asked the driver who were his friends, the tramps. But a stop at the spa town of Sveterack provided some consolation — a British subaltern gave them two empty sandbags, allowing them to dispense with their newspaper parcels.

At the grand British HQ in Salonika they were rejected at one entrance, and then rudely told at another that 'dagoes like you' must use the back entry. Eventually one of the intelligence staff vouched for them, and for the last time they gave reports about guns, troops and the Bolsheviks in Odessa. But on leaving they were abused by another guard for using the 'officers' entrance'.

That night they sought a bed at the officers' rest house. After the guard demanded identity papers and also tested their English for further proof, a quartermaster appeared. 'You're the Greek caterer's sons, aren't you?' he asked. 'We heard you were coming.'

After a three-day stay they found the sandbags containing their belongings placed carefully outside their doors. But the clothing store promised relief at last. As White and Bott returned one day dressed in the beginnings of new uniforms, they asked directions to RAF headquarters from an airman who had been celebrating with friends.

'Hey boys,' the airman said, turning to his drinking mates, 'come and see what's going to join the air force now.' Then, shaking his head at the pair, he said, 'Take my advice, don't join the Air Force, we're a rotten lot of drunks.'

But try they did. In a handwritten application to military headquarters, White wrote: 'I beg to state that I hereby apply to be attached to any Naval or Military force which may be sent to Odessa or other southern Russian ports.

'I have had 8 years Commissioned service, and received my Captaincy in the Australian Military Forces (Infantry) Oct 11, 1913.

'I was in Odessa from October 6 to November 3 1918, having escaped there from Turkey, where I had been a prisoner-of-war for two years and 9 months.

'I can speak French, enough Russian and a little Turkish.

'I have forwarded reports on the political and military situations in Southern Russia to Intelligence Depts at Varna, Sofia and Salonika.'

A few days before the Armistice, when White was still wearing his colourful waistcoat, a joyful Tommy, mistaking him for one of the local Greek labourers, slapped him on the back, declaring in the pidgin-French of the troops in Salonika, 'La guerre est fini, Johnnie!'

It was. 'And then it came,' recalled White, 'to the accompaniment of gunfire from warships in the harbour and rattling of musketry in the streets — less than two weeks after our arrival in Salonika.'

It was a bittersweet occasion for them. Selfishly, they wished the end had not come quite so soon. 'Our thousand-mile journey seemed almost in vain, though it was some small satisfaction to know that we had outwitted the wily Turk.'

12A

'Skin and bones' to body politic

The end of the 'war to end all wars' was Tom White's opportunity to see something of the wider world after almost three years in captivity. In Cairo he met many fellow prisoners repatriated by the Turks. He thought ruefully that they had 'reached Egypt with much less trouble and expense'.

After visiting Palestine, where he caught up with old mates of the Australian Flying Corps, it was on to Paris, then feting President Wilson at the Versailles Conference, and finally to London. When White arrived in late December 1918, troops from every corner of the Empire filled London's streets.

Some of them looked remarkably different. There was the extraordinary Hill, now in a smart RAF uniform, totally transformed from the bearded 'madman' White had nursed in a Turkish hospital. Hill was now able to give him the full story of his crazy escapades, from spooking a prison camp commandant to convincing everyone he was a lunatic. White repaid the forty pounds Hill had loaned him in hospital to aid his escape.

A dapper Yeats-Brown, monocle firmly in eye, looked much more at home, thought White, steering his car through Mayfair than wasting away as a POW.

At breakfast one morning in his cheap hotel near Victoria Station, White fell to chatting with the navy officer sitting opposite.

Surprisingly, they found they had both served in Mesopotamia. White told him of his work for the navy, collecting information on enemy positions before a battle and dropping the maps in an old film tin to General Townshend on HMS *Espiegle* on the Tigris.

'Really,' replied the naval officer. 'I'm the one who picked up that tin!'

Another surprise was a meeting with Tommy Taylor, an Australian soldier captured on the western front who escaped from a prison farm in eastern Germany and amazingly made his way to Moscow. After harrowing experiences with the Bolsheviks, and surviving in Moscow selling soap and gambling, Taylor was repatriated to London with the help of the Danish embassy. He and White were the only two Australians to escape via Russia in the First World War.

Other brushes with the military were not so enjoyable. London saw the beginning of a long battle with military officialdom over salary, expenses, promotion and awards for his service, capture and escape. Between serving under Australian, Indian and British commands, pay responsibilities had become confused, with one service cutting him off because it thought another was paying. White also had to battle for compensation for expenses and bribes incurred in escaping.

Worse was the protracted wrangling over promotion and awards. White had remained a captain during his incarceration, a postwar recommendation of promotion from the India Office apparently falling between the various desks of his military masters. The battle over awards really rankled. White received the Distinguished Flying Cross for services in Mesopotamia and a Mention in Dispatches for his bravery as a POW and escaper. But both the India Office and Major General Kemball, whom White had rescued from under the nose of the enemy after his plane was forced down in Mesopotamia, went into bat for a higher Distinguished Service Order.

Kemball's letters to former fellow army chiefs in Mesopotamia revealed the suicidal nature of the mission by White and Yeats-Brown back in 1915. Kemball said he had made inquiries after the two failed to return and found that the orders to land in two different hostile and unknown areas to cut telegraph wires were not in accordance with standard military instructions. Even the two pilots' commander believed the mission was 'practically hopeless'.

'As both Captain White and Captain Yeats-Brown must have been well aware that the attempt to carry out the orders given them would in all probability end in their death or capture, I would submit that the way in which they volunteered and attempted to carry out their desperate task exhibited intrepidity and devotion to duty of the highest order,' he wrote, recommending both promotion and the DSO for White.

Richard Williams, White's fellow Point Cook graduate and a rising star in the new air force after the war, took a different view. In an undated note, Williams, then Acting Director Air Services, considered White had been treated 'extremely well'. Other officers who had done more for their country had not received as much recognition as White. Anything further would be an 'extreme injustice', he said, recommending no further action. Williams' note contributed to the love-hate relationship between the two over the years.

The issue of White's 'lost' DSO bounced back and forth between England and Australia for years, with pointed inquiries as to why British officers received such higher awards but White did not. This feeling that there was an anti-colonial bias had already surfaced elsewhere. Commander Stoker of the submarine *AE2*, the first to penetrate the dangerous Narrows of the Dardanelles Straits to attack Turkish supply lines to Gallipoli, received only a DSO, while the British submariner who preceded him and failed, and the two who successfully followed in his tracks, all won Victoria Crosses.

Winston Churchill put the issue to rest in 1921. As Secretary of State for the Colonial Office, he told Australia's Governor-General, Lord Forster, that White had received a DFC and Mention in Dispatches, and the Air Council 'do not propose to make any further award to him'.

Privately White was livid. 'Unfortunately, the DSO was confused with a DFC, which I had got, and . . . the matter was [held] up so long that so far I have got neither the DSO or the promotion,' he wrote to Fred Cutlack in 1920, when helping the journalist with details of Half Flight for Cutlack's air force volume of the official history of the First World War.

The incident, however, highlighted a new side to White, a determination to get on in life. He had always been ambitious, with a strong independent streak, as shown when he stood up to a superior officer during the petty smoko night affair before the war. In London, White realised he now had to run harder to make up for the years lost in captivity.

'I regret that I never had an opportunity to escape sooner, for my unfortunate capture spoilt all chances of my receiving a decoration and leaves me the same rank as I was before the war,' he wrote to Kemball, pushing his case for new gongs and promotion.

Apart from rounding up POW colleagues and senior Mesopotamia chiefs for his cause, he also leapt into print, publishing articles in a British weekly on his daring escape with Bott. White was keen to make a name for himself as the only Australian to successfully escape from a Turkish prison camp. Another turn of fate, however, steered White down a new path — romance.

In Afion he had generously used part of his mail allowance to correspond with the Australian Red Cross office in London. The Red Cross official who ultimately received all his details of sick or dead Australian POWs was twenty-seven-year-old Vera Deakin.

In prison White might not have appreciated Vera's pedigree — the youngest daughter of Alfred Deakin, a brilliant, introspective but idealistic Melbourne barrister who played a central part in federation and served three terms as prime minister in Australia's first decade as a Commonwealth. Born in 1891, three years after Tom White, Vera had a privileged, sheltered upbringing, educated at Melbourne Church of England Grammar School before going on to study music in Berlin and Budapest, with her aunt as chaperone.

The First World War brought out not only Vera's independent streak but her commitment to welfare causes, and a managerial flair as well. Unbeknown to her protective parents, in 1915 she sent a message to Norman Brookes, then Red Cross commissioner in Cairo, asking if he needed any assistance in his war work. Overwhelmed by the sick and wounded returning from Gallipoli, he replied, 'Come at once and bring as many like you as you can find.' Vera had already completed a Red Cross home nursing course and was awaiting exam results for more senior administrative duties. She and a friend, Winifred Johnson, booked steerage class cabins on the SS *Arabia*, showing enormous daring and confidence for sheltered young women in those days.

'My father was very hurt with me,' Vera recorded many years later. She had dutifully told him she would not go if he said 'no'. But if he just said she would only end up in a harem, she would definitely go. Deakin grudgingly relented, offering to supplement money from her mother to enable her to live more comfortably as a volunteer. A brother-in-law, Herbert Brookes (Norman's brother), also offered to help financially.

'With sinking heart, khaki coat and skirt,' but still without her Red Cross exam results, Vera set sail. In Egypt she quickly established the Australian Wounded and Missing Inquiry Bureau, later transferring the office work to London as Australia shifted its military focus from Gallipoli to the western front.

With her exam results through, Vera qualified for Red Cross VAD (Voluntary Aid Detachment). It was hard, demanding work, with constant battles against unhelpful military authorities. There were long hours in collecting details of the missing and wounded, sending parcels and newspapers to POWs in Turkey and Germany, meeting and visiting wounded in hospital, handling a deluge of inquiries from relatives and friends, and sending detailed reports back to Australia — all as a volunteer.

The energetic and intelligent Vera blossomed under the challenge, developing managerial skills that earned her an offer of paid work with the American Red Cross. She turned it down. 'No salary would lure me' from working for her fellow Australians in the army and navy, she replied. She was awarded an OBE in 1917.

Vera's feistiness belied her bluestocking upbringing. Once, when Prime Minister Billy Hughes used a dinner at his London home to pump her for details about the Red Cross to use for political purposes back in Australia she responded: 'I am an officer of the Red Cross, and whether you are the Prime Minister or the Governor-General I am afraid I must refuse to answer.' Hughes huffily left the room and retired to bed early.

Visiting France to check on Australian wounded, Vera encountered opposition from both Red Cross and military bureaucracies. When one Red Cross commander said he 'could never face her father' if he allowed her to go near the front, Vera responded: 'I am of age, and I've faced difficulties in Egypt and London. I have come to France and I am not going back without going to the places I said I would.' She went.

When she tried to see a wounded Australian in a French hospital, one officer proved a real obstruction. Australians, he humphed, were spoiled. Nothing ever satisfied them. 'Sir,' Vera demanded from her imposing height, 'I am here to service my compatriots. Will you let me do my job?' The officer stamped off, and Vera completed her mission.

As the war ended in November 1918, Vera heard from former Turkish POWs in London that Tommy White was expected soon. She wanted to meet him, if only to thank him for his generous efforts in helping her keep tabs on wounded and sick POWs. The Sunday in late December that White arrived in London, Vera had promised to take a group of former POWs, including White's Afion escape collaborator Lieutenant Les Luscombe, to a service at the Temple Church of the Knight Crusaders off Fleet Street to hear its famous choir. White arrived late.

'I saw an emaciated looking skeleton of a man, with the skin tight on his bones,' Vera recalled. They shook hands over the prone statue of one of the crusader knights clutching a sword, 'Goodness,' thought Vera, 'Is this the man who gave us all this information?'

It was. And there might have been a twitch in the crusader's sword as it witnessed the handshake. Vera, then approaching her twenty-seventh birthday, cut an imposing figure in her blue uniform with cream blouse, navy tie and the Australia flash on her shoulders. About White's height, with strong attractive features, brown eyes and wavy dark hair, she had the confident stamp of leadership and a warmth of character that clearly appealed to the returned POW. The attraction was mutual: it was love at first sight.

More than the electricity between the couple may have been in the air of Temple Church that day. The Knights Templar, the order of crusading monks founded to protect pilgrims against Muslim harassment on their way to and from Jerusalem, built the church in the twelfth century. It was the first London call for White, newly returned from the same area after fighting twentieth-century Muslims. It had been the fate of the Knights Templar that gave Friday the 13th — White's favourite superstition — its modern significance. On Friday, 13 October 1307, King Philip IV of France unleashed a reign of terror on the Templars that lasted for seven years, decimating the order. This historic catastrophe gave Friday the 13th its superstitious reputation.

There could also have been a quiver of anticipation around the Knights Templar Church. White not only followed in his father's footsteps in the Masons, but later rose to become one of the leaders of the lodge in Britain. The Knight Templar is one of the highest degrees of Free Masonry.

Such extraordinary coincidences escaped Vera Deakin and Tom White that day in 1918, even though White's antennae were usually sensitive to fateful events. The party, including John Latham, later to become leader of the National Party in Australia, returned to Vera's flat for lunch and then went on to Queen's Hall to hear a Mendelssohn concert. Later, Latham confided to Vera that the 'young man' who had escaped from Turkey interested him very much. 'But he needs a feed,' he said. Vera quietly agreed.

In the following days White haunted the Red Cross Bureau. He wanted typing help for magazine articles he was preparing on his escape. 'There are none to spare,' Vera told him. 'If you wait until after hours I might type up a bit,' she added encouragingly. White took to leaving his hat behind at the Bureau, giving him an excuse to return to see Vera, while claiming that in prison camp he had got out of the habit of wearing a hat.

When Vera hosted Christmas dinner at her flat for a large group of servicemen and friends, she found White at her side as she struggled to carve a huge turkey. On New Year's Eve in her office a wrapped parcel arrived for her, containing a copy of Keats's poems. Inside was another poem in White's handwriting, in which he declared that meeting Vera had been the best day in his life. 'This is very ominous, I thought,' Vera later confided.

A few days later White asked her if she was attending the afternoon tea party of Vera's Red Cross colleague Miss Chomley, White's main Red Cross correspondent from Turkey. Unfortunately not, Vera responded. She had to go to a Richmond hospital to check on an Australian patient.

Leaving the hospital on a misty winter evening she saw a familiar figure standing near a little pond outside. It was Tom White.

'Why did you come?'

'I will tell you in a minute.'

Vera's version of events (Tom's is not recorded) is that by the time they got on the bus back to London they were engaged. 'I am ashamed to say it was [only] three weeks after the day I met him,' she confided later with coquettish modesty. 'Three weeks! Wasn't that terrible,' she added with a laugh.

Certainly some in the family thought so. Initially, there was stiff opposition to the marriage. Current family folklore tells of phrases like 'wrong side of the tracks' and 'trade' being thrown around by some in the Deakin clan. And, worse still, wasn't he already engaged?

While that misconception could be easily disposed of — White had broken off his engagement with Flora Bien from prison camp — Vera's influential brother-in-law, the entrepreneur Herbert Brookes, was very overprotective of her. Family lore tells of a threatened 'duel' following Brookes' speech at the couple's 1920 Melbourne wedding. Brookes had indicated that while Vera had already 'proved herself' in life, it was still up to White to do so. Given White's war record, his flying corps colleagues at the wedding were naturally outraged, lining up to challenge Brookes to a few rounds over his thoughtless remarks. Fortunately, tempers were soothed and the wedding reception proceeded without further incident.

Vera had to return to Australia in April 1919 when her father became very ill. Alfred Deakin, who had been in poor health for some time, died later that year from a heart attack. Although White never met him, he would provide a role model for the aspiring young man. Later a close bond developed between White and Deakin's widow, Dame Pattie.

Before her departure, Vera and White and one of her Red Cross friends visited Scotland. They stayed in an Oban boarding house near a picturesque Scottish Castle that they were keen to visit after hearing that the laird had been a prisoner of war. White knocked on the castle door. When he explained to the butler he had also been a POW, a tall, thin man appeared calling out, 'Brother lag, come in'. The laird escorted them around, with the Australians then inviting him to their hostel for afternoon tea. The proprietress of the boarding house was panic-stricken at the news of a first-ever visit by the laird, but she need not have worried. Both the laird and White sat on the floor to take tea.

'They were not used to chairs,' laughed Vera at the behaviour of the two ex-POWs. They discussed the plight of Russian POWs still in camps after the revolution, and with no parcels from home. The laird revealed that he regularly sent parcels to them. 'That endeared him to Tom's heart,' said Vera. 'They kept up a correspondence.'

Even as a prisoner White's mind had turned to a future business career. Since his father had died in 1915, his younger brother Percy had run the family locksmith and hardware business. 'I will be glad to be back in business again,' he wrote Percy from Afion in 1918. 'After all, it is certainly the most fascinating and satisfactory walk of life.'

White took leave from the air force in London, and spent the rest of 1919 studying new opportunities for the family business in Britain and America. On his return to Australia in early 1920 to marry Vera, the new couple bought a home in Walsh Street, South Yarra. Later they moved to a bigger home nearby, which they called 'Kurna', after the Mesopotamian town where White first experienced shells fired in anger.

The Whites had four daughters: Lilian, born in April 1921; Patricia, in February 1923; Shirley, in May 1925; and Judith, in June 1929. For White they were his 'little darlings'. Not once did he express a desire for a son, though he joked when he left for trips that he was escaping 'petticoat government'. In this he was also following Deakin, who similarly had only daughters.

Settling into the job of managing director of C. J. White & Sons, he was anxious to build up the hardware business with new agencies he had secured abroad. He and Percy opened a city branch and a factory in the suburbs. But trade associations, unions and banks proved unexpected obstacles.

The powerful trade associations, which were then very active in promoting 'orderly marketing', told White that if he tried to sell below the association's recommended prices his imports would be cut off. 'You're nothing more than pot-bellied war profiteers, and we'll fight you,' an angry White responded, showing the feistiness he had brought back from the war. In the ensuing struggle C. J. White & Sons' buying power saw them win. Fights with organised labour followed, with unions demanding that White pay an as yet unapproved pay rise despite having just negotiated rates with his staff. Strikes and picket lines continued for six months before White brought in employees from interstate. The industrial turmoil, however, had shaken the little company, and White's bank demanded he reduce the firm's overdraft by fifty per cent. White arranged a new overdraft facility with another bank, then called at his old bank and, as he put it, 'spat on the manager's carpet'.

These experiences made White a strong small business supporter. He once described his entrepreneur brother-in-law as employing the techniques of the business bully — 'the coward who skulks behind all the social privileges and the protection of capital'. Perhaps he had not forgotten Brookes' opposition to his marriage to Vera.

Both writing and the military still held attractions for him. He rejoined the army reserve, rising to Commander of the 6th Battalion, City of Melbourne Regiment, in 1926 with the rank of lieutenant colonel. He also found time to write the full story of his wartime adventures, entitling the book *Guests of the Unspeakable*, adapting Gladstone's description of the Turks. No Australian publisher was interested, however, and the manuscript gathered dust through the 1920s until a British publisher finally picked it up in 1928. It was an instant hit, prompting Angus & Robertson to publish an Australian edition, which then ran through several print runs. 'Compelling,' said *The Times*' reviewer, while *The Bulletin* in Australia judged it a 'great book'.

Perhaps the most poignant review was in the London *Spectator*. 'Colonel White sometimes ran great risks, and frequently went hungry himself in order to help our sick and wounded soldiers,' it said. 'The present writer can vouch for this, as he was there.' The reviewer was Yeats-Brown, who had found a job with the magazine.

While the combination of business, part-time military commitments and authorship might satisfy most, White was still keen to tackle other goals. Politics became a driving aim. Prison camp debates had awakened something in him, while his month in Odessa had instilled a horror of communism that he worried his fellow Australians did not share. Mixing with the Deakin family and its wide range of influential business and political friends, from the Brookes family to John Latham, who had entered federal politics for the National Party, opened new horizons for the small businessman from North Melbourne.

What Vera thought of this new aim is not clear, but there is an interesting letter White sent her in 1926 after the couple had had a minor spat, in which Vera must have made some comment about his career. 'The job I am after is not found in the situations vacant but on the hustings — and there I intend to find it — so there!' he wrote. It was a make-up letter rather than one of recriminations. 'Let's have a best lover competition,' he suggested, adding, 'in spite of all you say I do love you more than you love me.'

From the mid to late 1920s White made three unsuccessful bids to enter politics under the Nationalist banner, the predecessor of today's Liberals. In 1925 he gained preselection for the federal seat of Maribyrnong, regarded as safe for Labor. His campaign material said White was 'going to the electors on the straight-out question of communism or ordered government', stressing his experience in Russia. Organised groups tried to wreck his rallies, with police called to eject hecklers. One heckler made a sneering reference to his war service.

White responded, 'You remind me of the Arabs, when I was brought down behind Turkish lines, I was surrounded by Arabs who spat on me and struck me with sticks and other weapons. Mob rule — that's what it was, and it is mob rule which you and these stupid and noisy interrupters are trying to bring about.'

A newspaper account of another meeting full of imported hecklers reported White as shouting back that if they saw a little bit of Russia they would change their views. 'He had seen a little of Russia and God forbid that Australia should be like it (cheers),' the newspaper reported. 'There were men in Australia, parlour Bolsheviks, who had never seen anything more violent than a football match, who were hoping for some of the jobs which Lenin and Trotsky snapped up in Russia. The big obstacles to the communist movement were the church and the British Empire (cheers).'

White lost, but he pegged back Labor's vote, drawing himself to party attention and winning preselection for a crack at another safe Labor seat, Prahran, in the Victorian state elections of 1928. He ran as the 'business and resident' candidate. Losing again, he still performed well, although it was not sufficient to gain National preselection for a Senate berth. But in 1929 he gained preselection for the safe National seat of Balaclava, including bayside St Kilda, vacant after the sudden retirement of W. A. Watt, a former premier of Victoria.

Elected in an August by-election, White had to face the voters again in October at a general election called by the Bruce–Page National Government in a climate of industrial turmoil. He was re-elected — going on to hold the seat for twenty-two years — but Labor under James Scullin was swept to power, with even Prime Minister Bruce losing his seat. One consolation for White was that John Latham now became Leader of the Opposition.

White's entry to federal politics was quiet — at first. His maiden speech was devoted to a topic dear to his heart, completing the construction of the Australian War Memorial in Canberra. With the depression deepening there was talk of abandoning the project. 'We must not fail in this duty to the soldiers who passed over,' declared White. The War Memorial opened in 1941, just in time to start collecting material from another war.

The initially quiet MHR for Balaclava was a surprise package, however. Other parliamentarians just couldn't believe that this smallish, baby-faced man with a cowlick of hair dangling across his face was who he said he was — a lieutenant colonel. 'He looked like a cadet,' wrote the *Sydney Mail* (White was then in his early forties). 'Labor members thought "the Colonel" was a joke. Nobody quite believed he was the man he said he was.'

As the Scullin Labor Government ended universal service training and abolished the preference given to ex-servicemen in public employment, White became more and more aggressive. Ex-servicemen would never forgive this sell-out, he thundered.

This aggression drew attention. 'He was always jumping up — or if he wasn't jumping he was throwing what ministers called "insulting interjections" at them', said the *Mail*. 'He just couldn't help himself; there was the enemy, and he must be firing. It was the way they had at the war.'

White's aggression and his colourful wartime escapades made good newspaper copy. The reward came after the election of December 1931, when a re-energised Opposition rode back into power with a new party, the United Australia Party, and a new leader, the Labor defector Joe Lyons (Latham went off to the High Court). In January 1933, while relaxing with his family at Point Lonsdale, the Deakin family holiday home, White received a telegram from Lyons asking him to be the new minister for trade and customs.

Media speculation singled out White as future leadership material. *To-Day Magazine* in September 1933 reported that White had conquered the weakness of allowing political opponents to rattle him, and claimed his rapid advancement had 'astonished' politicians and the public. As well, said *To-Day*, he had Deakin family tradition on his side, and might well inspire a new proverb — 'A man is known by the wife he keeps'.

If that was the positive side, *To-Day* also outlined what it saw as White's negative qualities. 'He is a little man and, like many little men, not excluding Napoleon, is apt to have a great idea of his own importance and infallibility.' Such a description of course fits many politicians, large and small, but *To-Day* added to this White's 'sins' of snap statements and fast talking.

Even White conceded he had a short fuse. In a letter to Vera he said he usually was not the first to criticise, but when roused was quick to come to the boil. White's penchant for the explosive remark that backfired soon landed him in hot water with Prime Minister Lyons.

Returning from abroad, Lyons called him in over a growing turf dispute with the minister for commerce, F. H. Stewart, on handling trade negotiations. After the meeting White unwisely sent a letter to Lyons saying he had hoped that the prime minister would not have listened to tittle-tattle in White's absence. Lyons instantly rebuked his new minister. 'I desire to say at once that I resent your suggestion that I have listened to tales and undermining of yourself,' he replied. 'As head of the government it is my duty to listen to a complaint from any minister and to investigate it — that is all I have done in this case.' Lyons said he was returning White's letter 'in the hope that you will on calmer consideration review your attitude'.

Realising he had overstepped the mark, White quickly back-tracked, replying that he regretted giving Lyons the wrong impression. Let's move on, he said, noting 'there are bigger things to worry us all than this'.

Not that White was unsupportive of Lyons, who became the great election winner of the 1930s, racking up three wins in a row for the UAP. In March 1937, as Lyons was leaving Flinders Street Station for the coronation in London, White spotted a trouble-maker wearing swastikas and a cocked hat. He bumped the man aside, calling in a policeman. But he was also ambivalent about the great vote winner. In a clipping of a 1930 newspaper article on Lyons, White had underlined phrases such as 'country school master' and 'a few simple, deep-seated convictions, more moral than political'.

Menzies placed him in another quandary. The brilliant Melbourne barrister and state attorney-general entered federal politics in 1934, virtually guaranteed as Lyons' successor. White admired Menzies' oratory, but privately was very cutting about his lack of service in the Great War. This simmering feeling that Menzies was not up to scratch on White's pet subject of defence eventually erupted into the open in the early years of the Second World War.

Newspapers continued to canvass White's leadership potential. *The Star* in 1934 described him as a 'tiger' in defence of his party's principles and in verbal combat with opponents. Cuttingly, the newspaper added that he was also 'kind' as he had 'often lifted a weak platitude to its feet in the House of Representatives'.

A test of White's leadership aspirations came in December 1935 when the UAP voted for the vacant deputy leadership post. Menzies won easily, beating both White and the other rising star of the party, Treasurer Richard Casey.

Canberra was a hardship post in the 1930s, with few amenities outside Parliament House, which had opened in 1927. White stayed at the Hotel Canberra, where non-Labor politicians congregated (Labor were across at the Hotel Kurrajong), playing tennis with Casey and Menzies.

Vera visited occasionally, the media seeing her as 'the Colonel's keenest critic'. *The Star* noted that, 'during the dullest debates in the House she may be seen in the speaker's gallery, especially when the business concerns her husband'. The four attractive girls were also spotted in the parliamentary galleries. The *Sydney Mail* reported that 'nothing delights the youngsters more than a verbal battle between their father and the occupants of the Opposition benches'.

Still, White's heavy ministerial load in Canberra and frequent domestic and overseas travel as trade minister meant he was away from home a lot. He compensated by sending a stream of letters and poetry home to the girls. For Patricia's fifth birthday he wrote, to her great delight:

> My dearest Pat
> How is it that
> You look so tall
> And Stately
>
> It cannot be
> A girl of three
> (or is it four)
> could lately
>
> These presents tell
> The story well
> You're five years old
> To-day

White also sent the girls autographed menus and other mementos he collected on his ministerial round. One batch included autographs of the Governor-General, Lord Gowrie, and Don Bradman, telling the girls they would have 'to settle who keeps them'. Doubtless Bradman's was the prize in that offering.

His youngest daughter, Judith, remembers him as great fun, always trying to find time for his girls. One of her happiest childhood memories was going to meet him at the train station when he came back from Canberra. In those days travel to and from Canberra meant tiring train journeys, with a change at Albury for the switch between Victorian and New South Wales railway gauges. White estimated he spent a year on that train, but although he advocated a switch to air travel, an ear problem kept him on the train. Patricia says somewhat sardonically that her father was great 'when he was at home'.

Tariffs, censorship and ex-servicemen's issues dominated White's agenda through his ministerial years. With Australia's high trade protection walls, the minister for customs was a powerful post. He was effectively an industry regulator, and ministerial decisions could make or break companies.

White's tariff role was not just day-to-day administration. His predecessor, Henry Gullett, had negotiated the deal at Ottawa for a new system of imperial preferences. After Gullett fell ill, White as the new minister had the job of drafting the complex legislation and steering it through Parliament.

For Australia, the spirit of Ottawa involved mounting two levels of tariffs — a prohibitive one against 'foreigners', and a preferential tariff for British imports, giving them an advantage in the Australian market. Basically, Australia supplied the raw materials and foodstuffs, while Britain supplied the manufactures. But Ottawa also allowed Australia to set the preferential British tariffs at a rate that helped some local industry to grow. The trick was to get the balance right — setting levels that did not unduly upset Britain and jeopardise Australia's open agricultural entry to that market, while encouraging growth of local industry and jobs through the depression-racked 1930s.

White was very proud of the growth of Australian secondary industry under his Ottawa umbrella. Output rose by 75 per cent in the six years to 1936–37, while employment was up from 337,000 to 525,000. 'There is scarcely a secondary industry that has not benefited in the greater volume of business,' he declared.

Tariffs and British preference also enabled White to tread in the footsteps of Deakin, who had first broached the idea of an imperial preference system. He quoted Deakin on the relationship with Britain — 'Not an empire of the sword, of coercion, or centralised domination, but of voluntary and intimate unity'. It fitted White's own strong support for the social mores of the time, the Empire and White Australia. 'We need never apologise ... for being Britishers,' he said.

In White's view, tariffs were bread and butter for Australia. 'Protection is patriotism,' he declared in the 1920s, saying anyone who bought the goods of former enemies could not be called a patriot. Free trade, he often said, would not permit Australia to maintain its population (then about six and a half million) or its industry.

While tariffs dominated White's portfolio, he was also embroiled in electorally sensitive book and film censorship, then far more draconian than current standards. His department directly administered book censorship, involving White in endless public furores over particular books and comics ending on the banned list. White was a strong censorship supporter, arguing that chemists could not freely sell poisons, so why should books spread 'moral contagion'? Even 'fine writing' was no excuse. Privately, White called James Joyce's *Ulysses* 'the foulest novel yet, in spite of the author's much vaunted new techniques'.

Customs' seizures of allegedly censored material were a constant embarrassment, with Labor quizzing him as to why even John Stuart Mill's 'An Essay on Liberty' was seized in a Perth raid. Seeking to distance himself from the censorship fray, White appointed a special board headed by Sir Robert Garran to vet publications and advise whether they should be banned. But this created its own problem when the board's reports were kept confidential. 'Secret censorship', cried the media.

Despite such pressures, White did not neglect defence or ex-servicemen. In a 1934 reshuffle he lobbied Lyons for the defence portfolio, but was again offered trade and customs. A confidential note in Legacy's historical records, contained in the National Library's White papers, reveals extraordinary generosity by White to some ex-servicemen impoverished in the Depression. The note tells of one ex-digger who could not find work. White gave him his own pension card, saying, 'Look, old man, there's my pension card, go down to the office and draw all there is on it.'

The digger did, noticing that White's was not among all the signatures on the withdrawal card to receive the pension. 'The inference which he drew and which apparently is a true one is that Tom has at all times administered his pension as a trust for the less fortunate of our ex-service comrades,' the Legacy report said.

The high and low of White's ministerial career came in 1938. In March that year Cabinet authorised him, Attorney-General Menzies and Earle Page, the Country Party leader and commerce minister, to visit London to renegotiate the Ottawa Treaty. Together with their wives, officials, secretaries and an accompanying group of industry lobbyists, the party departed on the liner *Strathmore* on 22 March 1938. They would be away four months, a not unusual period for a ministerial trip in those days.

The ministers had a tough negotiating task. Cabinet wanted them to strike a revised Ottawa deal that would achieve almost contradictory aims — increase Australia's agricultural access to Britain; allow Australia to cut back on British tariff preferences to enable faster local industry growth; and enable Australia to cut new trade deals with countries such as the United States.

Negotiations dragged on in London against the background of the Czechoslovakian crisis and Hitler's demands for German *lebensraum*. Whether the British side was more diverted by the growing Nazi threat or the pressure of their own manufacturers to maintain access to the Australian market, it proved very stubborn.

White wrote to a friend in June: 'The negotiations are getting a move on, but it is surprising how in England Australia's effort of doing her best to buy all she can from Britain seems to be taken for granted, and as I noticed when addressing the Birmingham Chamber of Commerce last week many of the leading businessmen think we should still be hewers of wood. Between ourselves I am not very hopeful of a good agreement.'

He was right. In the end the two sides agreed just to renew the old Ottawa agreement, while White and Menzies trumpeted the signing as well of an innocuous new 'charter' of UK–Australian relations acknowledging Australia's right to develop its industry.

White's former Turkish prisoner colleagues provided some light relief to the dreary round of negotiations and formal dinners. Yeats-Brown, Bott and others hosted a party for him at London's Café Royal, where they toasted each other with raki, reminiscing about White's performance as Charlie Chaplin in one of the camp reviews.

After an emotional visit to the opening of the Villers-Bretonneux Memorial for fallen Australians of the First World War, White had good reason to recall prison camp life during a visit to Nazi Germany.

At the Potsdam opera house he and Vera had the use of Gestapo chief Hermann Goering's box. While White admired the music (*Faust*), he found the Nazi regime quite odious. His hosts gave him a bodyguard of thirty 'blackshirts', complete with swastika armbands. White protested when the bodyguard started brusquely sweeping people out of his path, but to no avail. It was an honour, he was told. He played a game with the blackshirts. As they linked hands around an exhibition at an industrial fair he would deliberately go to another, forcing them to rush and form again many times as he walked on.

One incident saw White in rare criticism of English royalty. Visiting a German hospital, he noticed that the Duke of Windsor had also signed the visitors' book, but as Graf von Windsor, with his wife who had caused the abdication scandal signing with her German title. 'I should have thought that Edward, with his 50,000

A teenage Vera Deakin

In her twenties, the patriotic Vera Deakin served as a Red Cross VAD officer in Egypt and London.

Wedding portrait, 1920

The four White daughters. From left: Lilian, Judith, Patricia and Shirley.

On the campaign trail when standing as Nationalist candidate for Maribyrnong in 1925

White visited Nazi Germany in 1938 as Minister of Trade and Customs. His constant efforts to evade his Nazi guard annoyed his hosts.

With Australian Air Force colleagues at Somers in 1941 (White third from left)

Inspecting the troops, 1941. During the Second World War White served in both Australia and Britain.

Entertaining the celebrated writer and actor Noel Coward at Somers base, 1941

The High Commissioner to London arrives at Tilbury on board the ***Oransay*** in 1951, flanked by daughter Shirley, wife Vera, and daughters Lilian and Judith.

Sir Thomas White with the young Queen Elizabeth at the Royal Festival Hall, 1954

Sir Thomas as High Commissioner in London. An illustration in ***The Tatler***, January 1955, by Wyndham Robinson.

Sir Thomas revelled in the High Commissioner's role.

At home in their Melbourne garden, 1951

Vale, Sir Thomas White.

White's three surviving daughters in 2004. From left: Judith Harley, Shirley Wadman and Patricia Sharp. *Source:* Elizabeth Brenchley.

pounds a year, now in retirement, might have stuck to his English title wherever he went,' he noted angrily in his diary.

The Nazi 'Heil Hitler' salute particularly annoyed him. 'I found it almost contagious and nearly did it myself once, after which I decided to place my right hand in my right pocket whenever I met [officials],' he commented.

Nazi officials pressed for a trade deal, particularly barter, saying they needed raw materials. But White was not keen on barter. He was much more interested in aircraft production. Visiting the Junkers works in Dessau, he asked pointed questions about the speed of the new Fighting Scout aircraft, and production numbers. He wrote in his diary that the British secret service had not been able to discover numbers. His German hosts told him the information was secret. 'I failed to learn what I wanted to know, namely its speed,' his diary noted. Nor could he learn production numbers.

This is an intriguing incident. Was White on a spying mission? He had reported to British intelligence after his wartime escape. A ministerial visit to New Guinea in the 1930s was a thinly veiled effort to examine Japanese threats. In Germany, apart from pressing his hosts for aircraft secrets, he also used field glasses to study army barracks for military aerodromes. In the coming war his diaries show he attended intelligence courses.

Before leaving Germany his and Vera's bags went missing. White was certain their papers were searched before the bags were eventually 'found'. A postcard of Hitler on which he had unwisely scribbled some sarcastic remarks (he had intended to send it to a friend) mysteriously disappeared.

White felt 'a load off his shoulders' leaving Germany. 'The leopard has not changed its spots and the old ruthless policy is being carried out more tyrannically now than even in the Kaiser's day,' he wrote presciently to an Australian friend. 'We breathed freely when we came to less efficient countries which preserve their liberty.' But he now came face to face with one of the consequences of Hitler's policies: the massive outflow of Jewish refugees.

President Roosevelt had called a special international conference at Evian in France to address the mounting Jewish exodus. White was not the immigration minister — in fact Australia did not then have such a portfolio — but as he happened to be in Europe he was instructed to attend the conference to represent Australia. However, he had no authority to boost Australia's small intake of Jewish refugees even if he had wanted to. Back in Australia the Lyons Cabinet had made up its mind, and final instructions — basically, sympathy but little practical action — were cabled to Evian the day White arrived.

Lyons was in no doubt about the growing urgency of the problem as 1938 progressed. Stanley Bruce, the London High Commissioner, cabled him that the British Foreign Office wanted 10,000 more Australian entry forms to handle the flood of refugee applications at their European posts. Jewish groups in London wanted to send a delegation to Australia to investigate relocating large numbers of refugees in the remote Kimberleys. Sympathy in Australia, however, was sparse.

Between the traditional preference for British immigrants and a fear that large numbers of Jewish refugees could threaten local jobs already much reduced by the Depression, there was little agitation to prise open Australia's entry door. Immigration officials were put on watch for would-be Jewish refugees arriving by ship as tourists. In the three years to 1937 only some 1670 Germans and 230 Austrians entered Australia as migrants. *The Bulletin*, which long stood for 'Australia for the White Man', said 'good Australians' were uneasy about the 'Jewish question' because many were coming in as Germans, Austrians, Hungarians, Estonians, Yugoslavs and 'what not'.

Lyons' cables to Bruce reflected this mood. On 8 April 1938 he stipulated a limit of 500 Jewish refugees a year, provided they were sponsored by Jewish welfare societies and that no more than twenty arrive on any one ship. By 22 June this had been improved to 300 a month unsponsored, but given the large number already applying 'applicants should be warned [there was] little prospect

... of being granted during the present year excepting in very special circumstances'.

The cable awaiting White in Evian took the same hard line. Ceilings would be 2500 refugees a year with guarantors (including the 500 he mentioned earlier) and 300 a month for those without, and these would need to pay two hundred pounds each. 'Limitation is necessary in view of Australia's restrictive absorption capacity and need for careful regulating of alien immigration,' the cable said. 'Applications on hand and now being received at rate 600 persons per week are more than sufficient to provide numbers eligible for admission during the next 12 months.'

With these orders, White called on the British delegate, Earl Winterton. Britain, Winterton said, was proposing to offer sanctuary in East Africa, What will Australia do?

'I told him that Australia did not intend to give the open door to any number of migrants but would go on taking a considerable quota under our present arrangements for aliens,' said White.

At the conference next day White repeated this line, saying Australia had no racial problem, and did not want to import one. Australia would cooperate (in refugee resettlement), but its performance already compared favourably on a pro rata basis with other countries — a conservative argument that would find echoes in the people smuggling issue some sixty years later.

The *Daily Telegraph* reported that the French delegate, M. Berenger, was unimpressed. 'Australia owes its development to migration from the old world,' he said. True, replied White, but this migration was predominantly British, and Australia did not want to depart from this policy 'while British settlers are forthcoming'.

Appointed the chair of a subcommittee, White heard what he described as 'heart wrenching' stories of the plight of refugees from the Nazis. The committee itself reported on a 'great human tragedy' that called for 'early amelioration'. But White's overriding orders from Cabinet meant his hands were tied.

Later that year, after White's report back to Cabinet and as the Nazis pushed into Czechoslovakia, Interior Minister John McEwen announced a final decision that Australia would take 15,000 unsponsored Jewish refugees over three years, a slight improvement on the 300 a month White had been instructed to offer in Evian. It was not Australia's finest hour. White later became an advocate of the Zionist cause to create a Jewish state in Palestine.

White's European visit and his personal inspection of the Nazi regime heightened his fears about Australia's defence preparedness. Back in Australia he became a firm supporter within Cabinet for the reintroduction of universal military training. You don't send an amateur into the ring against a professional, he argued. 'We seem to believe that we are a race of supermen who without training would be more than a match for any who may oppose us,' he warned.

It was not just universal training that agitated him. He wanted more than the planned doubling of army enlistment to 70,000, as well as increased pilot training and a new capital ship for the navy. 'If we fail our present generation, we will deserve the contempt of posterity,' he warned with considerable foresight.

In late 1938, as Lyons contemplated a major Cabinet reshuffle, White made another bid for his prized Defence portfolio. 'Most of the odium that Government carries and the attacks upon yourself are due to Defence policy and Defence administration,' he wrote to Lyons, staking out his claim for the portfolio then held by H. V. Thorby. White thought defence would naturally operate better under an ex-serviceman, and told Lyons he would 'gladly undertake' the ministry.

White was quite scathing about the defence portfolio being held by politicians who had not served in the military. 'Thorby cannot of course be expected to understand the ramifications of his department without any experience,' he wrote in his diary. 'Like Menzies and some others in our Cabinet, he did not volunteer during the war and has no service experience.'

Lyons was under enormous pressure, and not only over defence. A comment by his deputy, Menzies, that democracies could not survive in a world of growing totalitarianism without 'inspiring leadership' was widely seen — certainly by Mrs Enid

Lyons — as a direct attack on Lyons and a bid by Menzies for the leadership.

Intrigue around Cabinet was high, as White's diaries reveal. In September, when Munich saw British prime minister Neville Chamberlain agreeing — with Australian endorsement — to the dismemberment of Czechoslovakia to appease Hitler, White was horrified.

'I think we should all hang our heads that we did not stand up to the bully of Europe.' It meant the political expansion of Nazism, he wrote. Peace, but at what price? 'One can expect this attitude from M [Menzies] but Casey is inexplicable.'

In Cabinet White upbraided the veteran Billy Hughes, who as prime minister during the First World War had battled unsuccessfully for conscription. Why was he not now supporting universal service, when returned soldiers were calling for it? Hughes, said White, snarled and shouted, 'realising this could destroy his image amongst returned soldiers'.

In such an atmosphere Cabinet met on 1 November. It was Melbourne Cup day, and there was some grumbling about a meeting on this holy day of the Australian sporting calendar. Debate swirled around the reintroduction of national service, and sentiment began to turn against it. Lyons had promised at the 1937 election that Australia would rely on a voluntary military, not conscription. White's anxiety about the state of Australia's defences overrode a politician's normal sense of self-preservation. He declared that 'I could not remain in a Cabinet that did not support universal service, and that I had thought it over and intended to withdraw, and I left the room.'

Back in his office, White began drafting his letter of resignation. 'For some time now I have been in disagreement with the government on the matter of defence. This is a subject to which for many years I have devoted considerable thought and service. I feel, however, that the inadequacy of our . . .'

The letter trails off. Cabinet ministers, including Page and Casey beseeched him to come back. With a Labor no-confidence motion in the Parliament, his resignation could mean the end of the government and an election. Casey claimed he would lose his seat. 'I decided for the sake of the government I would return, but made it perfectly clear where I stood,' said White.

He deserves credit for his foresight in ringing alarm bells about the state of Australia's defences in the complacent period leading up to hostilities. Within a year Australia would be at war with Germany, and in three years Japanese troops would be on our northern doorstep. But for White, his near resignation was the calm before the storm that would see his political life take an entirely new turn.

14

Stormy petrel

White's withdrawal of his Cabinet resignation lasted all of one week.

Prime Minister Lyons unveiled his new Cabinet the following Monday, November 8. White was again offered the Trade and Customs portfolio. Defence went to a new minister, grazier Geoffrey Street.

As Cabinet assembled for Lyons to run through some of the detail of portfolio arrangements, White detected that something was amiss when Casey's name was read out before his. In the previous Cabinet he had been listed above the Treasurer. White tried to ask a question, but in the bustle as ministers left for Government House for the Governor-General's swearing-in he could not pin Lyons down.

At Yarralumla, the residence of the Governor-General, Lord Gowrie, there followed one of the most bizarre swearing-in ceremonies of any federal ministry before or since. With ministers assembled in the drawing room, Bibles in hand, the order of ministerial precedence was again read out, with Casey still above White. Breaking protocol, White interrupted the ceremony, openly quizzing Lyons on the Cabinet pecking order.

The assembled ministers were stunned as White asked why Casey was now listed above him? Was it an error or had Cabinet seniority been changed?

Lyons remained silent, but he was livid. White asked again, and again Lyons did not reply. The atmosphere must have been electric: the full new ministry assembled in Lord Gowrie's drawing room with one minister openly challenging the prime minister on precedence. The Governor-General could only stand by and wait.

Eventually, after White pressed the question a third time, Lyons responded. There was no error. He had placed Casey senior to White because of the importance of the office Casey held. White thanked Lyons for the information, and the swearing in proceeded.

The incident illustrates another side to White — that of a man very conscious of position. On a separate occasion he complained to Government House about the seating order in relation to himself and Vera at an official dinner, and was told that a mistake had indeed been made.

White was obviously prepared to swallow the minor humiliation of being listed below Casey, whom he regarded as a shallow opportunist, but the arrival of the newspapers the following day launched him on an explosive path.

Tuesday's papers carried news about the ministerial reshuffle that had not been revealed until late Monday night: Lyons planned to divide the ministry into an inner and outer Cabinet. While this is commonplace today, it had never been done before 1938. 'Senior group to decide high policy', stated one morning newspaper headline of Lyons' late-night revelation. 'New Methods in Cabinet Reconstruction', read another. The rest of Cabinet would be divided into two subcommittees, each presided over by one of the most senior Cabinet ministers, Lyons, Menzies or Page.

The initial reports suggested the new inner Cabinet would consist of these three, plus Casey (Treasurer), Hughes (External Affairs) and Thorby (Civil Aviation and Defence Works).

White consulted Lyons, and was informed he was to be a member of the inner group. But Lyons then talked with other ministers and had a change of heart. If the inner Cabinet was to be expanded, the minister for defence, Street, should be the one added. When newspapers reported this in the next few days, White scrawled in the margin, 'Who made these representations? RGM [Menzies]? Conveyed this to the press.'

Lyons called White back to his office, explained the dilemma and told him Street would be added to the senior group. White was now in the outer group.

Something inside White must have snapped. From his early military run-in with 'Pompey' Elliott over the smoke night, to the rejection of awards and promotion after the war, and then Casey being put above him, White must have seen himself as the quintessential outsider battling authority. Now he was to be excluded from the Cabinet 'club' as a result of the plotting of some of his colleagues. It was too much. He dashed off his resignation and sent it to Lyons.

As Parliament met for Question Time, the lobbies buzzed with excitement: a minister had resigned less than twenty-four hours after the new Cabinet had been announced. Inside the House of Representatives the crisis was clear: White, a minister only the day before, now sat on the backbench, while Menzies sat supportively alongside Lyons at the prime minister's front dispatch box position.

In the clubbier atmosphere of the smaller Old Parliament, White rose to read out his letter of resignation amid jeers of delight from the Opposition. 'My dear Prime Minister,' he began. He outlined his 'surprise' at the news of the new inner Cabinet, continuing:

'I had intended to question the wisdom of such action in putting Government policy into the hands of a coterie as being a departure from the best democratic principles, and did suggest, after you had mentioned that I was to be a member of such a Cabinet group, that if expedition in attention to Cabinet matters was the objective, it could be attained by more ordered discussion.

'Immediately after the Cabinet meeting you sent for me and informed me that a mistake had been made, and that I would not be one of the ministers taking the responsibility for policy. I pointed out to you that to allow Australian tariff matters and the welfare of secondary industries to be subordinated to a group on which the Customs Minister was not represented was to make this important branch of Government, responsible as it is for the protection of Australian industries and the welfare of so many of its citizens, as well as for the collection of the bulk of Commonwealth revenue, merely an administrative department, dominated by an inner group.

'In justice to these considerations, and the preservation of a protective policy, which I have endeavoured to carry out for nearly six years, I feel that I could no longer hold the Trade and Customs portfolio under such conditions.

'As you are aware, I have also been in disagreement with the Government's policy on defence for some time past, but, as you know, I did not wish to embarrass the Government by resigning during the period of the censure motion.

'Your recent action, so soon after the reconstruction, in subordinating so important a branch of Australia's economy to an inner group of Cabinet, makes my position now untenable, and consequently I tender my resignation. Yours faithfully, Thomas W. White.'

White's logic was a bit shaky. He had been prepared to accept an inner Cabinet despite his defence views if included in it, but not if he was on the outside. Lyons was quick to spear the inconsistency, reading to the House his letter of reply above interjections from both the Labor Opposition and White. Any thought of a dignified exit from Cabinet disappeared, as the prime minister and his former senior minister exchanged verbal blows on the floor of the house.

'I had hoped that the honourable member would have waited until he received my reply accepting his resignation before he made a statement to the House,' said the prime minister.

White: 'You had it at two o'clock, and had plenty of time to reply before the House met.'

Lyons: 'This is the letter I intended to send to the honourable member —

'Dear Colonel White. I am in receipt of your letter tendering your resignation from the Cabinet. I have no desire to enter into a public controversy with you, but certain of the statements in your letter call for blunt comment. You refer to the proposal for a policy committee of cabinet as something which is designed to put government policy into the hands of a coterie. You know this to be quite untrue.'

White: 'It is true, and the right honourable gentleman knows it.'

Lyons: 'You know this to be quite untrue, for only this morning in cabinet in your presence I made it clear that while for reasons of promptness and time-saving matters of policy would in the first instance be thrashed out by the committee, the results of their deliberations would in all cases be brought to cabinet, to which the final responsibility for decision would attach.'

White: 'We know what that means.'

Lyons: 'It means what it says.'

Labor interjector: 'A new dictatorship.'

Lyons (reading again): 'Moreover, it is interesting to note that your resignation was not tendered while you were (as was tentatively decided before this morning) a member of policy committee, but was tendered only when you discovered that there was to be a change, and that the Minister for Defence was to take your place.'

White: 'I made my protest in cabinet.'

Mr James (Labor): 'You put him in the dunces class. It was not fair.'

Lyons: 'The letter continues. The welfare of Australia's secondary industries will in no sense be prejudiced by the decision to have a policy committee.'

Mr Clark (Labor): 'Just the lost legions of the government.'

Lyons (continuing letter): 'The policy of the Government in relation to secondary industries remains unchanged, and the Minister for Trade and Customs will — as in the past — have every opportunity of submitting recommendations and contributing to decisions.

'I should add that your attitude comes as no surprise after the discreditable manner in which only yesterday at Government

House you indicated your annoyance at the Treasurer being placed above you in the order of precedence in the cabinet.'

White (angrily, said the press): 'This is despicable. You never told me about it.'

Lyons (reading): 'Your statement that you did not wish to embarrass the Government by resigning during the period of the censure motion is inexplicable to me. You did not resign when the censure motion was determined. You in fact accepted office in the new administration.'

Mr Gander (Labor): 'It is only a face-lifted administration.'

Lyons (finishing the letter): 'You, in fact, accepted office in the new administration, and were duly sworn in. No new matter of policy has been decided by the Government since then, and your resignation can therefore be related only to the personal issues to which I have already referred. I am forwarding your resignation to His Excellency the Governor-General with a recommendation that it be accepted as on and from today.'

Lyons' letter, delivered to White in the Parliament as the prime minister read it, was not only blunt. Unusually, it omitted the standard appreciation for ministerial service, normally extended in even the most difficult resignation. Stung by Lyons' reference to the Government House incident, White jumped to his feet again, waving Lyons' letter.

'Mr Lyons has referred to a discreditable incident,' he said. 'I did not think any Prime Minister would bring to Parliament a matter that occurred at Government House during a swearing-in ceremony. I questioned the names when they were read out as to seniority, as the change had not been pointed out to me, and I asked if there had been a mistake. The Prime Minister assured me there was no mistake. I pointed out that it was embarrassing personally, and I was sworn in. I read the policy of the Government in the newspapers.

'My resignation has nothing to do with the incident of yesterday, and I am surprised that the Prime Minister should try to drag it in to discredit me.'

With Labor members making merry with charges of 'the inauguration of a fascist dictatorship', the chamber fell into argument about whether the acting leader of the Opposition, Frank Forde, could speak. The upshot was that both White and his old friend Henry Gullett voted with the Opposition, but the Government still won the vote.

It was the start of an inevitable alienation of White from his ministerial colleagues and the UAP government. Why did White do it? Was it just impulsiveness and his notoriously short fuse after two slights in two days, first demoted in the Cabinet pecking order and then ejected from the inner group? Or were there deeper waters running? The politics of the time were particularly Machiavellian. Domestically, Menzies was trying to win the leadership from Lyons. White felt that his first resignation on defence spiked Menzies' guns on that issue. He could see Menzies' hand behind the new Cabinet 'coterie', and felt strongly that the whole idea of a small inner group was a step towards dictatorship. Lyons' widow later told White that her husband was 'at breaking point' at the time.

Internationally, dictators were on the rise. Press cartoons of Lyons' new Cabinet structure had ministers in an 'inner cabinet' room trying on their new Nazi uniforms. Did White believe that his stance on democratic principles coupled with his ardent support for Australian defence and secondary industry could propel him into the prime ministership ahead of Menzies? White himself had quoted Montrose in the past:

> He either fears his fate too much,
> Or his deserts are small,
> That dares not put it to the touch,
> To gain or lose it all.

Certainly, friends and business allies urged him to go for the top job or head a new party. One public relations executive, George Fitzpatrick, lobbied top businesspeople for money to provide staff and media help so that White could make a bid for the deputy leadership. White's assertion that Australia's protectionist policy required an inner Cabinet voice hit a target within the ranks of the UAP, forcing Lyons to reaffirm that his departure meant no change in tariff policy.

White's reply to a POW friend, Claude Vautin, who wrote reminding him of his prediction when the two were standing on Canberra railway station that White would one day become prime minister is revealing about the post-resignation climate.

'Yes, I remember your prediction, Claude,' he replied. 'There are many people now saying what you said then. From several quarters I have been invited to come forward as the leader of a new party. I am not being led aside by these suggestions, however, but intend to pursue the line I have always followed, in trying to bring Australia ahead nationally and economically so that it may take a better place among the nations.'

With the favourable press response after his resignation, White embarked on a round of public talks. 'Mr White took the right course,' said Keith Murdoch's influential *Melbourne Herald*. His good ministerial service meant 'he has earned something better than the treatment he received upon his resignation. In resigning he gave an example of independence and courage that might prove to be of value.'

The Bulletin, which had maintained friendly contacts with its former prison camp correspondent, found a new angle on the resignation relating to White's superstition with dates. In its usual racy style, the magazine reported on a 'joint in Tommy White's armour'. November 8, 1915, found him volunteering for the aerial expedition that cast him into exile for three years. November 8, 1938, saw him starting a period of exile from the ministry because Mr Lyons had weighed White against some ministerial colleagues and 'found him wanting'.

'One might have imagined that in an "inner cabinet" there would have been a place for him at a time when defence policy, and particularly aerial policy, was due for continuous discussion,' the magazine lamented. 'That he went out fighting in a blaze of unusual episodes was characteristic of Tommy White.'

The *Geelong Advertiser* was one of the few newspapers to take a dim view of White's action, labelling it a 'childish outburst' due to 'personal pride'. White took exception, writing to the editor that it was 'a matter of vital principle and not of personalities', and regretting that the *Advertiser* had 'missed the point'.

At an enthusiastic St Kilda rally in his electorate a few days after the resignation White, accompanied by Vera, laid down his 'democratic beliefs'. His speech notes read, 'British community — believe in maximum freedom, peace and justice', as well as 'Government ... through elected representatives. Any deviation from that path contrary to our democratic principles'. On his resignation, his notes said, 'British precedent must be rule in all cabinets', and that policy by cabal was 'retrogressive and reactionary'.

White also stressed his defence, industry and White Australia themes, asking his audience, rhetorically, whether they wished to 'hold this country', or whether Australia was just a 'nine day wonder'. He drew a solid 'yes' from the crowd when he asked them, 'Do you support the stand I have taken?'

The Protect Australia League, probably one of those groups urging him to start a new party, also drew his firm endorsement. The League stood for everything White embraced — strong defences and industry, loyalty to the British throne and empire, democracy as opposed to dictatorship, and White Australia. In a December 1938 radio broadcast for the League he said it would do 'great work' for Australia if it stirred well-wishers to a greater realisation of the need for greater national and economic security. 'Its laudable aims are to be commended.'

Letters of support poured in. 'I will come back stronger than ever,' he replied to one. 'I am sure a time will come,' he told another of the calls for him to start a new party. To another, he said Lyons was worried to death by plotters. A common response was that he could not tolerate a 'junta' in Australia.

'I now know that the person responsible was not Lyons, but Menzies,' he told a sympathiser. 'I would not consent to be the "rubber stamp" to a policy served up by an inner group,' he told another, adding that Cabinet 'should not resort to storm-chamber [sic] methods'.

With his resignation coming only six weeks after Munich, with its overtones of the growing Nazi menace, White tried to build on his anti-totalitarian stand. Columnist Alan Moyle interviewed him at his South Yarra home, finding him in a study surrounded by 'two piles of letters and telegrams', all from supporters. 'I believe that secret conclaves in the Federal Cabinet, that has a common responsibility, are the first sign of something dangerously approaching dictatorship,' White told him.

If White believed the Australian public would not stand for anything that 'tended towards dictatorship', he was to be disappointed. His resignation certainly caused a sensation, but was soon overshadowed by the growing European crisis. Then, in April 1939, Lyons died suddenly.

When United Australia Party parliamentarians met in Canberra on April 18 to select a new leader, there were four candidates — Menzies, Casey, Billy Hughes and White. Attempts to draft Bruce back from London failed. All four candidates told the meeting that everything should be subordinated to defence. White, Menzies and Casey declared their support for the reintroduction of compulsory military training, while Hughes equivocated.

White reportedly told the meeting that his sole reason for standing was to stake a claim to the deputy leadership, should such a position be created. In the subsequent ballot White was the first eliminated, with Casey next. Menzies beat the veteran Billy Hughes (then seventy-six years old) in the final ballot by just four votes.

Menzies did not invite White to join his new ministry. Another role now unfolded for White — as rebellious backbencher. A *Sydney Morning Herald* report in May 1939 said White, 'One time leading light in the Lyons ministry, was now well on his way to earning the title of "the stormy petrel of the House of Representatives".

'Since he stepped down from the ministerial ranks he has become a changed man,' said the *Herald*. 'Gone is the suave, restrained, impressive — in fact pontifical — manner. In its place is a barely concealed insurgence.'

White, said the newspaper, regularly got in 'three or four tough' questions to ministers each parliamentary sitting day. Most of his shafts were directed against Menzies.

'Of late he has taken to voting with the Labor Party, although it must be admitted that this is not Mr White's interpretation of the position. His argument is that he does not vote with the Labor Party — the Labor Party votes with him. That, however, is by the way. The essential fact is that Mr White is out to harass the ministry, and is likely to become a serious thorn in its side.'

Three and a half months later Australia was at war. White continued to hound Menzies on defence preparedness. He wanted an expeditionary air force to aid Britain, an end to domestic political bickering and a national government of both sides of politics to run the war effort. Openly attacking the Menzies Government for not doing enough, he declared: 'If Britain is defeated in this conflict, our position will be serious: our fate may be decided on some distant battlefield, and if it is defeat, Australia will be bartered away in some treaty like so many sacks of potatoes.'

White remained a thorn in Menzies' side right up to September 1941, when, faced with internal jockeying for the leadership and a disintegrating government, the prime minister resigned 'to bleed a while'. In early 1941 Menzies had undertaken a four-month trip to England, where he quarrelled with Churchill over the high leadership of the war but failed to secure British help in the Pacific.

Shortly after his return White again pinned him in Parliament, asking when Menzies would accelerate war efforts and bring Australia into line with Britain and New Zealand. A tired-sounding Menzies replied that he was still sorting out ideas and impressions of his journey, and would consult with colleagues on what action was necessary. But his government collapsed in September. Labor's John Curtin became prime minister forty days later, after the Country Party's Arthur Fadden failed to keep the coalition government afloat. Billy Hughes was elected leader of the now crippled UAP.

By then White was already on active war service in England. He wrote to a friend in December that had he delayed his departure for another few weeks he might have had 'a chance' at the leadership, believing he would have put up a strong showing against Hughes. 'However, one has to do what seems right at the moment, and I feel that it is good service helping the splendid youngsters in the air crews,' he wrote.

No other sentence better illustrates the man. White had no regrets at not having another shot at the party leadership; he was doing the right thing by serving his country instead.

White had tried to sign up for service the day war broke out in September 1939, just as he had in 1914. However, whether it was his age (fifty-one), former reserve officer status or current position as a parliamentarian, he fell between the cracks for active service and could not secure a posting. He found this very frustrating.

'So far I have not been permitted to go abroad, and as apparently there is no room for me in the [war] Cabinet, I am doing practical work in training air crews, and meanwhile am neither indulging in speeches or criticisms, as much of what I advocated is now operating, but am hopeful of being of more service still overseas,' he wrote to a friend in mid 1941.

White was a crackerbox of ideas of how he could serve. He volunteered for a string of missions, including the proposed expeditionary air force for Britain before it was converted into the Empire Air Training Scheme. He also offered to lead an Australian contingent to help Finland against the Russians, or to help defend Singapore, or to serve in the Middle East.

His June 1941 application for Middle East service was a masterpiece of understatement. 'I have had unusual opportunity to know Irak, Palestine, Asia Minor, Greece, Bulgaria and the Ukraine during the last war, and having a working knowledge of French and Russian, and slight acquaintance with Turkish,' he wrote, tongue in cheek.

His break came when the Air Force asked him to command Somers, an introductory base outside Melbourne for trainees in the Empire Air Training Scheme. Then, with leave from Parliament, in September 1941 he sailed to England, where until May 1943 he filled several roles, first at Bournmouth, where RAAF crews were pouring into Britain after final training in Canada under the Empire scheme. Later he was temporarily attached to the staff of Foreign Minister H. V. Evatt in Britain, before going on to run an RAF base at Brighton including airmen from Australia, New Zealand, Czechoslovakia and Poland.

Peter Isaacson, one of the trainees, said later that all the young airmen who passed through Somers or Bournemouth revered White. 'Because of his age, his rank and his command, Tommy was father confessor, disciplinarian and fighter for the rights of his men,' said Isaacson.

White's journey to Britain was not undertaken without some trepidation, brought on by his innate superstition. Some time before departure a fortune teller at a church fete told him he would twice go to England, but the second time he would not return. 'Well, I went in 1938 and returned,' worried White, 'now I am going again and there is a war on!'

In England, White devoted much energy to the welfare of Australian air crew. Many arrived from Canada without proper equipment. White tried to meet each contingent at the Bournmouth railway station, briefing them on dress, discipline and punctiliousness. The disorderly reputation of Australian airmen was quickly turned around.

One of White's tasks was to counsel airmen as they bid for postings and transfers. Bruce Daymond, an Australian airman, recalls White writing to him after a failed bid to get into flying boats. 'A useful slogan I have found is: it's all for the best', White wrote.

Another task was to sit on court martials. One case involved two Australians charged with 'shooting up' Bournmouth by flying too low over the town. White thought the service police who spotted them had wrongly estimated the height, and pleaded successfully for the two to be given the benefit of the doubt. The aircraft sergeant was a kangaroo shooter from Alice Springs, while the pilot was the famous war ace Paul Brickhill, who later wrote *The Great Escape* from his own experiences in Stalag Luft 111, as well as *The Dam Busters*. Brickhill later sent him a copy of his 'great escape', with a personal note to White acknowledging 'One of the greatest escapers and the best darned judge who ever acquitted me'.

Keen to see some action, White wangled a seat on board a bomber for a raid on the Ruhr in Germany. In a BBC broadcast he described the scene as the bomber fought its way through the flak after dropping its bomb load:

'Looking back we saw bundles and clusters of searchlights, and huge columns of grey smoke rolling up from the holocaust below, and merging into a huge bent pillar, among dark clouds stacked with hundreds of wicked flickering flashes where flak shells were bursting among the planes following us. Altogether an appalling and bewildering sight.'

When the bomber landed, ground crew found it had been hit six times, with one flak fragment penetrating the nose and then passing through a cushion on which the bomb aimer was lying, just missing his foot. The BBC's payment to White for the broadcast was passed to the crew of the Lancaster *G for George*, later flown out to Australia and now on display at the Australian War Memorial.

Some of White's wartime broadcasts made it to Australia, and Vera wrote that she and the girls were 'thrilled to hear his voice'. Vera returned to the Red Cross as in the first war, working long hours as Honorary Director of the wounded and missing enquiry bureau and as Victorian Divisional Commander from 1939 to 1945. Lilian became a teacher and Patricia gave up university to work in a munitions factory. 'I am so proud of them,' White wrote in his diary. He missed Vera badly. 'I feel a lost sheep without you,' he wrote poignantly early in the war.

The war rekindled White's literary aspirations. While commanding RAF Brighton he wrote 'Sky Saga', a 15,000-word epic poem in blank and rhymed verse that follows the career of an air trainee from Australia to bombing missions over Europe. The British Poetry Club selected 'Sky Saga' for a London reading, while the BBC broadcast it. Typically, White directed royalties from its publication by Hutchinson and Co. to the RAF–RAAF benevolent fund. 'Sky Saga' has recently been set to music and performed both in concert and for CD release.

England also brought out another side of some of White's former political colleagues. White heard that Bruce, the former prime minister and now London High Commissioner, blocked his appointment to a British War Council. 'I know he does not like me,' White wrote scathingly in his diary. 'I do not fawn; and he is afraid he may be shown up for the little interest he has taken in RAAF affairs.'

White suspected Bruce had not forgiven him for using the Ottawa Empire preference scheme to also benefit Australian industry. Bruce had once told him that Gullett would have implemented the scheme differently, had he not taken ill. 'I believe that agricultural countries should turn more to agriculture, and industrial countries should turn to industry,' White said Bruce told him.

'Meaning that Australia should stand still industrially?' asked White.

'Exactly.'

'Then it is a good thing Gullett went ill.'

At one meeting in London, Casey, who had been elevated from Cabinet to Australia's representative in Washington, and then to the British War Cabinet, where he was to be minister in the Middle East stationed in Cairo, was quite brusque with his former ministerial colleague.

White shugged it off, recalling that Casey was the 'consummate wrangler' who would 'stoop to almost anything to attain his ambitions'. He recalled Casey's mother telling him once how she had helped her son's advancement in the First World War by presenting a motor car to a general with the proviso that young Casey must drive it. 'Before long he had his commission and finished with DSO and MC whilst being a staff officer right through the war,' White commented, but added: 'I hope personal wrangling is unnecessary [in the new job] and his gifts of charm, good looks, wealth and moderate ability will be used for the good of the empire, not forgetting his native Australia. Best wishes to his work.'

White vented his anger against politicians who chose Canberra rather than join the war effort in several ways. At a lunch with the young Australian pilot Peter Isaacson of the RAF's Pathfinder bomber command, he suggested Isaacson run against Harold Holt after the war. Dennis Warner, Isaacson's biographer, said Holt had probably upset White because he opted for politics rather than the army. Isaacson won Liberal preselection for a State seat after the war, but lost by forty-seven votes.

White tried his own form of wrangling to get back to Australia. When Japan entered the war with the surprise attack on Pearl Harbor on 7 December 1941, he immediately applied to return home. 'Australia is more directly threatened,' he wrote in one application to authorities. 'I hereby apply for duty in or near Australia where I can give more useful service.'

His pleas went unanswered. White wrote to one friend that he had been 'unjustly sidetracked'. To another, he wrote from 'exile'. White felt his presence and military credentials would embarrass some coalition members of Australia's War Council.

He suspected Menzies' hand. 'I cannot help feeling that our mutual bete-noir may have a hand in this, as I see from the press what pressure he is putting on a come-back, and I have learned since I wrote to you last, that, when originally my name was put forward for a bigger post in another theatre of war, he had it struck out.'

Finally, in mid 1943, he received approval to return. But not before an unusual incident at RAF Brighton. White had taken a cut in rank from army colonel to squadron leader in the RAAF to run Somers base in Victoria. In Britain he was an acting wing commander, and to run Brighton he had been promised wing commander's rank. It came through only on the day he left to return to Australia. Even then, the RAAF stipulated that the rank must be relinquished upon leaving the station, which was, said White, 'some minutes later'.

It was not until 1944, when White had been back in Australia for almost a year that he discovered the likely explanation for such strange behaviour. An RAAF inquiry into 'certain losses' at Somers reported that year that it was 'impossible to pass over the apparent neglect of Wing Commander White'. White rejected this, producing a certificate from his successor that everything was in order at the time of the handover.

Another report, by Air Commodore Adrian Brownell, assessed White as 'inclined to view things from the political rather than the service angle', and that his unit had not been 'as efficient as it should have been' at handover. White tackled Brownell for this damning report, contending he had never raised these criticisms on the several occasions the two had met in Australia and overseas.

'Perhaps it is too late for you to rectify this now, but your report is a blot upon my long military and air force career,' he wrote. In yet another challenge to authority, he appealed but was unsuccessful.

Back in Australia in time for the 1943 elections — when Curtin's Labor Party demolished the conservative forces — White stood again for the party leadership. But Menzies was returned, ousting the venerable Billy Hughes.

As White joined with Menzies in working for a new Liberal Party a curious thing happened: relations between the two began to improve. Whether this was due to the long haul both realised they were in for to oust Labor, or the old political maxim that after a certain time in politics even your enemies become your friends, is not clear. Not that they became close friends. White always viewed Menzies as the 'Machiavellian one'. However, by 1944 Menzies himself awarded 'particularly good marks' to White and other former critics for their parliamentary performances. Certainly, White found no problem in attacking the socialist tendencies of Labor.

Prime Minister Ben Chifley's postwar nationalisation campaign revived White's longstanding hostility to communism. He offered to pay the fare of any Australian wanting to go to Russia so they could see what communism was really like. When one accepted, White offered him the money as soon as he could produce a passport and other formalities, adding: 'I have no doubt, having seen something of the country myself, that you will soon appreciate that Australia is an infinitely better country and the British Empire something worth preserving. If there are any communist union leaders that you know who wish to go, I would be prepared to give double in their case.'

Friends quizzed Vera when White went off to speak in the Sydney bastion of left-wing Labor firebrand Eddie Ward. Why did she let him do it? 'Let him?' asked Vera. 'I could not stop him.'

Serving in the Opposition provided time to devote to the many causes that Tom White seemed to accumulate, including Legacy, the Royal Flying Doctor Service and the Royal Life Saving Society. After the war he helped form an Australian branch of the RAF's Escape Club, as well as chairing the Free Libraries Movement.

When the 1949 swing of the pendulum swept the newly formed Liberals into power, Menzies generously offered White the ministry of air and civil aviation. White had long complained about 'snobs' in the RAAF, saying a sergeant pilot could remain just that despite wartime service because of his social or educational background. He seized the opportunity of the ministry to rejuvenate the Air Board, telling Menzies it was 'too old' and 'too slow' on rotation. One member had been there for fifteen years, and another for eight years.

As air minister, White helped negotiate for the RAAF's selection of the American F86 Sabre jet fighter to be fitted with British Rolls-Royce jet engines. Although this delayed the fighter's introduction, it gave the Australian version of the Sabres added fighting punch.

In 1951, when Menzies offered him the post of Australian High Commissioner in London, he took it. He was sixty-three. Menzies was newly returned to office and unassailable, with younger future leaders like Harold Holt and Paul Hasluck in the wings. White's domestic political horizons were limited. He left Parliament after twenty-two years as the member for Balaclava 'without a swansong'.

In London, White was his usual energetic self, urging all the State agents-general to operate from Australia House. He even proposed renaming his post as 'ambassador'. Neither happened. He and Vera patronised Australian art and culture, and he created a novel services unit to cater for the flood of young Australians then descending on London. These were busy times for the London post as Australia's postwar migration gathered pace. More than 40,000 British migrants left for Austalia in 1953.

Like many occupants of the post, White was criticised for overdoing the social side of the London high commissioner's role. Douglas Brass, the *Adelaide Mail*'s London correspondent, sprang to his defence. 'This tireless and pleasant-tongued little man does more to keep Australia in the British limelight than any ten others combined,' he wrote in his 'London Diary'.

When Menzies declined an extension of the five-year term, and also Privy Council membership (although a knighthood came his way in 1952), the Whites returned to Melbourne in 1956. Interviewed aboard the liner *Oronsay* at Adelaide on the way home, White showed he had lost none of his old political spark. A reporter asked if he would consider standing for Parliament again if Menzies got an overseas post. The *Melbourne Argus* reported:

'Sir Thomas rubbed his chin, reflected for a second and answered the reporter who asked the question: "Lad, when you get that definite, give me a ring and I'll give you a quick reply."' Another comment about political standards seemed to be aimed straight at the government. Yes, he might re-enter politics. 'I am anxious to see if the standards of Australian politics have fallen before deciding,' he said.

At sixty-eight, however, there were no serious prospects of any political second wind. White settled into a routine of writing and broadcasting, drafting the early parts of an autobiography. He had battled emphysema for some time. In October 1957, while walking to post a letter, he suffered a sudden heart attack. He died at home later that day — the 13th of October.

Tributes poured in, but perhaps the most eloquent came from Vera. A feature of their marriage, she said, was that everywhere they went they always bumped into someone Tom had helped during his prisoner or air force days. 'It is a marvellous monument he has — not in stone but in the hearts of people,' she said with quiet pride. Sir Edward 'Weary' Dunlop described him as 'perhaps the best loved man of his generation'.

Following a state funeral he was buried at Point Lonsdale near the family's Ballara holiday home built by Alfred and Pattie Deakin. White had loved the place, chopping wood for the stove fire and looking after the bushland around the house.

Vera chose a Crusader's sword for his tombstone in memory of their first meeting, and for the many causes White championed in his life. When she died in 1978, Vera's ashes were buried next to him.

Epilogue

Some final twists of fate

The cast of characters in the story of White's flight scattered far and wide after the war ended in November 1918.

When the Young Turk regime collapsed, Theodore the Greek waiter was released from prison, only a few days before he was due to hang. He often talked of using his wartime earnings as an intermediary to move to London to open a restaurant, and he was promised strong patronage by the British prisoners he had helped.

White later heard that the crew and officers of the *Batoum* were thrown into jail a few days after the ship arrived in Odessa. Apparently their greed knew no bounds, and by the end they had even sold the ship's anchor chains. He learned that Titoff, the greedy chief engineer, was killed in the subsequent Bolshevik uprising when the mob threw open the jails. Hatton, the English tanner, escaped to London with his family; but Franzovitch, the Ukrainian who sheltered them, was believed to have been killed when the Bolsheviks re-entered Odessa.

Cedric Hill, the Australian half of the great partnership of prison malingerers, joined the rush to become the first airman to fly solo from England to Australia. Unfortunately, his plane crashed on take-off on Timor as he was leading Charles Kingsford-Smith. Hill reportedly kept up his interest in conjuring, and remained on the permanent officer list of the RAF until 1944.

His partner E. H. Jones joined the Indian Civil Service before becoming involved in moves to establish an international police force. Later he became Registrar of the University College of North Wales.

Lieutenant Robert Paul became a police chief in Damascus before assuming his Irish baronetcy and marrying Miss Whitaker, the Englishwoman who so nobly assisted escapees in Constantinople. Fulton and Stone returned to Constantinople to work for the British government.

White's escape partner Alan Bott later made a special pilgrimage to Syria after the war to try to find George, the Syrian whom he had bribed to help him escape, but who then confessed all to the Turks. Bott last saw George at the railway station, pathetically pleading for his pardon. He found no sign of him in postwar Damascus.

After his success in writing about his and others' air force exploits in the war using his 'Contact' pseudonym, Bott took up drama criticism for newspapers before being appointed editor of *The Graphic* magazine in 1926. He went on to found The Book Society in 1929 and Pan Books in 1944. Bott died in 1952. White spoke at his funeral, recalling how his fluency in languages had saved them in several awkward situations.

Turkish prison camps seemed to inspire a literary bonanza in the inter-war years. Captain Dacre Stoker wrote the highly acclaimed *Straws in the Wind*, before going on to a successful London stage and film career. Jones and Hill's *Road to En-Dor* became a bestseller — and remains one of the most intriguing prisoner-of-war yarns. E. H. Keeling's *Adventures in Turkey and Russia* told of his escape via Russia to England, while Johnston and Yearsley's *Four-Fifty Miles to Freedom* related the story of their escape to Cyprus.

The siege of Kut and its aftermath took a high toll on Half Flight. Nine Australian mechanics were captured at Kut, but only two survived captivity, Flight Sergeant J. Sloss and Air Mechanic K. L. Hudson. Sloss made two unsuccessful escape bids. Corporal T. M. N. Soley died at Nisibin, and Air Mechanic D. Curran near Mosul. Air Mechanics F. L. Adams, W. H. Lord, J. Munro, W. C. Rayment and L. T. Williams died at Belemedik in the Taurus Mountains.

Captain Petre transferred to the RAF, while the remaining Half Flight members were absorbed into Australian flying units in Palestine and France.

Nogales, the South American soldier of fortune who saved White and his fellow officers from assassination after leaving Mosul, found that being a good Samaritan can pay dividends. Fulton and others of the group took him under their wing as the Young Turk regime collapsed, recommending him to British authorities. This helped Nogales gain passage back to South America.

Nogales also turned to literary pursuits, writing *Four Years Beneath the Crescent* and *Silk Hat and Spurs* about his colourful life. After reading White's book he said he was glad to be remembered. 'He never suspected the mess I got myself into in my efforts to be of service to himself and his fellow prisoners,' Nogales said in 1934.

In 1931 Nogales wrote to White congratulating him on his new political career. 'I am glad that you got to be a big "somebody" in Australia,' he said. 'Bully for you.' Despite his high-risk life as a soldier of fortune, Nogales died in his bed at home in Venezuela.

Perhaps the most successful literary career of all was that of the odd Francis Yeats-Brown, the monocled aesthete who shared White's misadventure behind enemy lines in November 1915. Yeats-Brown became an associate editor of *The Spectator* magazine before going on to write the classic *Lives of a Bengal Lancer*, later made into a hit movie starring Gary Cooper. In the 1930s Yeats-Brown became involved in right-wing politics, supporting Franco's regime in Spain and delightedly meeting Hitler, who told him he had seen *Bengal Lancer* five times. As White acidly noted during the early 1940s, this was high praise indeed in 1938, but it 'doesn't sound much now when the Führer's sun is setting'.

White and Yeats-Brown maintained a regular if occasionally heated correspondence over the years. White took strong exception to Yeats-Brown's description of their capture in his 1932 book *Golden Horn*, accusing him of literary licence and even pinching episodes from White's own book, as well as treating White as some sort of chauffeur on a mission in which Yeats-Brown claimed he was senior. Yeats-Brown had not been hit with a sword, or knocked out, and neither was he wearing his monocle at the time. 'This is a long way from the truth,' said White, 'hysterical rather than historical'.

Yeats-Brown fired back in the same vein. Wasn't White just the 'chauffeur' on their flight, ordered to deliver Yeats-Brown so that he could destroy the telegraph wires? 'Your job was to land us safely, which you failed to do,' he pointed out. 'I have never blamed you, but you force me now to remind you that I have never heard from you one word of regret or apology for having been the cause (unwilling, of course and largely blameless) of a brother officer spending two and a half years in captivity. We didn't quarrel at the time. Why should we do so now?'

Tempers cooled, and the two remained guarded friends. Yeats-Brown confided in one letter that he regarded White more highly than he believed White regarded him.

Yeats-Brown's tilt to the right and his admiration for totalitarian leaders took him into dangerous waters in the late 1930s. He believed Britain needed a new political order to deal with unemployment and slums. 'He realised that a supreme moment in Europe's destiny was at hand,' said his biographer Evelyn Wrench.

Indeed it was, but unfortunately for Yeats-Brown it was not what he might have desired. When war broke out he joined Britain's Home Guard, but he died in 1944. White wrote to his widow, Olga, who responded, 'There existed a deep and wonderful friendship between you both, and Francis often spoke about you with the same love and understanding as you put in your letter.'

One final turn of fortune would be added to those that kept popping up through Tom White's superstition-strewn life. Only three parties of British prisoners successfully escaped from Turkish prison camps — one led by White, another by Archibald Cochrane and a third by Edward Keeling. All three were knighted during their postwar careers, and all became members of parliament, White in Australia, Cochrane and Keeling in Britain.

Sources

Books

Adam-Smith, Patsy. *Prisoners of War*. Penguin, Ringwood, VIC, 1992.

Bott, Alan. *Eastern Nights and Flights*. William Blackwood & Sons, Edinburgh and London, 1920.

Brenchley, Fred and Elizabeth. *Stoker's Submarine*. HarperCollins, Sydney, 2001.

Brogden, Stanley. *The History of Australian Aviation*. The Hawthorn Press, Melbourne, 1960.

Clarke, C. M. H. *A History of Australia*, Vol. IV. Melbourne University Press, Melbourne, 1978.

Cooper, Bryan. *The Story of the Bomber 1914–1945*. Octopus, London, 1974.

Cutlack, F. M. *The Official History of Australia in the War of 1914–18*, Vol. V111, *The Australian Flying Corps*. University of Queensland Press, St Lucia, 1984.

Fitzhardinge, L. F. *The Little Digger 1914–1952*. Angus & Robertson, Sydney, 1979.

Gillison, Douglas. *Royal Australian Air Force*. Australian War Memorial, Canberra, 1962.

Isaacs, Keith. *Military Aircraft of Australia, 1909–1918*. Australian War Memorial, Canberra, 1971.

Jill, Duchess of Hamilton. *First to Damascus, The Story of the Australian Light Horse and Lawrence of Arabia*. Kangaroo Press, Kenthurst, NSW, 2002.

Johnston, Captain M. A. B. and Captain K. D. Yearsley. *Four-Fifty Miles to Freedom*. William Blackwood & Sons, Edinburgh and London, 1919.

Jones, E. H. *The Road to En-Dor*. John Lane, The Bodley Head Ltd, London, 1921.

Joy, William. *The Aviators*. Shakespeare Head Press, Sydney, 1965.

Kerr, Greg. *Lost Anzacs: The Story of Two Brothers*. Oxford University Press, Melbourne, 1998.

Martin, A. W. *Robert Menzies: A Life 1894–1943*, Vol. 1. Melbourne University Press, Melbourne, 1993.

——— *Robert Menzies: A Life 1944–1978*, Vol. 2. Melbourne University Press, Melbourne, 1999.

McMullin, Ross. *Pompey Elliott*. Scribe Publications, Victoria, 2002.

Moore. J. H. (ed.). *The Mesopotamia Campaign 1914–17*. Australian Army, Sydney, 1980.

Morgenthau, H. *Ambassador Morgenthau's Story*. Doubleday, New York, 1919.
—— *Secrets of the Bosphorus*. Hutchinson, London, 1928.
Morrow, John H., *The Great War, An Imperial History*. Routledge, London and New York, 2004.
Nogales, Rafael de. *Four Years Beneath the Crescent*. Charles Scribner's Sons, New York, 1926.
Sandes, Major E. W. C. *Kut and Captivity*. John Murray, London, 1919.
Saundby, Robert. *Air Bombardment — The Story of Its Development*. Chatto & Windus, London, 1961.
Schaedel, Charles. *Men & Machines of the Australian Flying Corps 1914–19*. Kookaburra Technical Publications Pty Ltd, Melbourne, 1972.
Shann, Edward. *An Economic History of Australia*. Cambridge University Press, Cambridge, 1948.
Stephens, Alan (ed.). *The War in the Air 1914–1994*. Air Power Studies Centre, Fairbairn, ACT, 1994.
Stoker, H. G. *Straws in the Wind*. Herbert Jenkins Limited, London, 1925.
Wackett, L. J. *Aircraft Pioneer*. Angus & Robertson, Sydney, 1972.
Warner, Dennis. *Pathfinder, The Peter Isaacson Story*. Information Australia, Melbourne, 2000.
Warner, Philip. *World War One, A Narrative*. Cassell Military Classics, London, 1998.
White, T. W. *Guests of the Unspeakable*. First published in Australia by Angus & Robertson, 1928. Republished by Little Hills Press, NSW, 1990.
Williams, Richard. *These Are Facts*. Australian War Memorial and Australian Government Publishing Service, Canberra, 1977.
Woolley, C. L. *From Kastamouni to Kedos*. Oxford University Press, Oxford, 1921.
Wrench, Evelyn. *Francis Yeats-Brown 1886–1944 (Bengal Lancer)*. Eyre & Spotiswood, London, 1948.
Yeats-Brown, Francis. *Caught by the Turks*. Edward Arnold, London, 1919.
—— *Golden Horn*. Victor Gollancz, London, 1932.

Papers/Manuscripts/Oral History

White, T. W. Antipodean — An Australian Autobiography. Unpublished manuscript. Undated. White family collections.
—— Notes for Fred Cutlack for his *The Australian Flying Corps*, Vol. VIII of *The Official History of Australia in the War of 1914–18*. Australian War Memorial.
—— Papers of Sir Thomas White. National Library of Australia. MS 9148.
—— Diaries of Sir Thomas White, Australian War Memorial.
Recordings of Vera Deakin White. National Library of Australia. TRC 4802.

Private papers, letters, photographs, books and war memorabilia held by Sir Thomas White's daughters and grandchildren:
Judith Harley
Patricia Sharp
Tom Harley
Roger Harley.

Acknowledgements

When we knocked on Judith Harley's South Yarra door that day we felt some trepidation. This was a granddaughter of Alfred Deakin and the keeper of the flame for her father, Sir Thomas White. But Judith and her husband Geoff proved to be relaxed and hospitable, prepared to give over their living room for several days so that we could wade through some of the family's copious records of Tom White's career. Our heartfelt thanks.

Judith's sister Patricia Sharp and her husband Tim were also generous in the access they gave to their 'Turkish box', a chest that White himself had brought back from Turkey and that still contains, amongst other records and memorabilia, the boots in which he hid the pages of his prison diary. Our thanks.

A third sister, Shirley Wadman, joined Judith and Patricia one day to share their collective memories of their father. It was a formidable array of Deakin granddaughters to face across a table, but the experience proved very lively and entertaining as they recalled their parents and departed sister, Lilian Bennett. Again, our thanks.

In Canberra, the research staff at the Australian War Memorial and in the manuscript room at the National Library were unfailingly supportive as we worked our way through a mountain of White material. The manuscript room people even found documents that had not yet been archived.

With the exceptions noted below, all photographs were drawn from the Harley–White family collections. Many of those from the war years first featured in White's original narrative of his wartime adventures, *Guests of the Unspeakable* (1928), as did the map reproduced at the beginning of the book. The photograph of Francis Yeats-Brown disguised as a German governess is borrowed from Yeats-Brown's own memoir, *Caught by the Turks* (1919). The illustration of White as Australian High Commissioner first appeared in the London *Tatler*, on 26 January 1955. The 2004 photographs of the surviving White daughters and of White's accommodating wartime boot were taken by Elizabeth Brenchley.

Charles Schaedel's *Men and Machines of the Australian Flying Corps 1914–19* (1972) was the source for some descriptions of the planes used by the Australian Flying Corps in training. Air Marshal Sir Richard Williams' recollections of the early days at Point Cook (pp. 20–3) are drawn from Keith Isaacs' *Military Aircraft of Australia, 1909–1918* (1971) and Williams' autobiography, *These Are Facts* (1977). The quotation on the aircraft used by the AFC in Mesopotamia (pp. 28–9) is taken from Fred Cutlack's official history of the AFC (1984).

Our gratitude to Ambassador Tansu Okandan and Lemis Okandan, Deniz Cakar and Kadri Caner of the Turkish Embassy, and to Charles Schaedel.

Thanks also to Peter Lundy, Peter Isaacson, Angus Houston, Kirk Alexander, Bruce Daymond and Denis Saunders for their encouragement and support.

Fred and Elizabeth Brenchley
September 2004

Index